Our exper

partners in your horticultural proje

At BOTANIX, we are gardeners first and foremost. As such, we love to share our passion for gardening and our knowledge of horticulture. This is why it would be an understatement to say that it's a pleasure for us to release this 10th edition of the BOTANIX Guide.

All the expert gardeners at BOTANIX are keenly interested in the environmental impact of our work, finding ways to lessen it, and finding products and services that will allow our clients to do the same. We also want to make it easy for you to follow our advice and carry out the environmentally-friendly practices we promote. Hence the last section in this new guide deals with specific, concrete methods for "green" gardening. Our specialists are always ready to help you benefit from their know-how, and partner with you in your projects.

As always, the BOTANIX Guide includes an impressive selection of high-quality plants. Here again, our overriding concern for the environment has resulted in the choice of plants that are hardier and more disease-resistant. We've gone through great lengths to make this 10th edition even more easy and pleasant to consult. I'm sure you'll find our exclusive turnkey gardens, that reflect the latest gardening trends, to be more than inspiring. Herein, you'll find invaluable advice on landscaping and garden maintenance, whether you're a rank amateur or a seasoned gardener.

Proud to count BOTANIX as a part of the RONA family for over a quarter-century now, I wish you a blooming gardening experience.

Robert Dutton
Robert Dutton
President and CEO
RONA inc.

BOTANIX Experts by nature

1. Lifestyles, Garden Styles

2. Trees and Shrubs

3. Flowers in the Garden

BOTANIX Experts by nature

4. Vegetable Gardens

5. Living with Nature

6. Indexes

Classification system for flowering periods:

December	January	February	March	April	May	June	July	August	September	October	November
early winter	mid-winter	end of winter	early spring	mid-spring	end of spring	early summer	mid-summer	end of summer	early autumn	mid-autumn	end of autumn
Winter			**Spring**			**Summer**			**Autumn**		

Flowering period:
Period during which a given plant usually flowers. Some plants have an extremely long flowering period; others, a short one; others yet again, have more than one flowering period. Significant variations in bloom time and duration may exist between one hardiness zone and another, which is why we define them seasonally rather than by giving specific months/dates.

Legend

Reference

| full sun | partial shade | shade | width | height | flowering | scented | pruning | winter protection | attract butterflies | attract birds |

Trees

| weeping | round | oval | pyramidal | columnar | spreading |

Conifers

| upright | pyramidal | ball | spreading | creeping | bushy | small cone | weeping |

Shrubs

| round | upright | spreading | creeping | bushy | tree-like | flared |

Grasses

| clump | mound | upright | open upright | arched upright |

Monarda 'Petite Delight' —————— Latin name
'Petite Delight' Beebalm/Bergamot —————— English name

global village style

This mark indicates that the variety is part of the BOTANIX Gardens by Design — GLOBAL VILLAGE style.

NB: product offering and availability may differ from one store to another.

Available colour*

*The colours are given for illustration purposes only and the hue shown may not be exactly the same as that of a given plant.

| ☼ | ☁ | ↔ 45 cm | ↕ 40 cm | ✿ Summer | ZONE 4 | 🦋 | 🐦 |

Attract butterflies and birds
Hardiness zone
Flowering period (season)
Height
Width
Sunlight exposure

OK,

everybody outside!

Living outdoors is becoming a more important part of our lifestyle, and gardens are becoming important areas in everyone's outdoor life.

Every year, the *Garden Media Group* publishes North Americans' landscaping and lifestyle trends. As having a healthy, quality life becomes a priority, so too does embellishing our immediate environments. We're all interested in getting more out of our gardens, and looking for plants that not only beautify, but that are also strong, resistant, quick to mature and low-maintenance.

This outdoor living trend is so strong, it seems everyone's rushing out to get the most sophisticated garden furniture: cooking appliances, bars, weather-resistant furniture, outdoor fireplaces, fire pits and the various concomitant accessories. Style, chic and comfort are becoming watchwords for our yards, just like they have been for our homes, and the role of plants in creating smooth transitions between one garden area and the other is growing.

A 2-year study commissioned by *Maclean's House & Home*[1], shows landscaping as the fourth priority for Canadians on their residential-improvement hit-parade. The good old backyard is now an extension of the house, and the home of outdoor living.

---

[1] Macleans's House & Home (PMB 2006)

The latest trends

Your garden reflects your personality and meets your needs, just like your house does. And here's where it's going:

Outdoor living

People want to spend longer days and more months outside, so patios and balconies are virtually becoming three-season dining rooms, and landscaping improvements are a major priority.

Escaping and centreing

The need to escape is increasing as our lives become more stressful, and what easier way to escape than escaping in our own backyard? Yes, our garden can become a peaceful refuge welcoming us to release the daily stress of the day amidst the soothing sounds of water and the comforting sight and scents of carefully chosen plants.

No pain but lots of gain

Sure, we want the joys of our garden, but we don't want the constant responsibility of continual maintenance, so why not have plants that are ornamental and useful? Increasingly, plants are being bred and purchased for their hardiness, disease resistance and prolonged flowering. So we can be surrounded by our garden, not immersed in the dirt.

Small spaces are big

As the population grows and urban density increases, gardening is growing... smaller. Rooftop, balcony and patio-gardens are increasing in popularity, and with them, the popularity of not only annuals and perennials in pots, but also vegetable gardens in containers. As part of the same trend, perpendicular structures that support upright and climbing plants allow us to create vertical green spaces where we have little room on the ground.

A better structured garden

The importance of balance and structure in landscaping is beginning to make an impression on more people. Gardens are becoming really organized and carefully planned, with more cleanly defined surfaces, better-delineated borders and more striking contrasts.

Ecology

The deleterious effects of man-made chemicals and the growing scarcity of potable water are common knowledge. Hence, ecologically-balanced gardening techniques are growing in popularity and people are increasingly demanding plants that require less watering and fertilizing.

Preternaturally large

Instead of cluttering their yard with many tiny plants, more gardeners are looking for a few spectacular specimens. Canna Lilies, Agaves, Castor Oil Plant and some conifers fit the bill, inevitably leading to larger pots and accessories, too.

BOTANIX Experts by nature

Foliage rules

For many years, being a gardener meant growing flowers. Nowadays though, there is a large choice of textures, colours, shapes and behaviours among leaves, too. And every year the available variety grows.

Luxurious and exotic

There is no doubt, rare plants are taking off. It's getting easier every year to find those plants you remember from exotic locations: Bananas, Palm Trees, hardy Hibiscuses, Cacti and Oleander are now within reach in the great white north.

Good enough to eat

It's no longer unusual to see edible plants interspersed with ornamentals, in fact, it's no longer unusual to see edible plants that are, themselves, highly ornamental.

Original vegetables

The popularity of the vegetable patch is undeniable. Combined with our foundness for the original, unusual edible plants are becoming almost commonplace, and that's a good thing! Expect to see more miniature vegetables, heritage seeds, strangely coloured vegetables, unusual-tasting fruits and veggies...

The return of the colour wheel

Masses of colourful shrubs and perennials are major attractions. Huge heaps of same-old, green foliage have given way to a full range of colours in foliage and flowers, including flowers such as Roses and Hydrangeas that bloom continuously or on and off until the first frosts. This means that plants with spectacular flowers like a Hibiscuses, Magnolias and Forsythias are all the rage.

Perfumes and feathers

As the odour reclaims the ground it lost to sight, gardens seduce with their amazing aromas emerging from flowers, foliage and stems – and the popularity of placing touch-sensitive plant textures near a busy pathways is growing, giving a new dimension to gardening.

Birdwatching, too, is a natural, ecological activity for which the garden is becoming an increasingly popular venue. Birdbaths, ponds, and plants that attract wildlife are springing up everywhere.

BOTANIX

Planting good ideas

We, at BOTANIX have long made it our mission to demystify gardening trends and clarify horticultural advances for our clients. This year, we've gone even further by creating three exterior landscape projects – turnkey gardens – just to make it easier for you to create a garden in your image. These three different arrangements, which reflect the most promising new gardening trends, are presented on the following pages. We are convinced that this latest avant-garde initiative is an extremely useful tool for our clients, so we've made the BOTANIX Gardens by Design the theme for this 10th edition.

Our prime motivation in creating the gardens was to encourage and guide you in growing a garden that fits your personality. You can choose to reproduce it inch by inch, or take inspiration in various aspects, ideas and juxtapositions to tailor your own garden to your own needs. Which resembles you most: OASIS, SPIRIT or GLOBAL VILLAGE? Get creative, and grow the plants *you* want for *your* enjoyment... and remember, at BOTANIX, the choice is yours!

BOTANIX Gardens by Design

The allure of
tranquility

If this garden appeals to you, you prefer elegance, composition and minimalism. This garden is a good example of the growing popularity for creating an oasis of peace in your yard, where one can get away from the stresses and strains of everyday life and recentre on the essential. It is structured, classical and formal, much like the quintessential French garden, integrating traditional plants, often symmetrically placed and evenly numbered. This style is also characterized by the creative, conscious placement of foliage.

In this arrangement, where all the seasons are given importance, conifers are planted in the four corners: two Canadian 'Smaragd' Cedars in the back, and two Japanese 'Capitata' Yews in the front, ensuring an overlaying harmony and creating a structural mirror image down the centre of the garden. At the same time, they define the space in every season with their perpetual greenness, and maintain the balance of the whole. The Hydrangeas and Roses were selected for the subtle tone of their flowers, while the 'Palibin' Lilac standards guarding each side of the entry were pruned into a sphere befitting the parameters of this garden type.

Round and round the rounds

An **OASIS** style garden is usually oriented to receive over six hours of sun a day, and features a stripped-down design style emphasizing curves, highlighting textures and bringing out forms. The little path, leading to a circular surface, sets the characteristic style for this type of garden, while the black cedar mulch adds an unmistakable tone of righteous sophistication.

The round blue 'Globosa' Spruces add subtle contrast with their shape and leaf-texture, while the 'Little Lamb' and 'Limelight' Hydrangeas with their subtly curving branches and the 'Morden Blush' Roses, boast globular

flowers and rounded leaves for conceptual continuity. The 'Catlin's Giant' Bugleweed, the Lamb's Ear and the Mountain Sandwort together form a carpet of interesting, diverse foliage and textures in each garden section.

All elements of this decor – materials, foliage and flowers – contribute to the structure and the perception of roundness. No straight lines or intersecting angles create a harsh element in this fluid, receptive and welcoming environment.

An invitation to contemplation

This garden exudes a serene atmosphere inviting contemplation. An idyllic port in the storm where one can rest, admire the beauty of plant life, listen to the water flowing peacefully and observe the birds wandering happily.

The carefully chosen plants contribute to this soft beauty in all seasons with their subtle mix of shades, going from green to grey to purple to cream... and white with delicate hints of pink. The two Red Twig Dogwoods stand in slight juxtaposition with their leaves sporting cream patches, while the Hydrangeas

and Roses compete in their own beauty contest until the first frosts. The white 'Vision in White' Astilbes – available only at BOTANIX – contribute their down-like softness to the scenario. The Fairy Candles, accompanying other perennials in the urns, dance about in the wind, attracting the eye, while the ball-shaped topiaried Eugenia adds an exotic note. The creeping plants with their discrete flowers complement this charming montage.

A garden that would gracefully embellish any classic home, contributing to an air of quiet dignity and resolute relaxation.

The **BOTANIX** Gardens by Design - The OASIS style

Traditional materials

Non-living materials also play an essential role in an **OASIS** style garden, with cement, cast iron, and compacted stone-dust for pathways being particularly appropriate, in keeping with the classical French inspiration. In this garden, the majestic fountain, curved opening of the arbour and the refined lines of the vases and their bases all obey the dictates of the style and add omnipresent elegance.

The **OASIS** style is a continental garden from the classical period: chic and elegant.

BOTANIX Experts by nature

Trends without end

Better structured gardens

The alignment, symmetry, integration of plants in even numbers and ubiquitous roundness are good reflections of the mounting trend for planning, care for the overall effect and search for balance in gardens. Everything in this garden emanates from a carefully thought-out aesthetic that's increasingly drawing support from gardeners everywhere.

The comfort of foliage

This particular arrangement is a perfect example of the growing popularity for foliage and the play of texture, but also the reasons behind that popularity. The conifers and foliage in this garden, bring a broad and striking range of various shapes and textures, creating a visual richness without overpowering the other elements.

Getting away and getting centred

The obvious serenity, beauty of the plants, and the life added by the tinkling fountain with its visiting birds are characteristic elements of a secluded utopia that invites relaxation, encourages objectivity and calms the wild beast. In an increasingly wired, linked, networked and hectic world, this garden answers the obvious desire for one's own quiet little hideaway.

The BOTANIX Gardens by Design - The OASIS style

The OASIS style garden layout

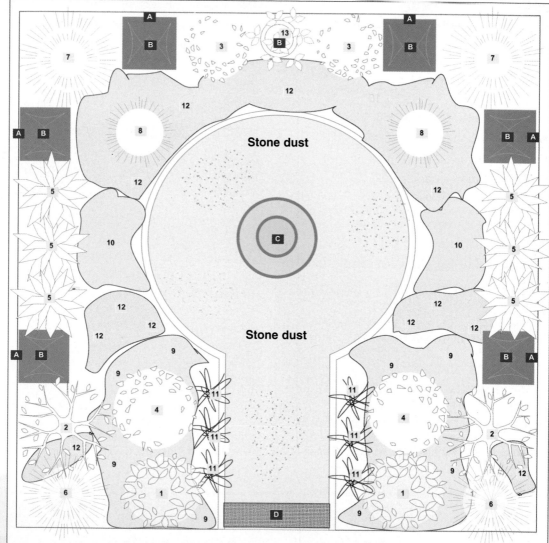

Stone dust

Stone dust

BOTANIX Experts by nature

Plants used for the OASIS style garden

Trees:
1. Dwarf Korean Lilac on stem (2) p. 63

Shrubs:
2. Red Twig Dogwood (2) p. 105
3. 'Limelight' Hydrangea (2) p. 108
4. 'Little Lamb' Hydrangea (2) p. 108
5. 'Morden Blush' Rose (6) p. 158

Conifers:
6. 'Capitata' Japanese Yew (2) p. 83
7. Emerald Green Cedar (2) p. 92
8. 'Globosa' Dwarf Spruce (2) p. 82

Perennials:
9. 'Catlin's Giant' Bugleweed (18) p. 170
10. Mountain Sandwort (14) p. 172
11. 'Vision in White' Astilbe (6) p. 177
12. Lamb's Ear (36) p. 228

Tropical Plant:
13. Eugenia on stem (in the urn) (1) p. 267

Materials for building this garden:
6 m x 6 m (20 ft x 20 ft) of land

- Geotextile sheet
- Pebbles (3/4 po)
- Stone dust
- Black plastic border for the stone-dust path

A) 6 bases
B) 7 urns
C) 1 fountain
D) Black cedar mulch

Interesting alternatives

All the plants in this garden were carefully chosen to best represent the **OASIS** style. This garden could be reproduced completely, of course, but there's no reason not to add your own personal touch in your own garden. Other varieties of Roses, Hydrangeas and Conifers that are also true to this garden style could be used to create an equally attractive version. Remember, however, to verify their hardiness in your zone before purchasing.

To re-create this garden faithfully, download a printable plan and technical explanations from **botanix.com.** A colour plan and the required materials are available at your BOTANIX centre, where they're specially identified.

A contemporary
concept

If you are the **SPIRIT** style type, you're looking for an outdoor environment that's obviously modern and comfortable. You love living outside, and take pleasure in your garden but aren't interested in working in it very much. This garden style, which is a response to the increasing popularity of small urban gardens belonging to busy people, comprises a few elements virtually unique to this style.

In the small city garden illustrated here, the grass has been replaced by inert materials, as is typical of the SPIRIT style gardens. The duckboard overlaying the decorative river pebbles replaces the ground itself and guarantees low maintenance. The plants – including 'Camelot White' Foxglove, Ruby Masterwort, 'Superba' Astilbes, Iris and Grasses – were selected for their militarily erect form which gives the garden an attentive, disciplined look, while being rather original.

Right angles

This south-southwest-oriented garden gets over six hours of sun every day. Its contemporary design with refined lines, the right angled composition and the clear, basic and svelte forms are all telltale signs were dealing with an **SPIRIT** style garden. This style also marries well with a vegetable garden.

The Flame Amur Maple, 'Purple Robe' Locust, Emerald Green Cedars, 'John Cabot' Roses, 'Henryi'

Clematis and Showy Stonecrop Sedum unobtrusively structure the garden while effectively fulfilling their functions: privacy screen, border, verticality... A Cedar hedge provides a welcome contrast to the brown colour of the fence all year round. All elements in this arrangement contribute to a dominant characteristic of this garden type: geometry.

The **SPIRIT** style garden is structured and undemanding: a pleasant surrounding for living at today's fast pace.

Energy and vitality

In this dynamic decor, everything inspires movement and energy; this garden was obviously designed for full enjoyment and pleasant intimacy. A long-lasting garden, with its varieties of cheerful colours blooming until late in the season.

Islands of green

The garden has areas reserved for perennials near the duckboard. Blue Flag Irises with their leaves thrust upwards like so many Excaliburs being held aloft by The Lady of the Lake, flower in the spring, when the purple flowers can also be brought indoors to be placed in strategically situated vases. A little farther, the azure spheres of the thistles are surrounded by the highly dentated foliage resembling artichoke plants. From the end of July into autumn, they add surprising shapes and originality to the garden. In the next area, the 'Fuji White' Balloon Flower ornament the garden with their little white balloons that appear at the same time, while the 'Munstead' Lavender does its thing all summer long. As summer's hottest days draw to a close, the 'Purpurescens' will be over 4 feet high, masking the alleyway entrance to the garden, whence only the sound of water betrays the presence of a fountain secluded within their feathery branches.

The vegetable garden

Here we have a practical, ecological aspect of the garden, where vegetables rub shoulders with aromatic plants, and the liquorish scent of Basil wafts gently on the slightest breeze.

A comfortable garden

The structural elements of the garden form a typical arrangement, creating a desired intimacy and bringing an unobtrusive beauty. The autumnal foliage of the Amur Maple and the summer flowering of the 'Purple Robe' Locust create the perfect balance between practicality and beauty. A comfortable garden for dynamic people who believe in living spontaneously, and don't want to spend their time caring for a garden.

Functional materials

Technology, of course, means constantly new materials that work better than those they are replacing. This garden opens the way for new materials like these slim pots arranged to accentuate the geometry of the duckboard. The patio corners are filled with such perennials as the Euphorbia de Corsica, the Hen-and-Chickens, and the Pennisetum. A bistro set at the centre of the little courtyard adds the final touch to the decor with a round table top displaying a blue and beige mosaic.

The floor, with its modular sections, can be moved to change its outline by adding, relocating or removing squares. These forms are picked-up by the modern fountain, accentuating the geometry of the duckboards and the patio itself.

Trends without end

The increasing popularity of small gardens

With the primacy of the climbing plants and the Cedar hedge, this arrangement perfectly reflects the growing trend for gardening in small spaces and the concomitant popularity of vertical structures. This garden is very much about the patio, as is shown by the many pots of perennials, which are a useful way to make the most of limited space.

No pain but lots of gain

This garden was created for people with a busy lifestyle so they could enjoy a garden without having to spend too much time maintaining it. The prime mandate here was to allow full and relaxing enjoyment, hence the use of inert materials and hardy, resistant, vigorous plants. A formula that appeals to many people, nowadays.

A better structured garden

These gardens reflect the growing concern for a harmonious, structured environment with clearly delemited sections, sharp edging, and clean border bespeaking functionality. Our SPIRIT style garden plainly demonstrates that propensity.

Good enough to eat

Here, tomatoes and aromatic plants grow together, illustrating the trend for having ornamentals and edibles rubbing shoulders instead of being relegated to separate garden areas.

The BOTANIX Gardens by Design - The SPIRIT style

The SPIRIT style garden layout

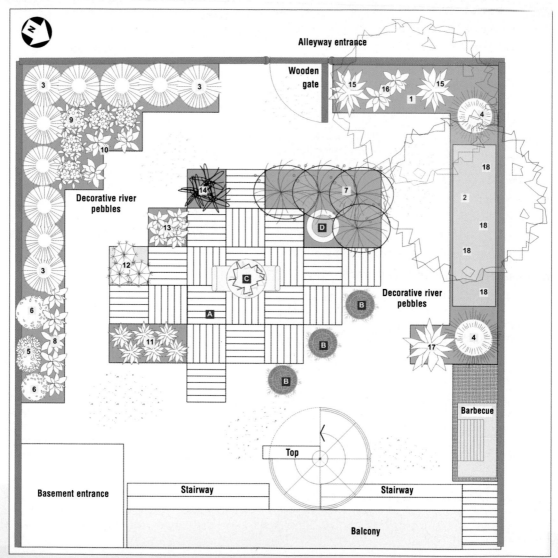

Alleyway entrance

Wooden gate

Decorative river pebbles

Decorative river pebbles

Barbecue

Top

Basement entrance

Stairway

Stairway

Balcony

BOTANIX Experts by nature

Plants used for the SPIRIT style garden

Trees:
1. Flame Amur Maple (1) p. 48
2. 'Purple Robe' Black Locust (1) p. 55

Conifers:
3. Eastern White Cedar (10) p. 92
4. Emerald Green Cedar (2) p. 92

Climbing plants:
5. 'Henryi' Clematis (1) p. 143
6. 'John Cabot' Rose (2) p. 156

Ornamental grasses:
7. Purple Silver Grass (4) p. 240

Perennials:
8. Showy Stonecrop (5) p. 226
9. 'Camelot White' Foxglove (5) p. 190
10. Ruby Masterwork (3) p. 178
11. German Iris (6) p. 207
12. Globe Thistle (3) p. 193
13. 'Fuji White' Balloon Flower (5) p. 222
14. 'Munstead' English Lavender (3) p. 210
15. 'Superba' Astilbe (2) p. 177
16. 'Royal Standard' Hosta (2) p. 205
17. Queen of the Prairie (1) p. 194

Vegetable Garden:
18. Tomatoes and aromatic plants

Materials for building this garden:
7.6 m x 7 m (25 ft x 23 ft) of land

- Geotextile sheet
- Gravel (3/4 po)
- Decorative river pebbles (beige)

A) 20 duckboards (2' x 2')
B) 3 modern pots

C) 1 bistro set
D) 1 fountain

Alternatives

The plants for this garden were chosen according to the main criteria of the trend. You can – if you wish – reproduce it faithfully. However, in order to create a garden that better meets your own tastes, it's possible to use other varieties that fit in with the concept. For instance, you could replace the Cedar, Clematis, Explorer Roses, Astilbes and Digitalis with other varieties of the same or similar species. To facilitate maintenance, simply spread a natural cedar mulch to discourage weeds and maintain soil dampness. It's your move, go!

To re-create this garden faithfully, download a printable plan and technical explanations from **botanix.com.** A colour plan and the required materials are available at your BOTANIX centre, where they're specially identified.

Act

naturally

If you're a globetrotter who enjoys authentic, exotic items, the **GLOBAL VILLAGE** style is for you. You love to spend your time in an informal, country-style garden to get away and get focused, and you like the fact that it's low-maintenance. You find natural materials like wood and stone appealing and you love watching birds playing and fighting over the feeders near your water feature. You make the most of the great diversity of plants and foliage, and appreciate the shade of a tree. Rich, refined and contrasting flower colours complete the scenery. Yes, the GLOBAL VILLAGE style is an amalgam of many garden trends, and the perfect blend for you.

The 'Sensation' Lilac that smoothes the transition between the pea-gravel sitting area and the water feature is the perfect example of how a rustic, country-style plant can perk up the environment. The vast range of foliage growing from the land and water plants reminds one of Manley Hopkin's winsome: "Long live the weeds and the wilderness, yet." The bright, contrasting foliage and flowers are also important, distinctive elements of this landscaping style.

Hey, Bungalow Bill...

To visit a **GLOBAL VILLAGE** style genuine garden is to take an intercultural voyage. This landscaping trend features a distinctively freestyle and unplanned look with a large variety of plants. The vibrant green of conifers and the many branches of deciduous trees structure the garden in the winter and maintain its balance all year long.

The plurality of little gravel paths – allowing free and easy access to all sections – links the garden areas via many whimsical detours, making it possible to access the most hidden corners in the garden and to appreciate it from many different angles.

The degree of sunlight varies from one area of the garden to another, abetted by the proclivity of diverse trees and bushes to create varying degrees of shades at different times of the day, giving most of the garden four to six hours of sun daily.

Relax, dawdle, hang about, mosey around and generally take the time to appreciate nature's riches at various times of the year. That's what the **GLOBAL VILLAGE** style garden is all about.

More sense than cents

This garden manages to create a joyful atmosphere with its coloured foliage and flowers, continuously thrilling the eye from spring to autumn. Bird feeders located near sitting areas allow unplanned bird watching interspersed with appreciating the visual beauty of your plants. Enjoy their varied aromas mingling with the fertile odour of the soil and the chocolate aroma of the cocoa-hull mulch that so effectively reduces weeds, amends the soil and conserves its dampness while minimizing maintenance. For background music, you have the water gurgling in the pond, punctuated by birdcalls.

The rich, refined shades of the plants bring light into your garden: 'Coppertina' Ninebark with its copper foliage, Dwarf Winged Euonymus with its reddish-pink foliage, 'Quick Fire' and 'Pinky Winky' Hydrangeas with their coloured flowers that really stand out in fall, 'Goldsturm' Coneflower, 'Blue Queen' Sage, Crocosmia and 'Petite Delight' Bergamot with their yellow, mauve and red flowers.

Amazing how a small-garden tour can turn into an outdoor hike full of adventure and sensory delight!

Raw materials

This trendy garden includes natural materials such as wood and stone. All accessories, including furniture and terrace are from raw materials taken from our natural world and chosen for their resistance to the vicissitudes of nature, as well as for their functionality. River rocks and a mulch of wood shavings carpet the sitting area and flower beds.

The water feature

Water is everywhere in this landscape. The water basin and its aquatic plants are naturalistic enough to make us think "pond," with its country-garden plants at the water's edge and tropical delights in the middle. The nearby grasses, including 'Red Baron', add both colour and pristine sublimity. Silver Falls and other ferns remind one of a forest floor. Aquatic plants including Papyrus, Waterlilys, large-leafed Butterburr, Elephant Plants and Spider Lily, add a touch of the exotic to your garden. Remember, though, these tropical plants must be brought inside at the end of the season.

If you can't go to nature, bring nature to you.

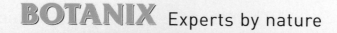

BOTANIX Experts by nature

Trends without end

Escaping and centreing

The wandering path, the abundance of plants and the natural-looking pond conspire to make of this garden a refuge for contemplation and repose that many only dream of. While the quiet lap and sprinkle of the ever-changing water induce peaceful thoughts, the exotic nature of the large-leafed aquatic plants speaks of faraway tropical shores.

The comfort of foliage

This garden also follows the trend towards increasing interest in foliage, with the quantity and variety of plants reminiscent of the flora on a forest trail. The diversity of colours, forms and textures creates a garden that's too natural to have been planned, and too beautiful to have occurred naturally.

Chunks of colour

Masses of colour with flowers that bloom into fall are also becoming increasingly popular. This joyful garden includes many bright, contrasting perennial flowers that assure continuous flowering throughout the clement weather.

Perfume and feathers

The olfactory aspects of the outdoor environment are also beginning to interest more gardeners, as this mini-estate demonstrates with its highly perfumed spring flowering bushes and the cocoa-hull mulch that gives off a tantalizing scent of chocolate. Meanwhile, the increasingly popular trend towards birdwatching on one's own backyard is represented here by abundant vegetation, the bird feeder near the seating area and the pond attract our feathered friends for drinking and bathing.

An ecological orientation

Thankfully, respect for the environment is beginning to influence our choices in our own backyards. This garden is an excellent example of that, with its emphasis on the birdwatching experience and use of stone, mulch and other natural materials to reduce maintenance and the carbon footprint.

Native wild plants

In keeping with the authentic, natural concept, indigenous plants could easily replace some of the extant plants in this garden. Those appropriate for shady areas will remind you of a walk in the woods. An advisor at your local BOTANIX can help you choose low-maintenance indigenous plants to vary the composition in your garden and help you enliven your yard with local life forms!

The GLOBAL VILLAGE garden layout

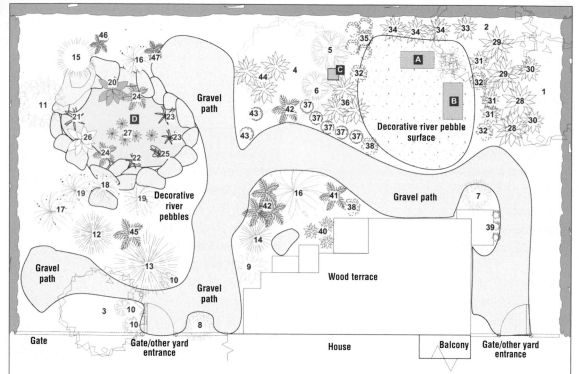

Materials for building this garden:
18.5 m x 10.6 m (61 ft x 35 ft) of land

- Geotextile sheet
- Gravel (3/4 po)
- Decorative river pebbles
- Cacao-hull mulch

A) All-purpose dolly (112.5 cm x 118.5 cm x 57.5 cm)
B) Storage bench (92 cm x 119.5 cm x 67 cm)
C) Birdfeeder
D) Water-feature kit

To re-create this garden faithfully, download a printable plan and technical explanations from **botanix.com.** A colour plan and the required materials are available at your BOTANIX centre, where they're specially identified.

Plants used for the GLOBAL VILLAGE style garden

Trees:
1. Northern Catalpa (1) p. 51
2. European Mountain Ash (1) p. 55
3. Shadblow Serviceberry (1) p.58

Shrubs:
4. 'Sensation' Lilac (1) p. 121
5. Dwarf Winged Euonymus (1) p. 106
6. 'Coppertina' Ninebark (1) p. 111
7. 'Quick Fire' Hydrangea (1) p. 109
8. 'Pinky Winky' Hydrangea (1) p. 109
9. 'Emerald'n Gold' Wintercreeper (1) p. 127
10. Bearberry (3) p. 126
11. 'Lancinata' Staghorn Sumac (1) p. 113

Conifers:
12. Weeping Larch (1) p. 88
13. Nootka False Cypress (1) p. 86
14. 'Blue Arrow' Juniper (1) p. 87
15. Dwarf Japgarden Juniper (1) p. 79

Ornamental Grasses:
16. 'Malepartus' Miscanthus (2) p. 239
17. 'Silberfeder' Miscanthus (1) p. 240
18. 'Red Baron' Grass (1) p. 239
19. Variegated Moor Grass (2)

Aquatic Plants:
20. 'Imperial' Elephant Ear (1) p. 278
21. Umbrella Plant (1) p. 279

22. Dwarf Papyrus (1) p. 279
23. Variegated Spider Lily (2) p. 280
24. Common Rush (2) p. 281
25. Corkscrew Rush (1) p. 281
26. Butterburr (1) p. 282
27. Water Lettuce (20) p. 283

Perennials:
28. Siberian Bugloss (2) p. 179
29. 'Frances Williams' Siebold Hosta (2) p. 207
30. 'Goldsturm' Coneflower (2) p. 224
31. Dwarf 'Blue Queen' Sage (3) p. 224
32. 'Crème Brûlée' Coreopsis (3) p. 185
33. Common Monkshood (1) p. 169
34. 'Petite Delight' Bergamot (3) p. 217
35. Salvia (5) p. 225
36. Crocosmia (3) p. 186
37. 'Tricolor' Chameleon Plant (5) p. 207
38. Lady's Mantle (2) p. 170
39. 'Blue Chips' Carpathian Bellflower (3) p. 180
40. 'Mardi Gras' Sneezeweed (3) p. 197
41. 'Ruby d'Oro' Daylily (1) p. 200
42. 'Stella de Oro' Daylily (4) p. 200
43. 'May Night' Sage (2) p. 225
44. Red Turtlehead (3) p. 182
45. 'Orange Crush' Daylily (1) p. 199
46. Common Maidenhair Fern (1) p. 234
47. Japanese Painted Fern (1) p. 234

Exterior decoration

rule

Although most people plan their interior decorating before they start, they usually treat gardening in a more haphazard fashion, even though landscaping is also an important investment. After all, we walk through at least part of the garden to get to the house, and plants can outlive us! Furthermore, good planning can save us a considerable amount of time and money.

Good planning requires long term vision. For example, if you're planning to put in a pool in a few years, it's best to plan for that possibility right from the beginning. Then, with the final arrangement in mind you can proceed step by step over the years, adjusting and improving as you go.

Different plants have different life spans. Sometimes, you can rejuvenate a flowerbed by simply rotating the plants. Every year, there are new arrivals, and adding them to your garden usually results in more than just a new look, because they're often hardier and more resistant.

Don't hesitate to ask a BOTANIX counsellor for advice. Like so many things, it's all about tricks – and one little trick can make your life so much easier, or vastly improve the look of your garden. Also, our **botanix.com** site has a plethora of landscaping information and horticultural techniques.

So, dig in!

The key to success

Planning and task scheduling are imperative for successful landscaping. Just like in life, if you fail to plan, you're planning to fail, so get organized... it will grow on you!

Know your soil:

Soil composition influences plant growth as well as resistance to insects and diseases. Do you know your soil? To find out what you need to know, please see our soil analysis section on page 318.

Understanding plant conditions:

To choose the appropriate plant, it's important to be aware of plant conditions such as:

- Light levels and sun-exposure
- The size of the lot

Understanding what your plants do:

- In a way, trees are the structure of your garden, giving it style and adding value to your property. Trees increase intimacy, create shade and generate fresh air. Use them as a star attraction, windbreak or visual screen.
- Being trees, conifers add structure to your garden, but they also bring beauty in shape and foliage and green year-round. Conifers are natural noise barriers, make great hedges and can reduce wind throughout your garden.
- Shrubs are the furniture of the garden; setting the tone of a flower bed; embellishing a building; creating a border, hedge or screen; dividing and defining space, and grounding your design.

- Though climbing plants improve any garden, they are particularly useful in a small garden where their verticality expands your green space, and harmonizes arbours and pergolas, unifying your garden.
- Perennials are the rhythm and harmony section of your garden, creating an important part of the decor whether interspersed or planted in masses, and their succession of flowering forms an ever-changing palette of colours and textures over the years.
- Annuals complete the decor with their floral beauty and vast range of colours pleasing the eye from early spring until the first frosts. They allow you to change your garden's look every year, and give you instant gratification – especially when they're potted.

Don't forget about tomorrow:

Watch out for the classic neophytes' error: buying and planting vegetation without knowing how big it's going to be at maturity, and without considering how that might affect the light reaching other plants.

Plant in an orderly fashion:

The structural elements of your garden – the deciduous and coniferous trees – should be planted first, then the shrubs followed by climbing plants. Once those are in, you're ready to place your perennials, annuals and bulbs.

Enjoy every season:

It's possible to create a garden that looks fantastic all year long. Think spring flowering, summer colours, autumn fruit, leaves or berries that remain on the stem in winter. Try to create contiguous flowering so that in every direction you look, there are attractive flowers or foliage for as long as possible.

Light, yes, but lighting too:

Being able to use your garden in the evening effectively extends the life of your garden, and you'll appreciate it in a whole different way once the sun has gone down. From mild solar-charged mood lights to spot and flood lighting, there are so many lighting options available to help you create exactly the mood and view you want.

Tips and Tricks

- A planning method that's really gaining ground is taking photos in your garden at different weeks over the season so you can remember exactly how each part of your garden looks at various times. With these photos on hand, it will be easy for you to determine which new perennials, annuals or structural plants you'd like to bring home from the garden centre.

- Scrapbooking is a popular new pastime that allows you to prolong your gardening pleasure if you use it to compile and display notes, cuttings, photos or other elements of gardening, and incorporate them into a scrapbook project. Just like gardening itself, it involves planning, colour and texture.

25°C in the shade...

deciduous trees

Trees are the lungs of the planet, creators of oxygen for the Earth. Can you imagine what the planet would look like without them?

In our local environment, trees play an important role. Whether it be for their beauty – as the anchor plants of an arrangement, as a windbreak, or to cover an unsightly intrusion – trees give structure to our garden and create freshness and a sense of intimacy.

Beautiful and functionally servile, they are amongst the first plants to show signs of life in spring. Their translucent green buds unequivocally announce the awakening of the new year in your garden.

Judiciously planted, trees add a lot of style and value to a property. Since trees usually take a few years to grow to their desired size, it's a good idea to plant them as soon as you move into a new house.

Because of the size and longevity of a tree, careful consideration must be put into making such an investment. Find out about the characteristics of your favourite species and its height when full-grown. Make sure it is right for the size of your property and remember to consider nearby the electric wires.

Acer platanoides
Norway Maple

Getting the most out of your outside area

When choosing a tree, consider the following: its shape, foliage density, flowering, seed-setting, autumn colour, hardiness, and fruiting.

- To bring diversity and rhythm into your garden, think about various colours of foliage, staggered flowering periods, diverse textures and complementary forms.

- Why waste your garden in wintertime? Some trees have remarkable bark or persistent foliage, others attract hungry birds with their fruit, bringing life to your winter wonderland. Snow-laden or frost-encrusted branches and the frozen fruit of some crabapples can turn your winter garden into amagical fairyland.

- Take into consideration the magnificent new arrivals that will bring a touch of surprise and originality to your exterior decor.

Grafted trees:
too much of a good thing!

As larger houses on small lots become more prevalent, and as the popularity of gardening increases even on postage-stamp parcels of land, the significance of grafted trees has increased. Many horticultural varieties are particularly appropriate for tight spaces. A relatively new phenomenon – developed especially for terraces, patios and container-planting – is the grafting of bushes onto standards to create beautiful miniatures.

Crabapple sound good?

No less beautiful because they have been familiar for generations. Shortly after a light spring pruning, you may well find that your Crabapple tree is almost buried in flowers that exhale an innervating perfume announcing the arrival of clement whether. Trees with fruits that hang on throughout the early months of winter are particularly rewarding. And Crabapple trees come in a vast range of textures and flavours, so just pick the one you prefer.

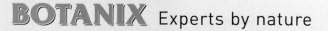

BOTANIX Experts by nature

Did you know?

- Some trees, such as silver maple, the large willows and poplars can cause damage to foundations, swimming pools or the public infrastructure, so before planting any of them you'll want to speak to a BOTANIX counsellor or a municipal official to find out about regulations.

- In many municipalities, permission is required for cutting down a tree on your own property.

- It's possible to plant a tree right after the last frost and right up till the first freeze in autumn. Don't use a tutor unless absolutely necessary, as a stronger root system develops without them.

Getting the most
out of your exterior decor means...

Gleditsia triacanthos var. inermis
Thornless Honeylocust

...eavesdrop on the susurrating leaves

"**Many of our clients ask for the classics because they want trees that remind them of their childhood, although the new varieties – which are often hardier and more disease resistant – are very popular too.**"

Étienne Bisaillon, BOTANIX
Ferme Florale, Saint-Bruno

Magnolia loebneri
'Leonard Messel'
Leonard Messel Magnolia

Malus 'Sir Lancelot'
'Sir Lancelot' Crabapple

...to see heaven in a wildflower

Sorbus aucuparia 'Cardinal Royal'
European Mountain Ash

...witness a birds' banquet

...breathe in spring's subtle scent

Acer freemanii 'Autumn Blaze'
'Autumn Blaze' Maple

Unquestionably one of the most beautiful Maples, with its large, dense, ovoid form and magnificent autumnal foliage, mixing shades of orange and scarlet. A vigorous but slow-growing tree that tolerates dry spells. For wide-open spaces.

☼	↔ 6 to 8 m	↕ 12 to 15 m	ZONE 4	◗

Acer ginnala
Flame Amur Maple

spirit
style

This globe-shaped Maple will make an interesting contrast with your garden — both in spring, with its scented flowers and in fall, with its rewarding colours. Tolerant of urban conditions.

☼	☁	↔ 6 m	↕ 6 m	ZONE 3a	♧

Acer negundo 'Flamingo'
'Flamingo' Boxelder

A small but rapid-growing tree with leaves that are sprayed in white and pink, and samaras that last into winter.

☼	↔ 6 m	↕ 6 m	ZONE 4b	◗

Acer negundo 'Kelly's Gold'
Golden Leaved Boxelder

Give it full sun to bring out the eponymous gold in the greenish leaves before they turn red in the fall. A rapid grower with several trunks that do not produce samaras.

☼	☁	↔ 5 m	↕ 5 m	ZONE 4a	♧

BOTANIX Experts by nature

Acer platanoides
Norway Maple

With its straight trunk and globular crown, this is a majestic and imposing tree. The many leaves emerge early to create an impenetrable shadow. Expect these qualities: quick growth, immunity to pollution, tolerance to dryness and disease resistance.

| ☼ | ☁ | ↔ 12 m | ↕ 20 m | ZONE 4b | ♀ | 🐦 |

Acer platanoides 'Columnare'
'Columnare' Norway Maple

A beautiful, erect, columnar tree with dark green leaves that turn bright yellow in autumn. Perfect for a small garden, this vigorous Maple can grow in mostly any soil and tolerates urban conditions.

| ☼ | ↔ 4.5 m | ↕ 15 m | ZONE 4b | ⬙ | 🐦 |

Acer platanoides 'Drummondii'
Silver Variegated Maple

As long as you remember to prune the branches that don't feature the remarkable white splattering on their leaves, you'll have a unique tree with its ascending, spreading branches incongruously supporting its remarkable foliage. Disease- and pollution-resistant.

| ☼ | ↔ 6 m | ↕ 10 m | ZONE 5 | ♀ | ✂ |

Acer platanoides 'Globosum'
'Globosum' Norway Maple

A grafted, spherical cultivar with a straight trunk and dense, shiny green foliage. A fantastic ornamental for small spaces and symmetrical gardens.

| ☼ | ☁ | ↔ 5 m | ↕ 4 m and + | ZONE 5 | ♀ |

Trees

Acer platanoides 'Princeton Gold'
'Princeton Gold' Norway Maple

'Princeton Gold' is definitely an attention getter. This hardy, oval tree sports thick chartreuse-yellow foliage – bringing both light and shadow to your garden.

☀ ↔ 8 m | ↕ 13 m | **ZONE 4**

Acer platanoides 'Royal Red'
'Royal Red' Norway Maple

Appreciated for the shade it provides, 'Royal Red' also has an interesting grey bark that splits open with age, and shiny, dark, round leaves that stay on till late autumn. Tolerates urban conditions, but needs wide, open spaces.

☀ ↔ 9 m | ↕ 12 m | **ZONE 4b**

Acer rubrum
Red Maple

In a natural, humid environment, this Maple produces flower bunches before leafing. Of equal interest are its reddish bark and red stemmed-tips, particularly in autumn when these colours complement the yellow, orange and scarlet leaves.

☀ ↔ 8 m | ↕ 15 m | **ZONE 3b**

Acer saccharum
Sugar Maple

The Sugar Maple slowly grows into a superb, gigantic tree that adds value to any landscape with its intensely coloured autumnal foliage. This is the tree that's normally tapped for its sap to produce maple sugar. In rich, well drained soil, it isn't troubled by urban pollution.

☀ ☁ ↔ 25 m | ↕ 25 m | **ZONE 4**

BOTANIX Experts by nature

Betula papyrifera 'Renaissance Reflection'
'Renaissance Reflection' Paper Birch

New

The Renaissance series was created to resist the Birch borer that is currently killing the Birch population. Given sufficient sun and damp soil, this oval cultivar grows quickly. The dark green leaves turn yellow in autumn.

☼ | ↔ 8 m | ↕ 20 m | ZONE 3 | ◯

Betula pendula 'Rocky Mountain Splendor'
'Rocky Mountain Splendor' European Birch

New

A vigorous, slightly weeping hybrid developed to resist insect damage and increase hardiness. Like most Birches, its leaves turn yellow in fall.

☼ | ↔ 9 m | ↕ 15 m | ZONE 4 | ◯

Catalpa speciosa
Northern Catalpa

global village *style*

Highly decorative: irregular form, heart-shaped leaves, and strongly scented white flowers. This quick grower is such a striking plant you definitely won't want to crowd it. The leaves emerge late in spring.

☼ | ↔ 10 m | ↕ 15 m | ❀ Summer | ZONE 5 | ◯

Celtis occidentalis
Common Hackberry

A particularly attractive tree, with its a symmetrical form, distinctively rugged bark and dark purple fruit that attracts birds and the usual small suspects. Very hardy and pollution resistant.

☼ | ☁ | ↔ 7 m | ↕ 15 m | ZONE 4 | ◯

Elaeagnus angustifolia
Russian Olive

With its silver branches, irregular profile, typical of this species, unique leaf colouration and texture, and abundant flowering of small scented blooms, this is a very seductive shade tree you'll want to give pride of place to in your garden. Hardy and resistant.

☀ ↔ 6 m ↕ 8 m ❀ Summer ZONE 3

Fraxinus americana 'Autumn Purple'
'Autumn Purple' White Ash

'Autumn Purple' was developed for better resistance and better fall colour. Non-fruiting, but it adapts well to all urban conditions and soil types.

☀ ↔ 7 m ↕ 16 m ZONE 4

Fraxinus pennsylvanica 'Northern Treasure'
'Northern Treasure' Ash

A large, hardy, highly adaptive and quick-growing Red Oak that likes damp soil. The samaras cling to its oval form throughout winter.

☀ ↔ 8 m ↕ 15 m ZONE 2

Ginkgo biloba
Maidenhair Tree

A colossal tree with distinctive, fanlike leaves. A slow-grower that lives for a long, long time. Pollution resistant and able to adapt to all soils. Give it lots of space, to better appreciate its superb yellow raiment in fall.

☀ ↔ 8 m ↕ 20 m ZONE 4

Gleditsia triacanthos var. inermis 'Skyline'
'Skyline' Thornless Honeylocust

The long, delicate and ethereal foliage provides that much-coveted filtered shade. Place it where you don't mind it growing quickly to dominate the landscape. Highly tolerant of urban conditions and any well-drained soil.

☼ ↔ 12 m ↕ 15 m ZONE 4

Gleditsia triacanthos var. inermis 'Sunburst'
'Sunburst' Thornless Honeylocust

This variety has telltale, yellow-gold foliage in early summer, an irregular shape and widespread branches. A great addition to your landscape that doesn't produce pods, and casts a very pleasant, light shadow.

☼ ↔ 10 m ↕ 12 m ZONE 4b

Liriodendron tulipifera
Tulip Magnolia

Its characteristic tulip-shaped foliage will add a hint of the exotic to your garden. Its upright branches gradually descend with age, so the older trees look more rounded. Casts a dense shade. Once the tree is about six years old, you'll be able to experience the pretty, scented, greenish-yellow flowers with their orange corolla.

☼ ☁ ↔ 7 m ↕ 10 m ❁ Summer ZONE 5

Prunus virginiana 'Shubert'
'Shubert' Choke Cherry

This attractively-formed tree is perfect for small gardens with its decorative foliage that starts out green and rapidly turns burgundy. Numerous pink bunches of small flowers transform into little black cherries that attract birds. Hardy, undemanding and tolerant of urban conditions.

☼ ↔ 4 m ↕ 7 m ❁ Spring ZONE 3

Trees

Quercus 'Crimson Spire'
'Crimson Spire' Oak

New

As its name implies, this is a narrow-columned, autumnal splendour wrapped in dark red leaves… that don't drop until following spring! Resistant to fungal diseases, but needs a deep, well drained rooting medium.

☼	↔ 3 m	↕ 15 m	ZONE 4	⬙

Quercus macrocarpa
Bur Oak

An extremely hardy and long-living species that slowly becomes a gigantic tree scaled for large spaces. Its thick foliage provides shade whether the large crown is sporting shiny green leaves in summer or orange ones in autumn. Birds and sundry garden creatures love its acorns.

☼	↔ 20 m	↕ 20 m	ZONE 2b	◯

Quercus palustris
Swamp Oak

Prized for its pyramidal form and straight trunk, which, combined with the finely dentated leaves to make the quintessential tree. In autumn, birds and squirrels twitter and scurry among the bright red leaves, still clinging to its outstretched limbs in search of delicious acorns. Likes rich, damp soil and laughs at urban pollution.

☼	↔ 13 m	↕ 22 m	ZONE 5	⬠

Quercus robur 'Fastigiata'
Pedunculate Oak

An interesting columnar tree whose elegance and golden brown autumn leaves continue to thrill into winter, when it will make a pleasing contrast with the green of your conifers.

☼	☁	↔ 3 m	↕ 15 m	ZONE 4b	⬙

Quercus rubra
Red Oak

Give this tree enough space and it will grow to amazing heights and outlive you by a few decades. Valued also for its horizontal branches and spreading habit, this hardy tree adapts well to urban conditions if provided with depth for its roots. Its leaves turn red in fall.

| ☼ | ↔ 12 m | ↕ 25 m | ZONE 3 | 🌳 |

Robinia pseudoacacia 'Purple Robe'
'Purple Robe' Black Locust

spirit
style

A straight-stemmed tree with attractive clusters of fragrant flowers, and alternate leaflets that emerge as bronzed-red buds from the slightly spiny branches before opening to dark green. The elongated pods last into winter.

| ☼ | ↔ 7 m | ↕ 9 m | ✿ Summer | ZONE 4-5 | ♀ | 🌰 |

Trees

Salix alba 'Tristis'
Golden Weeping Willow

The magnificent weeping form, and large, rounded, irregularly-flared crown will add a touch of nobility to your garden. A swift-growing tree with vigorous roots that need a lot of room, and raw-sienna branches that scrape the ground.

| ☼ | ↔ 15 m | ↕ 15 m | ZONE 4a | 🌿 |

Sorbus aucuparia 'Rossica'
European Mountain Ash

global village
style

This variety is coveted for its beautiful, white spring flowering and subsequent red berries. The dark green leaves with their velvet-textured undersides turn red in autumn. A hardy Ash that resists bacterial attack and thrives in well-drained soil.

| ☼ | ↔ 6 m | ↕ 8 m | ✿ Spring | ZONE 3 | 🌲 | 🐦 |

Sorbus thuringiaca 'Fastigiata'
'Fastigiata' Mountain Ash

This Ash is admired for many factors, not the least of which are its orange-yellow bark, corymbs of white flowers in May, lobed foliage that turns red in fall, and orange berries. Well loved, also, for its short trunk and narrow shape by those with small yards.

☀	↔ 3 to 6 m	↕ 6 to 8 m	❀ Spring	ZONE 4		

Syringa reticulata 'Golden Eclipse'
'Golden Eclipse' Japanese Tree Lilac

Gorgeous, creamy white panicles adorn the light green leaves at the end of spring and beginning of summer. At the same time, the leaves' centres gradually become darker green, and gold spreads out from the toothed leaf margins, like a time-lapse eclipse. One of the top Japanese Lilacs.

☀	☁	↔ 4 m	↕ 7 m	❀ Summer	ZONE 4			

Syringa reticulata 'Ivory Silk'
'Ivory Silk' Japanese Tree Lilac

In early summer you'll probably notice the enticing perfume of the spectacular, creamy white blooms before you even see them. Deadhead to stimulate further flowering. With its svelte, limbless trunk and round crown, it works very well growing out of the centre of a flower bed. Hardy. Tolerates dryness and pollution.

☀	☁	↔ 4 m	↕ 8 m	❀ Summer	ZONE 2			

Tilia americana 'Redmond'
'Redmond' American Linden

Redmond's dark foliage doesn't quite hide the little flowers that delight your sense of smell from afar. A sure bet, tolerant of urban conditions and quite hardy.

☀	☁	↔ 10 m	↕ 15 m	❀ Summer	ZONE 3		

Tilia cordata 'Corzam'
'Corzam' Littleleaf Linden

New

A narrow, pyramidal tree with dense, thick and shiny foliage. Valued both for its shade value and the highly fragrant, yellow flowers. A proud tree that adapts to all soils and will enhance any environment.

☼ ☁ ↔ 5 m ↕ 15 m ZONE 3a

Tilia cordata 'Glenleven'
'Glenleven' Littleleaf Linden

This hardy, quick grower needs little maintenance to grow its many large, thick leaves into a pyramidal form that creates a dense shadow. In early summer, small, white flowers give off a powerful perfume.

☼ ☁ 5 to 7 m 10 to 15 m Summer ZONE 3

Trees

Tilia cordata 'Greenspire'
'Greenspire' Littleleaf Linden

Despite its relatively small leaves, this Basswood grows so big that it can still cast a considerable portion of your garden into deep shade. In early summer, small creamy-white pendant flowers give off an attractive, powerful aroma. Hardy and pollution resistant.

☼ ☁ 10 m 15 m Summer ZONE 3

Ulmus 'Pioneer'
'Pioneer' Elm

Place it where there's a lot of space so it can grow to its colossal size and show off its large spherical crown. The dark green leaves adopt a bronze tint in the fall. Very hardy, disease-resistant and unfazed by urban conditions.

☼ 10 m 15 m ZONE 3a

Amelanchier canadensis
Shadblow Serviceberry

global village style

This little multi-trunk tree is the hardiest Amelanchier. Its green leaves with white undersides, turn orange yellow in the fall. Shadblow's highly decorative, dark, juicy and sweet berries attract birds.

| ☀ | ☁ | ↔ 3 m | ↕ 7 m | ❀ Spring | ZONE 4 | | | |

Betula pendula 'Youngii'
Young's Weeping Birch

A beautiful addition to a small garden or waterscape, with its irregular cascading branches bending down to the ground. Attach to a tutor from where you want the branches to droop in order to avoid a low sprawl and maintain its majestic beauty.

| ☀ | ↔ 6 m | ↕ 4 m | ZONE 3 | | |

Caragana arborescens 'Lobergii'
Siberian Pea Tree

In the spring, this Caragana's fairylike foliage and numerous yellow flowers are quite astonishing. Its irregular, slightly weeping form will bring originality to your garden throughout the year. A hardy tree that adapts to all soils.

| ☀ | ↔ 2.5 m | ↕ 3.5 m | ❀ Spring/Summer | ZONE 2b | |

Caragana arborescens 'Pendula'
Weeping Peashrub

You'll love the abundant yellow blooms that emerge from the bright green foliage as the warm summer days begin. Very hardy and undemanding, particularly when planted in full sun. Its little berry bunches attract birds.

| ☀ | ☁ | ↔ 1.5 m | ↕ 2 m | ❀ Spring/Summer | ZONE 2b | | |

Caragana arborescens 'Walker'
'Walker' Peashrub

Feathery, finely dentated leaves, similar to a fern. Branches that start out erect, then droop like a Weeping Willow. Generous flowering, and a highly tolerant character. What's not to like?

☀	↔ 1.5 m	↕ 2 m	✿ Spring/ Summer	ZONE 2b	⌂

Catalpa bignonioides 'Nana'
Umbrella Catalpa

Its straight, slim trunk and dense, wide crown give this tree its charm and its common name. A quick-growing dwarf variety with large, heart-shaped leaves, perfect for a small garden... when protected from strong winds.

☀	↔ 3 m	↕ 2 m	ZONE 5b	♀

Cercidiphyllum japonicum 'Pendula'
Weeping Katsura

New

A delightful little tree with rounded, dentated foliage that goes from bronze, to aquamarine, to a golden orange in fall. As a last hurrah, the falling leaves actually exhale a slight caramel aroma.

☀	⛅	↔ 5 m	↕ 10 m	ZONE 5b	⌂

Fraxinus excelsior 'Pendula'
Weeping Ash

A small but vigorous Ash, grafted onto a straight trunk, leaving its drooping branch-ends to support a delicate foliage. Likes deep, fertile and loose soil.

☀	↔ 3 m	↕ 4 m	ZONE 5	⛲

Ginkgo biloba 'Mariken'
'Mariken' Maidenhair

New

This small, compact tree can definitely be considered original. Its tender green, slightly dentated fan-like leaves will add a decidedly exotic touch to your patio or small garden. It's a slow grower, proven to be resistant to diseases, insects and urban pollution.

		↔	↕	❀		
☼	☁	1 m	2 m	Spring	ZONE 3a	

Halimodendron halodendron
Salt Tree

A graceful, bushy tree with gently arching branches covered in silver green leaves, which are joined, in summer, by pinkish mauve flowers that give off an aroma reminiscent of almonds. Tolerates difficult conditions and all well-drained soil.

	↔	↕	❀			
☼	1.5 m	2 m	Summer	ZONE 2		

Ginkgo biloba 'Pendula'
Weeping Maidenhair

This cultivar will definitely stand out in your garden, with its irregular form, parasol silhouette, weeping branches and fan-shaped leaves. Its soft-green leaves turn gold in fall. Resists urban pollution.

	↔	↕		
☼	2.5 m	2.5 m	ZONE 3	

Maackia amurensis
Amur Maackia

With its globular form, shiny bark, attractive foliage and odoriferous flowers that smell like freshly cut hay, this Maackia is an interesting tree. Better yet, it's so highly tolerant that you can plant it nearly anywhere under the sun.

	↔	↕			
☼	6 m	8 m	ZONE 3b		

Magnolia loebneri 'Dr Merrill'
'Dr. Merrill' Magnolia

A fast-growing but not huge Magnolia with a large canopy and a rounded top. With its numerous, large, scented white flowers that come out before the leaves, it's ideal for a sunny spot in your garden. Requires winter protection.

| ☀ | ☁ | ↔ 3 m | ↕ 3 m | ✿ Spring | ZONE 5b | ♀ | ⚰ | △ |

Magnolia loebneri 'Leonard Messel'
Leonard Messel Magnolia

A superb, round-shaped Magnolia with slightly spreading, grey-tinged branches and large, 12-petalled flowers that precede leafing. Prefers rich, loose soil and requires winter protection.

| ☀ | ↔ 6 m | ↕ 5 m | ✿ Spring | ZONE 5b | ♀ | ⚰ | △ |

Magnolia soulangiana
Saucer Magnolia

This popular Magnolia has a distinctive spreading form. Before leafing, beautiful, tulip-shaped flowers with nine petals emerge to dazzle you with their shades of white, pink or purple. Pollution-tolerant but requires winter protection.

| ☀ | ☁ | ↔ 3 m | ↕ 3 m | ✿ Spring | ZONE 5b | ♀ | △ |

Magnolia soulangiana 'Susan'
'Susan' Magnolia

This variety with its many spreading branches and rounded crown produces a plethora of crimson buds that generate reddish purple, highly scented flowers before foliation. Give it lots of room to appreciate the complete spectacle of its unparalleled flowering and prune regularly forthwith.

| ☀ | ☁ | ↔ 3 m | ↕ 4 m | ✿ Spring | ZONE 3 | ♀ | ⚰ | ✂ |

Grafted Trees

Magnolia stellata 'Royal Star'
'Royal Star' Magnolia

The erect, branching limbs of this Magnolia form a rounded silhouette as it ages. Before foliation, innumerable pink flower-buds open to magnificent, scented, pure white double flowers. Although it's one of the hardiest Magnolias, you're better off protecting it in winter.

☀ ☁ ↔ 2 m | ↕ 3 m | ❀ Spring | ZONE 5b

Morus alba 'Pendula'
Weeping Mulberry

Kids love this tree – not only for its edible raspberry-like fruit that varies from creamy pink to purplish red, but also for its weeping dome that makes a great secret outdoor playhouse. You'll love it for its tolerance to pollution and dry spells, as well as its ability to fit into a small space.

☀ | ↔ 3 m | ↕ 3 m | ZONE 4b

Prunus cerasifera 'Newport'
'Newport' Cherry Plum

New

A study in contrasts: the purple spring leaves turn copper in autumn, and the scented white spring flowers give way to small burgundy fruit. Striking and highly resistant if given a well-drained soil.

☀ | ↔ 5 m | ↕ 5 m | ❀ Spring | ZONE 5

Robinia pseudoacacia 'Twisty Baby'
'Twisty Baby' Black Locust

Great for small spaces with its slightly twisted branches and leaves, limited crown-spread and the light shade it casts. Unlike other Robinias, this variety does not flower, but is definitely an interesting addition to a small urban garden.

☀ | ↔ 1.5 m | ↕ 2.5 m | ZONE 4

BOTANIX Experts by nature

Salix caprea 'Pendula'
Kilmarnock Willow

A classic addition to small gardens and waterscapes thanks to its weeping branches, rounded form and dark green leaves with gray undersides that flicker playfully in the breeze. An undemanding rapid grower.

☀		↔ 1.5 m	↕ 1.5 to 2 m	❀ Spring	ZONE 4	⋔

Syringa juliana 'Hers'
Weeping Lilac Standard

Here's a heart-stopper that features abundant drooping lavender panicles on the weeping branches in spring... and sporadically through-out the summer. Its leaves, being small and finely toothed, will bring character and novelty to your garden throughout the season.

☀	☁	↔ 2 m	↕ 1 m	❀ Spring/Summer	ZONE 4b	⋔

Syringa meyeri 'Palibin'
Dwarf Korean Lilac on stem

oasis
style

You'll have a hard time noticing anything else in your garden in the springtime — when this Lilac becomes a mound of fuchsia-pink, perfumed flowers that hypnotize butterflies. This slow grower tolerates dryness and urban pollution, but appreciates well-drained soil. A solid addition to any garden.

☁	↔ 2 m	↕ 2 m	❀ Spring	ZONE 3	♀	⚘	🦋

Ulmus glabra 'Pendula'
Weeping Wych Elm

This tree has a rare shape that could serve you well if you're looking for horizontal branches with drooping tips to occupy a space that's wider than high. An excellent choice when you're looking for a squat umbrella near a water feature or over low perennials.

☀	↔ 6 m	↕ 3 m	ZONE 4b	⋔

Grafted Trees

Malus 'Brandywine'
'Brandywine' Crabapple

☀	↔ 5 m	↕ 3 m	❀ Spring	ZONE 4
				Applescabs resistance: Average

Malus 'Centurion'
'Centurion' Crabapple

☀	↔ 4 m	↕ 5 m	❀ Spring	ZONE 4 a
				Applescabs resistance: Excellent

Malus 'Coccinella'
'Coccinella' Crabapple

☀	↔ 3 m	↕ 5 m	❀ Spring	ZONE 3 a
				Applescabs resistance: Good

Malus 'Dolgo'
'Dolgo' Crabapple

☀	↔ 4 m	↕ 7 m	❀ Spring	ZONE 2
				Applescabs resistance: Excellent

Malus 'Harvest Gold'
'Harvest Gold' Crabapple

☀	↔ 4 m	↕ 5 m	❀ Spring	ZONE 3
				Applescabs resistance: Excellent

Malus 'Madonna'
'Madonna' Crabapple

☀	↔ 3 m	↕ 5 m	❀ Spring	ZONE 4
				Applescabs resistance: Excellent

Malus 'Red Jade'
'Red Jade' Crabapple

☀	↔	↕	❀	ZONE
	5 m	3 m	Spring	2
				Applescabs resistance: Good

Malus 'Royal Beauty'
'Royal Beauty' Crabapple

☀	↔	↕	❀	ZONE
	3 m	2 m	Spring	3 b
				Applescabs resistance: Excellent

Malus 'Royal Splendor'
'Royal Splendor' Crabapple

☀	↔	↕	❀	ZONE
	5 m	6 m	Spring	3a
				Applescabs resistance: Excellent

Malus 'Sir Lancelot'
'Sir Lancelot' Crabapple

☀	☁	↔	↕	❀
		2 m	2.5 m	Spring
ZONE 3				Applescabs resistance: Good

Malus prunifula 'Rinki'
'Rinki' Crabapple

☀	☁	↔	↕	❀
		1.5 m	5 m	Spring
ZONE 3a				Applescabs resistance: Good

Malus sargentii 'Tina'
'Tina' Crabapple

☀	↔	↕	❀	ZONE
	3 m	2 m	Spring	3
				Applescabs resistance: Excellent

Living in Abundance

Fruit trees have been part of our horticultural tradition for generations. One never tires of fruit trees: from admiring the delicate flowers and appreciating their fragrant perfume in the spring to gathering the delicious fruit at harvest time. The ultimate marriage of beauty and utility!

The species in this guide were selected, of course, with gardeners in mind, so hardiness and disease resistance were paramount, but fruit trees offer many other, equally important joys:

- Spring flowering
- Ornamental value
- The gratification of picking fruit in one's own garden
- The olfactory, gustatory and tactile pleasures of freshly picked, sun-ripened fruit
- The joy of cooking your own sinful fruit desserts
- Sharing the harvest

The golden rules

It's easy to grow fruit trees, as long as you're mindful of the following:

- Disease resistance
- Hardiness
- Pollination requirements
- Size at maturity

For a good harvest, you'll want to respect these conditions:

- Maximum sunlight
- Annual fertilization
- Annual pruning

At **botanix.com** you'll find a cornucopia of advice on planting and pruning fruit trees.

Malus 'Liberty'
'Liberty' Apple Tree

BOTANIX Experts by nature

Did you know?

- Fruit trees are either **self fertile** or **dioecious**. The first has both staminate (male) flowers and pistillate (female) flowers on the same plant, so they are fertilized by their own pollen and produce fruit even if grown in isolation. Dioecious fruit trees, meanwhile, must be fertilized by another variety of the same species. To produce fruit, the two trees must be within 200 to 300 m of each other.

Name	Zone	Width	Height	Fruit Colour	Fertility	Use	Comments and Use
'Bing' Cherry	5	4 m	4 m	Golden-red. Sweet.	S	Raw/Cooked	Pollinated by 'Van' or 'Stella'. Prune in autumn.
'Carmine Jewel' Cherry	3	2.5 m	2.5 m	Red. Red flesh.	F	Raw/Cooked	Very hardy. Prune in autumn.
'Evans' Cherry	3	3 m	3 m	Red. Orange flesh.	F	Raw/Cooked	Very productive. Prune in autumn.
'Meteor' Cherry	5	2 m	3 m	Red. Yellow flesh.	F	Raw/Cooked	Slightly acidic fruit. Prune in autumn.
'Montmorency' Cherry	3	3 m	5 m	Red. Yellow flesh.	F	Raw/Cooked	Slightly acidic fruit. Prune in autumn.
'Stella' Cherry	5	4 m	4 m	Black. Sweet black flesh.	F	Raw/Cooked	Large, sweet and juicy fruit. Prune in autumn.
'Reliance' Peach	5b	3 m	5 m	Yellow. Yellow flesh.	F	Raw	Ornamental value for flowers. Very hardy. Prune in autumn.
'Chojuro' Asian Pear	5	5 m	4 m	Orange-brown.	F	Raw	Pollinated by 'Bartlett' or 'Shinseki'. Prune in winter.
'Shinseiki' Asian Pear	5	5 m	4 m	Yellowish green.	F	Raw	Round fruit. Prune in winter.
'Anjou' Dwarf Pear	5	4 to 5 m	8 to 10 m	Yellowish green. White flesh.	S	Raw	Good pollinator. Prune in winter.
'Bartlett' Pear	5	5 m	6 m	Yellowish green.	S	Raw/Cooked	Subtle-tasting fruit. Pollinated by 'Clapp'. Prune in winter.
'Beauté Flamande' Pear	3	5 m	6 m	Yellow with ruddy.	F	Raw	Large, excellent fruit. The hardiest. Prune in winter.
'Bosc' Pear	5	5 m	6 m	Brown	S	Raw/Cooked	Quality fruits that are good for preserves. Prune in winter.
'Clapp' Pear	4	5 m	6 m	Yellow	S	Raw	Eat immediately after harvesting. Pollinated by 'Bartlett' or 'Beauté Flamande'. Prune in winter.
'Fleming Beauty' Pear	4	5 m	6 m	Yellow	S	Raw	Very productive. Prune in winter.
'Luscious' Pear	4	5 m	5 m	Yellow with pink highlights. Sweet.	S	Raw	Fruit resembles 'Bartlett'. Prune in winter.
'John' Pear	3	6 m	10 m	Yellowish green to yellow-red.	S	Raw/Cooked	Yellow, juicy fruit. Pollinated by 'Ure'. Prune in winter.
'Hardy Ure' Pear	3	5 m	6 m	Yellowish green. Sweet.	S	Raw	Highly applescabs resistant. Small pears. Prune in winter.
'Belmac' Apple	4	4 m	4 m	Red and green. Sweet white flesh.	S	Raw/Cooked	Keep well. Very resistant to applescabs. Slightly acidic fruit. Prune in winter.
'Britegold' Apple	3b	3 m	3 m	Yellow. Sweet.	S	Raw	Very resistant to applescabs. Prune in winter.

Fertility: S = self-sterile / F = self-fertile

BOTANIX Experts by nature

Name	Zone	Width	Height	Fruit Colour	Fertility	Use	Comments and Use
'Empire' Apple	4	5 m	5 m	Red	S	Raw/Cooked	Fruit resembles 'McIntosh'. Can be kept for a long time. Prune in winter.
'Honeycrisp' Apple	3b	5 m	5 m	Red-marbled yellow.	S	Raw	Exceptionally crunchy and juicy. Can be kept up to seven months. Prune in winter.
'Jonafree' Apple	4	8 m	6 m	Red	S	Raw	Crunchy, juicy fruit. Very resistant to applescabs and bacterial burning. Replaces the 'Cortland'. Prune in winter.
'Liberty' Apple	4	5 m	5 m	Red streaked with yellow.	S	Raw	Crunchy, juicy fruit. Very resistant to applescabs. Replaces the 'McIntosh'. Prune in winter.
'Lobo' Apple	3	5 m	5 m	Red	S	Raw/Cooked	Large, firm fruit that can be kept well. Prune in winter.
'McIntosh Savio' Apple	3	5 m	5 m	Red	S	Raw	Hardier than the 'McIntosh'. Prune in winter.
'Red Melba' Apple	3	5 m	5 m	Red	S	Raw/Cooked	Can be kept a short while. Vigorous and hardy. Prune in winter.
'Redfree' Apple	4	5 m	5 m	Red	S	Raw	Very resistant to applescabs and very hardy. Replaces the 'Paula Red'. Prune in winter.
'Richelieu' Apple	3	5 m	5 m	Red on green.	S	Raw	Crunchy, mild and slightly acidic fruit. Very resistant to applescabs. Replaces the 'Lobo'. Can be kept well. Prune in winter.
'Rouville' Apple	3	5 m	5 m	Red on green. Creamy white, sweet flesh.	S	Raw	Large, sweet and juicy fruit. Very resistant to applescabs. Replaces the 'Jersey Mac'. Prune in winter.
'Burbank' Plum	4	6 m	6 m	Dark red. Sweet yellow flesh.	S	Raw	Pollinated by 'Early Golden'. Prune in autumn.
'Damas Bleu' Plum	3	3 m	3 m	Blue. Sweet flesh.	F	Raw	Productive and very hardy. Prune in autumn.
'Early Golden' Plum	4	6 m	6 m	Dark yellow. Sweet yellow flesh.	S	Raw	Pollinated by 'Burbank'. Prune in autumn.
'Italienne' Plum	5	6 m	6 m	Black. Sweet greenish flesh.	S	Raw/Cooked	Pollinated by 'Mount Royal'. Prune in autumn.
'Mirabelle' Plum	4	6 m	6 m	Yellow-orange. Sweet pulpy flesh.	F	Raw	Small fruit of an excellent quality. Prune in autumn.
'Mount Royal' Plum	3	6 m	6 m	Blue. Firm yellow flesh.	F	Raw	Very popular. Prune in autumn.
'Reine Claude' Plum	4	7 m	8 m	Yellow	S	Raw	Round, juicy and sweet fruit. Prune in autumn.

Forever green

There is nothing quite like a conifer! In winter, when deciduous leaves disappear, conifers guard the fort and contribute a dash of green to the white landscape. After a snowstorm, the beauty of their burdened branches is unassailable!

Like all trees, conifers play an important part in landscaping. They structure the garden, add a variety of textures and foliage, or create a magnificent hedge that serves as a hiding place and larder for wildlife.

Our Nordic climate is particularly welcoming to conifers, whose hardiness is attested by their omnipresence in our boreal forests. Recent cultivars, which are even more hardy and disease-resistant, increase the available collection for evergreen-loving gardeners.

Evergreens make excellent windbreaks as they attenuate the cooling and drying properties of wind, and their dense, opaque foliage protects you from unwanted noise and intruding eyes.

Above all, conifers serve the greatest function: adding beauty with their charm and character, and calmness with their fine foliage.

Picea
Spruce

Conifers: a thousand and one uses

Whatever the season, whatever the reason, whatever their shape or whatever their height, conifers just keep on giving, and will always please your eyes.

- In isolation, they steal the spotlight. In groups, they add a deep-woods feel to group plantings, low walls, slopes or flower beds. In winter, they alone bear proud witness to the hidden delights of the summer season.

- Side by side, they form an impressive passageway or luxurious hedge. When carefully sculpted they evoke French gardens. Grown cheek by jowl, nothing gets through them.

- They provide structure when placed near other plants of various heights.

- As a ground cover, conifers offer a dense green carpet.

The play of form and colour

Although most conifers are naturally pyramid-shaped, like Fir and Spruce, there are many other forms, too: narrow, columnar, conical, globular, spreading, creeping and weeping. For visual and functional diversity, vary the plant shapes of your conifers.

The panoply of textures and foliage with subtle colouration, such as chartreuse, verdigris, silvered-green, dark-green, and golden yellow are a plus when planted separately, but when you these varieties are planted together, they form an unparalleled winter garden.

Small conifers grafted onto standards, which look so attractive in a small garden, porch or patio, are gaining in popularity. Please see the index at the end of this guide for our top-10 grafted-conifers list.

Thuja occidentalis 'Smaragd'
Emerald Green Cedar

Did you know?

- In autumn, the needles of some conifer varieties turn golden yellow before dropping. The European Larch, which is the only European conifer to lose its foliage in winter, is one of them, as is the Metasequoia.

Tips and Tricks

- The branch buds of some cultivars – such as Rainbow's End White Spruce – are brighter than their ancestors, creating a bicolour accent.

Conifers: a thousand and one uses

Picea sp.
Spruce

Great Presence

Choose your conifers carefully

If you're looking to have long-lasting conifers in your garden that add value in all seasons, you should do well to consider the following:

- Carefully choose their location, as they are sizable structural elements;
- Determine their size at maturity in order to avoid unpleasant surprises;
- Find out how hardy they are... and how demanding!

To get the inside story on planting, growing and caring for conifers, go to **botanix.com**, or consult an advisor at your BOTANIX garden centre.

Juniperus procumbens 'Nana'
Dwarf Japgarden Juniper

Luxuriance

Taxus cuspidata 'Nana'
Dwarf Japanese Yew

Texture

Pinus strobus cv.
White Pine

Conifers

Stability

Abies balsamea 'Nana'
Dwarf Balsam Fir

☼ ☁ ↔ 90 cm ↕ 60 cm **ZONE 3** ◯

This variety is slow growing and non-fruiting. With its compact, bushy and rounded form with a flat head, you'll want it to play a central role in your landscaping. Requires humidity.

Chamaecyparis pisifera 'Aurea-nana'
'Aurea-nana' False Cypress

New

☼ ↔ 1 m ↕ 90 cm **ZONE 4** ☁

The golden colour of the leaf buds contrasts nicely with the green of the mature foliage. In winter, it turns to bronze colour. This dwarf forms an irregular mound that's ideal for tight spaces.

Chamaecyparis pisifera 'Boulevard'
'Boulevard' False Cypress

☼ ↔ 90 cm ↕ 2 m **ZONE 4** △

A beautiful conifer with soft foliage that's bluish in summer and silver in winter. Perfect alone or in groups in a small garden, with its pyramidal form and restrained size.

Chamaecyparis pisifera 'Sun Gold'
'Sun Gold' False Cypress

☼ ↔ 1 m ↕ 60 cm **ZONE 4** ◯

A charming conifer, whose yellow early summer colour turns to olive green over the season. An attention-getter in a small garden that will thrive in well-drained soil.

Juniperus chinensis 'Blaauw'
'Blaauw' Chinese Juniper

☀ | ↔ 1 m | ↕ 1.5 m | ZONE 4a | ⌂ 🐦 ⌂

This attractive little funnel-shaped conifer has astonishing ascending branches with irregular blue-green foliage. Give it winter protection for the first few years and your garden will have a new star.

Juniperus chinensis 'Gold Lace'
'Gold Lace' Chinese Juniper

☀ | ↔ 1 m | ↕ 60 cm | ZONE 3 | 👑

The feathery leaves of the yellowest of all Junipers will not lose their colour throughout the year. The tips of its gracefully arching branches look like finely cut lace. With other Junipers or leafy trees it will make a pleasing contrast in your rock garden.

Juniperus chinensis 'Gold Star'
'Gold Star' Chinese Juniper

☀ | ↔ 2 m | ↕ 80 cm | ZONE 3a | 👑

Bluish green and gold-tipped foliage adorns this slim Juniper. Plant in a group or alone, in damp, well-drained soil.

Juniperus chinensis 'Mint Julep'
'Mint Julep' Chinese Juniper

☀ | ↔ 1.8 m | ↕ 1 m | ZONE 4 | 👑

When it reaches maturity it forms a large bush with semi-erect, intertwined and curving branches that will undoubtedly remind you of a fountain. Mint green needles adorn its drooping extremities. Looks good in every situation: on slopes, among other Junipers or with a variety of other plants.

Decorative Conifers

Juniperus chinensis 'Pfitzeriana Aurea'
'Pfitzeriana Aurea' Chinese Juniper

		↔ 1.5 m	↕ 1 m	ZONE 4	

A charming little Juniper with verdigris foliage and golden, drooping tips. By the end of summer, the needles have uniform, green-coloured tips. It's a strong and hardy plant that needs damp soil.

Juniperus communis 'Depressa Aurea'
'Depressa Aurea' Juniper

	↔ 1.8 m	↕ 60 cm	ZONE 2b	

The delicate foliage of this pretty little Juniper takes on a bright yellow colour that skews bronze at summer's end. It's a hardy plant that tolerates dry spells, but appreciates a well-drained soil.

Juniperus horizontalis 'Blue Chip'
'Blue Chip' Juniper

	↔ 1.2 m	↕ 25 cm	ZONE 3b	

'Blue Chip' grows into a stellar form. It's rampant branches with short silver-blue needles make it an ideal ground cover. Undemanding and hardy, as long as you give it a well-drained soil.

Juniperus horizontalis 'Ice Blue'
'Ice Blue' Juniper

	↔ 1 m	↕ 15 cm	ZONE 3	

This beauty will carpet a small wall with its tiny silver-blue foliage that turns violet in winter. Not only is it wind resistant, but it also it adapts to all soils – even the heaviest.

Juniperus horizontalis 'Limeglow'
'Limeglow' Juniper

☀	↔	↕	ZONE	
	2 m	60 cm	3	⌂

Its new lime-green buds rapidly turn bright yellow, then bronze at the end of the growing season. In a rockery or winter garden, it's simply magnificent. The fact that it's a slow grower makes it ideal for small gardens or tight spaces.

Juniperus horizontalis 'Plumosa Compacta'
'Plumosa Compacta' Juniper

☀	↔	↕	ZONE	
	1.2 m	40 cm	2	⌂

One of the most visually pleasing of the spreading conifers. In time, its foliage — grey-green in summer and purple in autumn — will form a sizable little mound. Very hardy and undemanding.

Juniperus horizontalis 'Wiltonii'
'Wiltonii' Juniper

☀	↔	↕	ZONE	
	1.2 m	15 cm	2b	⌂

The word «ground cover» seems inadequate to describe this Juniper: it forms an actual bluish carpet that would look great in your rock garden, covering a small wall or cascading over a slope. A very hardy plant that adapts to all soils and is unbowed by winds.

Juniperus procumbens 'Nana'
Dwarf Japgarden Juniper

global village style

☀	↔	↕	ZONE	
	1.2 m	20 cm	4b	⌂

A low-growing Juniper with few, thick, well covered branches. For maximum effect, let it trail over a low wall, cover a flat area or spread out in your rock garden. In order to preserve its beautiful greenish blue colour, cover with snow in the winter.

Decorative Conifers

Juniperus sabina 'Blue Danube'
'Blue Danube' Juniper

☀ ↔ 1.5 m ↕ 90 cm **ZONE 3** ☐

In the short time it takes to develop its mature, semi-erect, flared and bushy form, this hardy shrub will look like a bluish cloud with verdigris highlights.

Juniperus sabina 'Calgary Carpet'
'Calgary Carpet' Juniper

☀ ↔ 1.5 m ↕ 40 cm **ZONE 3** ☐

Bring a startling intensity to your garden all year round with this glorious moss-green foliage spreading out into the shape of a vase. Adapts to any condition, but appreciates well-drained soil.

Juniperus squamata 'Blue Star'
'Blue Star' Juniper

☀ ↔ 90 cm ↕ 50 cm **ZONE 4** ☐ △

A slightly flattened, compact, dwarf tree that will look great in your rock garden, even if ignored during dry spells, its blue needles will turn copper in late summer. Protect it in winter if your snow cover is not deep enough.

Juniperus squamata 'Holger'
'Holger' Juniper

☀ ↔ 1 m ↕ 40 cm **ZONE 4** ☐

'Holger' foliage starts with a contrasting yellow at the end of its branches. It will bring undeniable beauty and originality to a small garden area when used as a groundcover.

Microbiota decussata
Russian Arborvitae

☀ ⛅ ☁ ↔ 1.5 m ↕ 40 cm **ZONE 2** ♔

As its name indicates, it will tough out even the coldest winter. The soft texture of its foliage is reminiscent of a Thuja, with which it shares its common name: Arborvitae. On a low wall, in groups, on a slope, as a ground cover... wherever you put it, you'll love its copper tint in autumn and its forgiving nature!

Picea abies 'Little Gem'
'Little Gem' Norway Spruce

☀ ↔ 50 cm ↕ 50 cm **ZONE 3** ◯

This slow grower with short green needles that never fade is perfect for small gardens. Try this little ball of dense foliage, which turns conical with age, in your rock garden.

Picea abies 'Nidiformis'
'Nidiformis' Norway Spruce

☀ ☁ ↔ 1.5 m ↕ 80 cm **ZONE 3** ♔

A dwarf variety that spreads, and grows up to resemble a bird's nest. Though it seems to fit particularly well with other conifers, it also looks good with other shrubs and perennials. Tolerates light shade and requires damp, well-drained soil.

Picea glauca 'Rainbow's End'
'Rainbow's End' White Spruce

☀ ☁ ↔ 1.25 m ↕ 1.5 m **ZONE 3** ⌂

The young creamy-yellow buds of this dwarf variety create a marvellous contrast with the dense, dark green older foliage, forming a bicolour look that will brighten the rockery of any small garden. Tolerates urban pollution well, but fears wind.

Picea pungens 'Globosa'
'Globosa' Dwarf Spruce

| ☀ | ↔ 1.5 m | ↕ 1 m | ZONE 3 | ○ |

A compact, rounded dwarf that becomes pyramidal with age. A highly valued ornamental that will turn any garden bed or rockery into a success, yet is equally impressive when standing alone. A hardy Spruce that tolerates urban conditions well but needs cool soil.

Picea pungens 'Thume'
'Thume' Blue Spruce

| ☀ | ↔ 1 m | ↕ 1 m | ZONE 2 | ○ |

A compact Spruce that starts out rather flat, but becomes pyramidal with age. A slow grower that will work marvellously in a rockery or diminutive perennial-flower arrangement.

Pinus mugo var. pumilio
Swiss Mountain Pine

| ☀ | ⛅ | ↔ 1.2 m | ↕ 1.2 m | ZONE 2 | ☁ | ✂ |

This dwarf looks good in a rock garden or standing out from the landscape. Trimming its fascicles will keep it compact.

Pinus strobus 'Blue Shag'
'Blue Shag' White Dwarf

New

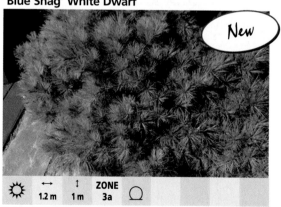

| ☀ | ↔ 1.2 m | ↕ 1 m | ZONE 3a | ○ |

This conifer forms a greenish-blue sphere that slowly turns silver. This compact dwarf is ideal for small gardens.

Pinus strobus 'Nana'
'Nana' White Dwarf

| ☀ | | ↔ 1.5 m | ↕ 1 m | ZONE 3 | ⌂ |

The answer for those looking for a pretty, compact bush with dense, greenish-blue needles and bright shoots. Wind resistant, it works well to structure a small garden, but it is not a city-dweller at all.

Taxus cuspidata 'Aurescens'
'Aurescens' Japanese Yew

New

| ☀ | ☁ | ↔ 1 m | ↕ 30 cm | ZONE 4 | ⌇ |

The golden shoots of this Yew – which are even brighter in full sun – make a felicitous contrast with the green of the mature foliage. Tolerates urban conditions, but be careful, humans don't tolerate ingesting its seeds.

Taxus cuspidata 'Capitata'
'Capitata' Japanese Yew

oasis style

| ☀ | ☁ | ↔ 2 m | ↕ 3 m | ZONE 4 | ⌄ | ⌂ |

The tufted, dull green foliage is sprinkled with lighter shoots in spring, and poisonous berries later in the year. Slow-growing and tolerant of pruning, but requiring protection from winter wind and cold, especially the first few years after planting.

Taxus media 'Densiformis'
'Densiformis' Yew

| ☀ | ☁ | ☁ | ↔ 2.5 m | ↕ 3 m | ZONE 5 | △ | ✂ |

A slow grower that makes an unusual hedge with its spreading habit and upright growth. Prune tips to maintain foliage density. Its fruit is non-comestible.

Taxus media 'Hicksii'
Hick's Yew

| ☀ | ⛅ | ☁ | ↔ 2 m | ↕ 1 m | ZONE 5 | ⌒ | △ |

Though it's upright branches are particularly well suited to create hedges, it will also look good elsewhere in your garden. A fast grower that needs winter protection. Its fruit is non-comestible.

Thuja occidentalis 'Danica'
'Danica' Arborvitae

| ☀ | ⛅ | ☁ | ↔ 60 cm | ↕ 1.2 m | ZONE 5 | △ |

This dwarf cultivar develops into a small sphere of thick, bright green foliage. Great for a rockery or small garden, easy to grow and tolerates all soil types.

Thuja occidentalis 'Golden Globe'
'Golden Globe' Arborvitae

| ☀ | ⛅ | ↔ 60 cm | ↕ 60 cm | ZONE 3 | ◯ |

With its erect branches starting at ground level and its evenly, rounded form, this is a highly decorative little shrub. To enjoy its golden colour at its best throughout the year, plant it in full sun but keep its trunk in the shade.

Thuja occidentalis 'Hetz Midget'
'Hetz Midget' Arborvitae

| ☀ | ↔ 1 m | ↕ 1 m | ZONE 4b | ◯ |

Superb, dense, storied and bright green foliage that never needs pruning. Grows slowly into a ball shape even in semishade, but put it in the sun and watch it really thrive.

Thuja occidentalis 'Little Giant'
'Little Giant' Arborvitae

| ☀ | ⛅ | ↔ 1.5 m | ↕ 1.5 m | ZONE 3 | ◯ |

A round, little bush, with a bright green colour that is maintained all year round. Since it takes well to pruning, use it for a border or low hedge. Tolerates semishade but does better in full sun. Likes cool, rich soil.

Thuja occidentalis 'Rheingold'
'Rheingold' White Cedar

| ☀ | ↔ 1.5 m | ↕ 1.25 m | ZONE 4 | △ | ◁ |

Rheingold's green foliage is intermingled with gold and bronze. Needs winter protection and deep, well-drained soil, but requires little maintenance.

Thuja occidentalis 'Teddy'
'Teddy' White Cedar

| ☀ | ↔ 60 cm | ↕ 60 cm | ZONE 4 | ◯ |

The delicate, bright green foliage of this Cedar is soft on the eye and to the touch. This slow growing little ball works well in a small flowerbed.

Tsuga canadensis 'Jeddeloh'
'Jeddeloh' Canadian Hemlock

| ☀ | ↔ 60 cm | ↕ 60 cm | ZONE 4 | ◯ |

This dwarf cultivar looks like it was developed especially for rock gardens. Shaped like a small, round heap with a flat top, its gently arching branches give it a graceful air. Tolerates sun, but prefers shade.

Decorative Conifers

Chamaecyparis nootkatensis 'Pendula'
Nootka False Cypress

global village *style*

This remarkable pyramidal conifer stretches out its branches and lets their tips cascade elegantly down. Protect it in winter, give it a rich, damp soil, then sit back and enjoy...

| ☀ | ↔ 3 m | ↕ 5 to 6 m | ZONE 5a | △ | ⌂ |

Juniperus chinensis 'Fairview'
'Fairview' Juniper

The superb, light green leaves with their blue highlights form a narrow pyramid. Grows quickly in a well-drained soil. Undemanding.

| ☀ | ↔ 1 m | ↕ 4 m | ZONE 4 | ⌂ |

Juniperus scopulorum 'Blue Heaven'
'Blue Heaven' Juniper

A magnificent, hardy Juniper that stays compact in its youth, then opens up over the years. Prune it to maintain density. Give it a well-drained soil, and winter protection for the first few years.

| ☀ | ↔ 1.5 m | ↕ 4 m | ZONE 2 | ⌂ | ✂ | ⌂ |

Juniperus scopulorum 'Moffet Blue'
'Moffet Blue' Juniper

A good choice for a small garden, as it is narrow and dense with a highly decorative blue-green foliage with silver highlights. Give it a well-drained soil, and winter protection for the first years.

| ☀ | ↔ 80 cm | ↕ 2.5 m | ZONE 4 | ⌂ | ⌂ |

Juniperus scopulorum 'Tolleson's Blue Weeping'
'Tolleson's Blue Weeping' Juniper

With its finely dentated blue-grey foliage that gives off a characteristic odour, and its majestic presence, you'll find this weeping Juniper will add a note of exoticism to the facade of your property or the edge of a watercourse.

| ☀ | ↔ 1.2 to 2 m | ↕ 2 to 3 m | ZONE 4b | ⋔ |

Juniperus scopulorum 'Wichita Blue'
'Wichita Blue' Juniper

This popular conical Juniper has the bluest foliage of any Conifer. Strikingly ornamental whether planted as a screen, alone, in groups, or mixed with other plants.

| ☀ | ↔ 90 cm | ↕ 3 m | ZONE 3b | ∩ |

Upright Conifers

Juniperus virginiana 'Blue Arrow'
'Blue Arrow' Juniper

global village style

With its elegant line, solid base and pretty little blue berries that last into winter, this bluish tree will anchor any landscape admirably and form an interesting contrast with so many other plants.

| ☀ | ↔ 60 to 80 cm | ↕ 2.5 m | ZONE 3 | ∩ | ◮ |

Larix decidua
European Larch

Grows rapidly until it becomes gigantic and striking, with its widespread branches and their down-turned tips. The soft, bright green needles turn golden yellow before falling. Give your European Larch lots of space, this beauty deserves it.

| ☀ | ↔ 8 m | ↕ 20 m | ZONE 3 | △ |

Larix decidua 'Pendula'
Weeping Larch

global
village
style

Being a Larch, its soft green foliage turns golden yellow in autumn. Its size varies according to the height of the graft. Works very nicely in a small garden with contrasting forms.

☀ ↔ 1 m ↕ 2 to 3 m **ZONE 3** ⬛

Picea abies 'Pendula'
Weeping Norway Spruce

Attach the head to a tutor to maintain its verticality, and allow the branches to reach down as far as the ground. Undemanding and hardy as long as it's grown in well-drained soil.

☀ ↔ 90 cm ↕ 3 m **ZONE 3b** ⬛

Picea glauca 'Pendula'
Weeping Spruce

This narrow tree with an undeniably eccentric shape, works uncannily well in a rock garden, small space or Japanese-style layout. It's short branches, covered in bluish green foliage grow downwards... until they reach the ground.

☀ ☁ ↔ 90 cm ↕ 2 to 4 m **ZONE 4** ⬛

Picea glauca var. albertiana 'Conica'
Dwarf Alberta Spruce

A wonderful addition to a small garden, thanks to its restrained conical shape, dense foliage and pale green leaves. Tolerates urban pollution but not winter winds.

☀ ↔ 90 cm ↕ 1.5 m **ZONE 4** △ ◭

Picea pungens 'Fat Albert'
'Fat Albert' Colorado Blue Spruce

A large, rounded pyramid with silver blue needles, on thick branches that look magnificent all year round. Very hardy and tolerant of urban conditions.

☀ | ↔ 2 to 3 m | ↕ 5 m | **ZONE 3** | △

Picea pungens glauca
Colorado Blue Spruce

It is hard to miss, this large, symmetrical, hardy spruce, with its vertical branches that spread out as it ages. The bright, soft needles on its branch tips contrast nicely with its older silver-blue foliage.

☀ | ↔ 5 m | ↕ 20 m | **ZONE 2** | △ | 🐦

Picea pungens glauca 'Baby Blue Eyes'
'Baby Blue Eyes' Colorado Spruce

New

A hardy semi-dwarf variety with needles that maintain their superb bright blue colour all year. With its large, regular conical shape and its upright trunk, this will no doubt be a major attraction in your small garden area.

☀ | ↔ 2.5 m | ↕ 5.5 m | **ZONE 3** | △

Pinus cembra
Swiss Stone Pine

This magnificent pine earns its place in your garden thanks to its pleasingly symmetrical, conical shape, its strong vertical branches and upright cones. Hardy and wind-resistant.

☀ | ↔ 4 m | ↕ 10 m | **ZONE 3a** | ⌂

Upright Conifers

Pinus nigra austriaca
Austrian Pine

Excellent as a standalone or wind-break, thanks to its uncompromisingly upright branches that create a dense pyramid. Undemanding, hardy and tolerant of urban conditions.

☀ ↔ 6 m ↕ 15 m **ZONE 4** △

Pinus strobus
White Pine

A huge fast grower that really wants a lot of space. Whether planted alone or as a windbreak, you'll love to see the way its shape is gradually transformed by the wind. Give this indigenous plant a damp, rich and well-drained soil and the urban conditions won't bother it at all.

☀ ⛅ ↔ 7 m ↕ 25 m **ZONE 3** △ 🦆

Pinus strobus 'Contorta'
'Contorta' White Pine

This hardy variety is unusual for its twisted, vertically oriented branches and stems, as well as for its curly greenish blue needles.

☀ ⛅ ↔ 3 m ↕ 6 m **ZONE 2b** ⋂

Pinus strobus 'Pendula'
Weeping White Pine

Whether it grows tall and thin or wide and low, the Weeping White Pine will astonish you with its singularity. Its branches, which drape down to the ground, are adorned with long, greenish blue needles. It's a botanical star that will give any garden an oriental look.

☀ ↔ 1.2 m ↕ 2 to 4 m **ZONE 4b** ⋔

Thuja occidentalis 'Boisbriand'
'Boisbriand' Cedar

A good choice for a group planting or rock garden, with its elongated oval form. Give it a humid environment and prune at will.

☀	☁	↔ 80 cm	↕ 1.5 m	**ZONE 3a**	⌂

Thuja occidentalis 'Brandon'
'Brandon' Cedar

Hardy, narrow and compact with a down-soft foliage that cries out to be caressed. Wind resistant and highly tolerant of pruning, easy to add a strong verticality to your yard.

☀	↔ 1.2 m	↕ 4 m	**ZONE 2a**	⌂

Thuja occidentalis 'Degroot's Spire'
'Degroot's Spire' Cedar

Give it a rich, damp soil and you'll have a narrow, columnar beauty with dense, textured, dark green foliage-spirals that form a rewarding contrast with just about any other plant you could have in your garden.

☀	☁	↔ 1 m	↕ 2 m	**ZONE 3b**	⌂

Thuja occidentalis 'Fastigiata'
Pyramid Cedar

This exceptionally beautiful cedar looks fantastic in groups, as a hedge, offsetting a permanent structure, or to frame a view. It is columnar, but occasionally develops two or three heads. Keep it in a humid area out of strong winds.

☀	☁	↔ 1.5 m	↕ 6 m	**ZONE 3b**	⌂

Thuja occidentalis 'Holmstrup'
'Holmstrup' Cedar

Frequently used to create a dense un-pruned hedge with its pyramidal, compact shape. Works well in small yards, too, when pruned. This variety resists very well to cold weather; the only acknowledgment it has of the winter months is the bronze tint its normally emerald-green foliage takes on in wintry weather.

☀ ☁ ↔ 80 cm ↕ 2 m **ZONE 3** △

Thuja occidentalis 'Pyramidalis'
'Pyramidalis' Cedar

The most popular of all Pyramidal Conifers. Similar to the Pyramid Cedar, although the base is wider. You might want to provide winter protection in order to safeguard its dense, soft foliage.

☀ ☁ ↔ 2 m ↕ 15 m **ZONE 3b** △ ⌂

Thuja occidentalis 'Smaragd'
Emerald Green Cedar

oasis style

The reason for Smaragd's popularity can be summed up very easily: it's simply beautiful. The upright branches produce a delicate, vibrant green, dense foliage that maintains its colour and soft tactile qualities all year round. Use it for a magnificent, luxurious hedge or as an excellent addition to an assemblage of Conifers.

☀ ☁ ↔ 1.2 m ↕ 3.5 m **ZONE 4** ⌂

Thuja occidentalis 'Sunkist'
'Sunkist' Cedar

'Sunkist' is a Pyramidal Conifer that you'll appreciate especially when its new yellow buds sprout out from the bright green foliage. Use it for unique hedge or as a contrast in a small garden.

☀ ↔ 80 cm ↕ 1.5 m **ZONE 4** △

Thuja occidentalis 'Unicorn'
'Unicorn' Cedar

New

In spring, watch its young buds go off in every direction, to create a dense, dark green foliage that turns olive green in winter. It naturally maintains a rather symmetrical, columnar form that needs very little trimming. Winter protection, however, is recommended.

☀ ☁ ↔ 60 cm ↕ 3 m ZONE 3

Thuja occidentalis 'Yellow Ribbon'
'Yellow Ribbon' Cedar

The aptly named 'Yellow Ribbon' maintains its dense, bright gold and yellow foliage throughout year, to form a narrow column that is best appreciated when it's not too crowded.

☀ ↔ 80 cm ↕ 2 m ZONE 3

Upright Conifers

Tsuga canadensis
Canadian Hemlock

A large pyramidal tree with gently falling branches that, with age, weep. It's an elegant indigenous tree that loves filtered light or any shady situation, as long as it's protected from the wind. Plant in well-drained soil and keep it damp.

☁ ☁ ↔ 8 m ↕ 20 m ZONE 4

Tsuga canadensis 'Pendula'
Weeping Canadian Hemlock

Gracefully weeping branches laden with dense, extremely dark green foliage cascade away from the trunk. Its height varies depending on how it's staked. Ideal in a Conifer garden or as the centre of a small arrangement. Protect from wind.

☁ ☁ ↔ 2 m ↕ 3 m ZONE 4

Beautiful...

in any season

In exterior decoration, shrubs are the furniture. They anchor the décor and give meaning to your flower beds. They serve many functions: focal point of the garden; giving curb value to your buildings, structure and garden accessories; bordering mass plantings; creating a visual screen near a pool; delineating flower beds by giving them a brief visual transition; defining spaces and providing landmarks. They're like living architecture in your garden, which is exactly why they're used to create hedges.

It's easy to find a reason to plant shrubs: masses of spring flowers, successive flowering, fruits that attract birds, autumn leaf colours, winter foliage... there's such a large range of ornamental shrubs on the market that you could practically create a garden with only shrubs and trees. Not only are they attractive to the eye, but they are also low-maintenance, so if you're looking for a way to create an intimate, attractive exterior space without investing much energy, shrubs are the way to go.

Come discover the new varieties of shrubs during your next visit to BOTANIX.

Syringa 'Tinkerbelle'
'Tinkerbelle' Lilac

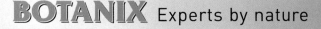

Variations on a theme

Thanks to the huge variety of species now available, you have your choice in terms of shape, foliage and successive flowering. In other words, shrubs help you create a garden that looks good all year round. Shrubs rule!

- In spring, many shrubs, including Lilacs, flower abundantly, generously perfuming the surrounding air, and allowing you to create successive flowering by mixing early and later flowering varieties. Some shrubs, such as Forsythia and Azalea, even flower before their leaves emerge.

- Midsummer shrubs not only bring a diversity of foliage to your garden, but also prolonged flowering, when such bushes as Hydrangea, Potentilla and Spirea attract butterflies and other insects to their pollen.

- Some shrubs – amongst which, the appropriately named Burning Bush and the indigenous Staghorn Sumac – save their most spectacular raiment for fall. At the same time, the Elderberry, Viburnum and others attract our feathered friends to your garden.

- One of the most exciting aspects of shrubs is their contribution to a winter garden, since some foliage, flowers and fruit refuse to be daunted by a bit of snow and subzero weather. The flowers of Hydrangeas – which often pass the entire winter dried on the branch – are perfect examples of this desirable phenomenon.

Grafted Shrubs

Fortunately for those of us with terraces, patios, porches and small gardens, shrubs grafted onto a standard are becoming increasingly popular with the gardening set, inspiring more varieties and greater availability.

Euonymus alatus 'Compatus'
Dwarf Burning Bush on sid

There is a limit

The ever popular hedge marks your property line and literally adds cachet to your yard. Many varieties naturally grow into a shape that's perfect for hedges, and some of the new ones are hardier and more resistant than ever. Other cultivars are startling for their beauty and originality: the beautifully flowering Dwarf Ninebark and the graceful Arctic Blue Willow are but two examples. For a low hedge or border, Dwarf Spirea could be ideal.

The freestyle hedge is also becoming more popular for both its beauty and its low maintenance requirements. Un-pruned shrubs can express their natural personality: you get a greater variety of shape and, often, more flowers. Why not plant other species near your hedge and add interest to its changing form and colour over the seasons? Even without accompaniment, though, Van Houtte Spirea makes a spectacular statement with its heavy load of flowers in spring, as does any flaming red bush in autumn.

Spiraea japonica 'Golden Carpet'
'Golden Carpet' Japanese Spirea

Equal rights for winter!

Don't forget about wintertime in your garden, after all, as we all know, it's a painfully long season to neglect. Bring living beauty into your winter garden by planting vegetation that retains foliage, has bronzed leaves, sports dried flowers clinging to shivering branches (think Hydrangea), delights with frozen fruit to attract over-wintering birds, or boasts scarlet branches (think Dogwood).

Shrubs

Hydrangea paniculata 'Grandiflora'
PeeGee Hydrangea

Ilex verticillata
Winter Berry

BOTANIX Experts by nature

Did you know?

- Trimming shrubs stimulates their flowering and controls their development, but it must be done at the right time.
  - Shrubs that flower in mid-summer or early autumn: prune in October, or in April/May before the buds appear.
  - Spring-flowering shrubs: prune from the end of May to early June, after flowering.
- To promote better growth, remove dead wood as soon as you notice it.

Variations on a theme

...your garden's strong point

BOTANIX Experts by nature

Ilex meserveae 'Blue Princess'
Blue Holly

Tamarix ramosissima
Russian Tamarisk

Salix integra 'Hakuro Nishiki'
Spotted Willow

...year-round beauty

...splendid foliage

...spectacular!

Acer palmatum 'Bloodgood'
'Bloodgood' Japanese Maple

	↔ 1.5 m	↕ 2.5 m	ZONE 5b	

A slow-growing, widespread bush that deserves a central place in your garden. The finely dentated leaves, which turn from pinkish red to purple at the end of the season, make it one of the best Japanese Maples, though it does need wind protection.

Aralia elata
Japanese Angelica Tree

		↔ 2 m	↕ 4 m	Summer/ Autumn	ZONE 5a		

Possesses one or several stems, and large, red autumn leaves on its spiny branches. Huge flower umbels appear at the end of summer, followed by black fruit that attracts birds. This exotic-looking bush provides a lot of bang for its size.

Aronia melanocarpa 'Autumn Magic'
Black Chokeberry

		↔ 1 m	↕ 1.5 m	Spring/ Summer	ZONE 4			

Aronie magnificently decorates gardens with its abundant, highly perfumed, white flowers, followed by black berries that attract birds all winter. In autumn, its leaves turn flamboyant red and gold. A hardy variety that loves damp, cool soil.

Azalea 'Rosy Light'
'Rosy Light' Azalea

		↔ 1.5 m	↕ 1.5 m	Spring/ Summer	ZONE 4		

The fuzzy leaves are followed in spring by a multitude of bright pink, perfumed flowers with dark highlights. A hardy Azalea in the form of an upright bush. The Light Series Azalea offers an interesting range of colours.

Berberis 'Aurea Nana'
Japanese Barberry

☀ ⛅ ↔ 80 cm ↕ 60 to 90 cm ❀ Spring/Summer ZONE 4 ◯ 🐦

A compact dwarf that will bring light into a semishade garden with its bright yellow foliage in spring that turns lime green in summer, then red in the fall. Discreet little bellflowers give way to small red berries that attract birds.

Berberis thunbergii 'Concorde'
'Concorde' Barberry

New

☀ ⛅ ↔ 60 to 90 cm ↕ 30 to 45 cm ❀ Spring ZONE 4 ◯ 🐦

This, the smallest Berberis, has purple flowers that would create an appealing contrast with lime green, yellow or speckled foliage. When grown in sunlight throughout the summer, it maintains its colour and then darkens in fall. Its small fruit attracts birds.

Berberis thunbergii 'Rose Glow'
'Rose Glow' Barberry

☀ ⛅ ↔ 1 m ↕ 1.2 m ❀ Spring/Summer ZONE 4 ◯ 🐦

This superb Berberis, with ruby-coloured, rose-speckled leaves on brown branches, is from Denmark. Despite dry soil and urban conditions, its fruit will cling on into winter, attracting birds to your garden. At maturity it is wider than high.

Berberis thunbergii 'Royal Burgundy'
'Royal Burgundy' Barberry

☀ ⛅ ↔ 1.3 m ↕ 1.4 m ❀ Spring/Summer ZONE 4 ◠ 🐦

The most beautiful Berberis, thanks to the spectacular colour of its dark burgundy, summer foliage and blackish-red fall leaves. Use it in a rockery, diverse plant group, or – taking advantage of its thorns – to make an impenetrable hedge. Its fruits attract birds throughout winter.

Shrubs

Berberis thunbergii 'Sunsation'
'Sunsation' Barberry

New

| ☀ | ⛅ | ↔ 1 m | ↕ 1 m | ✿ Spring/Summer | ZONE 4 | ♔ | 🐤 |

The bright yellow foliage of this dwarf cultivar turns a glorious orange in autumn. An excellent choice to create a lively contrast with other plants in a flower bed or small garden. Hardy and tolerant of the most impoverished soils.

Betula pendula 'Trost's Dwarf'
'Trost's Dwarf' Silver Birch

| ☀ | ↔ 1.5 m | ↕ 2.5 m | ZONE 3b | ◯ | 🐤 |

Plant it in full sun in a well-drained, sandy soil and you'll be charmed by the elegance of its finely toothed foliage and weeping branches. A slow grower that will definitely add value to your garden.

Buddleja davidii
Butterfly Bush

| ☀ | ↔ 1.5 m | ↕ 2 m | ✿ Summer/Autumn | ZONE 5 | 🌾 | | 🦋 | ✂ |

This Buddleja's long, arching shoots are covered with elongated, conical, flower spikes that are irresistible to butterflies, especially Monarchs and Viceroys. To stimulate this vigorous shrub's flowering, cut back severely in spring. It likes well-drained soil and winter protection.

Clethra alnifolia 'Ruby Spice'
'Ruby Spice' Summersweet

| ☀ | ⛅ | ☁ | ↔ 1 m | ↕ 1.5 m | ✿ Summer/Autumn | ZONE 4 | ◯ | | 🦋 | 🐤 |

A bushy little round shrub with upright branches that support highly perfumed, pale pink flowers. Its leaves turn yellowish-orange in autumn. Requires high humidity, and would do well in semishade.

Cornus alba 'Ivory Halo'
Red Twig Dogwood

☀	⛅	↔ 1.4 m	↕ 1.4 m	✿ Summer	ZONE 4	〰

A compact cultivar with magnificent, large, white-margined green leaves, as well as bark and branches that turn red in winter. A highly adaptive and ornamental plant that prefers damp soil.

Cotinus coggygria 'Golden Spirit'
'Golden Spirit' Smoke Tree

☀	↔ 4 m	↕ 4 m	✿ Summer	ZONE 4b	〰

Appreciated for its its golden, round leaves, and fascinating duvet-like flowers in summer, it will provide a welcome contrast with other garden plants. Hardy, bushy and undemanding, but grows best in dry soil.

Cotinus coggygria 'Royal Purple'
'Royal Purple' Smoke Tree

☀	↔ 3.5 m	↕ 3 m	✿ Summer	ZONE 5	〰

The most compact Cotinus, with burgundy foliage that darkens as the season progresses, until it turns quite purple. Many red flowers appear over the summer. Use it to create an excellent, opaque screen for intimacy.

Daphne cneorum
Rose Daphne

☀	↔ 1 m	↕ 20 cm	✿ Spring	ZONE 2b	〰	🜋	⌂

A slow-growing but very hardy, spreading and creeping plant that features attractive evergreen foliage and scented pink flowers. Plant in groups, as a groundcover, or to accompany your conifers. Mulch in summer and cover in winter to avoid having the roots dry out.

Shrubs

Euonymus alatus 'Compactus'
Dwarf Winged Euonymus

global village style

☼ ☁ ↔ 1.5 m ↕ 1.2 m **ZONE 4**

In fall, the foliage of this shrub takes on a fascinating, intense scarlet colour and sports a multitude of miniscule but highly decorative orange fruit capsules. Compact, undemanding and perfect in isolation or as a free-form hedge.

Forsythia 'Northern Gold'
'Northern Gold' Forsythia

☼ ☁ ↔ 1.5 to 2 m ↕ 2 m ✿ Spring **ZONE 3**

Makes a spectacular spring entry to your garden with its avalanche of yellow flowers that precede the leaves. The sun stimulates flowering and intensifies its colours. Its upright shape and the luminous colour of its flowers create an amazing contrast with conifers in the background.

Genista lydia
Lydia Broom

☼ ↔ 60 cm ↕ 35 cm ✿ Spring/Summer **ZONE 5**

The greenish blue, long-lasting flowers are buried in a multitude of little golden flowers at the end of spring. The slightly spreading, arched form of its verdigris branches render it an interesting subject for a rock garden. Prefers well-drained, acidic soil and requires winter protection.

Hibiscus syriacus 'Blue Satin'
'Blue Satin' Hibiscus

PW PROVEN WINNERS

New

☼ ↔ 90 cm ↕ 90 cm ✿ Summer/Autumn **ZONE 5**

A fascinating cultivar, due to its shocking-blue flowers with their purple throat and white stamens. Requires full sun and will tough out dog days. Adapts to any soil type, but flowers best when cut back rather severely at the end of autumn or early spring.

Hibiscus syriacus 'Blush Satin'
'Blush Satin' Hibiscus

New

☀	↔ 1.5 m	↕ 2.5 m	❀ Summer/Autumn	ZONE 5	◯

A popular Hibiscus, thanks to its superb, copious and prolonged summer flowering. Large, pale pink flowers with red throats contrast pleasingly with the bright green leaves. A decidedly tropical-looking variety that is sensational in a small garden. Tolerates heat and dampness.

Hydrangea macrophylla 'Blushing Bride'
'Blushing Bride' Hydrangea

New

☀	☁	↔ 90 cm to 1.5 m	↕ 90 cm to 1.8 m	❀ Summer	ZONE 5	◯	✂	△

Its whitish pink flowers grow on new and previous branches. It's a vigorous cultivar that will illuminate shady areas of your garden, and makes magnificent cut flowers. Disease-resistant, but requiring winter protection where snow coverage is insufficient.

Hydrangea arborescens 'Annabelle'
'Annabelle' Hydrangea

☀	☁	☁	↔ 1.5 m	↕ 1.25 m	❀ Summer/Autumn	ZONE 2b	◯	✂

The large white flowers of this cultivar provide an interesting contrast with the outsized, velvet-textured leaves. Bushy and rounded, this hardy Hydrangea will reward you whether planted in groups or alone, but must be cut back to within 30 cm of the soil in early spring.

Hydrangea macrophylla 'Endless Summer'
'Endless Summer' Hydrangea

☀	☁	↔ 1m	↕ 1m	❀ Summer/Autumn	ZONE 4	◯	✂	△

Flowers on new and old growth, so it provides a long blooming period. Cut back to half-size as soon as the leaf-buds appear, in order to stimulate growth. Flowers are pink in alkaline soil and blue in acid soil.

Shrubs

Hydrangea paniculata 'Grandiflora'
Standard 'Grandiflora' Hydrangea

| ☀ | ⛅ | ↔ 2 m | ↕ 2 m | ✿ Summer/Autumn | ZONE 4 | ⚜ |

If you're looking for a late-flowering, long-flowering and abundant-flowering tree, look no further. In summer, this rapid grower sprouts white panicles that turn pinkish before going bronze in autumn. A classic symbol of plenty, its branches bow down to the ground with the weight of its flowers.

Hydrangea paniculata 'Limelight'
'Limelight' Hydrangea

| ☀ | ⛅ | ↔ 2 m | ↕ 2 m | ✿ Summer/Autumn | ZONE 4 | ☁ |

The magnificent, faded, lime-green panicles of this Hydrangea will lend a spirit of erstwhile nobility and untenable romanticism to your garden throughout the year. In rich, acid soil, this vigorous plant will flower best.

Hydrangea paniculata 'Little Lamb'
'Little Lamb' Hydrangea

| ☀ | ⛅ | ↔ 1.5 m | ↕ 1.5 m | ✿ Summer/Autumn | ZONE 3a | ☁ |

The abundant flowers of this compact variety are the most delicate of all the Hydrangea Paniculatae. Will not lower the tone of even the most spectacular garden.

Hydrangea paniculata 'Pink Diamond'
'Pink Diamond' Hydrangea

| ☀ | ⛅ | ↔ 1.5 m | ↕ 2 m | ✿ Summer/Autumn | ZONE 4 | ☁ | ✂ |

Prune new shoots to foster abundant flowering of the elongated, creamy white inflorescences that turn dusty pink, then darker rose-coloured as the season progresses.

Hydrangea paniculata 'Pinky Winky'
'Pinky Winky' Hydrangea

| ☁️ | ☁️ | ↔ 1.5 m | ↕ 1.5 m | ❀ Summer | ZONE 3 | ⌂ | ✂ |

The bicolour flowers set this cultivar apart. In summer its ravishing panicles morph from creamy white, through dark pink, to vibrant red. Cut back in autumn, as it flowers on new growth.

Hydrangea paniculata 'Quick Fire'
'Quick Fire' Hydrangea

| ☀️ | ☁️ | ↔ 1.5 m | ↕ 2 m | ❀ Summer/ Autumn | ZONE 4 | ☁ | ✂ |

The earliest blooming of the Hydrangeas, has flowers that last until the first snowfall. Serious pruning encourages abundant flowering that starts out pink and gradually darkens.

Hydrangea serrata 'Arctic Blue'
'Arctic Blue' Hydrangea

New

| ☀️ | ☁️ | ↔ 1 m | ↕ 1 m | ❀ Summer/ Autumn | ZONE 4 | ◯ | ⌂ |

Bright, sterile flowers covering the entire plant encircle a mass of tiny, dark blue, fertile blooms, much like the 'Blue Bird'. The narrow leaves turn burgundy in fall.

Hydrangea serrata 'Arctic Pink'
'Arctic Pink' Hydrangea

New

| ☁️ | ↔ 1.2 m | ↕ 1.2 m | ❀ Summer | ZONE 4 | ⌂ | ⌂ |

As is the case with many other Hydrangeas, the acid-loving flowers change colour over the season: from white, to pink, to cranberry-red.

Shrubs

Hydrangea serrata 'Blue Bird'
'Blue Bird' Japanese Hydrangea

☁	↔ 70 cm	↕ 1 m	❀ Summer/Autumn	ZONE 5	◯	⊿

The superb flowers of this compact bush emerge creamy pink and become clear blue in acid soil. The pale blue sterile flowers surround a knot of dark blue fertile ones. Leaves turn copper-red in fall. Winter protection required.

Hypericum kalmianum
St. John's-wort

☀	↔ 90 cm	↕ 90 cm	❀ Summer/Autumn	ZONE 4a	◯	🐦	✂

An indigenous bush that attracts attention by its numerous, bright yellow inflorescences that grow on new wood. Its green leaves with silver-blue undersides are not unlike willow leaves. Cut back in spring. The little autumn berries attract birds.

Kolkwitzia amabilis 'Pink Cloud'
'Pink Cloud' Beauty Bush

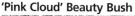

☀	↔ 3 m	↕ 2 m	❀ Summer	ZONE 4b	⊔

As spring turns to summer, the many pale-rose, yellow-throated bells appear on the lithe branches that grow out of the stem erect, then droop towards the extremities. The bluish-green foliage reddens in fall. Undemanding if provided with a rich, well drained soil.

Philadelphus coronarius 'Aureus'
Golden Mock Orange

☀	☁	↔ 2 m	↕ 1.5 m	❀ Summer	ZONE 3	◯	🔧

The golden foliage of this Philadelphus will brighten up a shady corner of your garden, but will itself be brighter in full sun. The breathtakingly scented white flowers appear in early summer. Bushy, dense and compact. Be careful not to water the foliage.

Philadelphus virginalis 'Snowbelle'
'Snowbelle' Mock Orange

| ☀ | ⛅ | ↔ 1.2 m | ↕ 1.2 m | ❀ Summer | ZONE 4 | ◯ | ⚘ |

The magnificent, double, white flowers stand out against the dark green foliage as soon as they surface in early summer. Grown alone or in a group, you'll be seduced by its aroma. Rounded, and more compact than most Philadelphuses.

Physocarpus opulifolius 'Coppertina'
'Coppertina' Ninebark

| ☀ | ⛅ | ↔ 2 m | ↕ 2.5 m | ❀ Spring/Summer | ZONE 3 | ⨆ |

When the foliage first appears, it is copper-orange, but it is reddens over the season until it becomes scarlet by mid-autumn if kept in full sun. Plant as a backdrop or, for a rewarding disparity, near green foliage.

Physocarpus opulifolius 'Dart's Gold'
'Dart's Gold' Ninebark

| ☀ | ⛅ | ↔ 1.5 m | ↕ 1.25 m | ❀ Spring/Summer | ZONE 3 | ☁ | 🦆 |

A delight in small gardens, with its compact, rounded dwarf form and golden leaves that provide a startling contrast among green or purple plants. Much to the delight of our feathered friends, the white flowers give way to red fruit. Resistant and unfussy.

Physocarpus opulifolius 'Diabolo'
'Diabolo' Ninebark

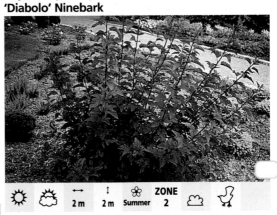

| ☀ | ⛅ | ↔ 2 m | ↕ 2 m | ❀ Summer | ZONE 2 | ☁ | 🦆 |

The well-deserved popularity of this bush may be due to its hardy character, its unusual, multi-lobed, dentated and purple flowers its white flowers that appear in early summer, or its little fruits that hang on into winter. Plant in any soil-type and enjoy.

Shrubs

Physocarpus opulifolius 'Summer Wine'
'Summer Wine' Ninebark

| ☀ | ⛅ | ↔ 1.2 m | ↕ 1.2 m | ✿ Summer | ZONE 3 | ☁ | 🦋 | 🐦 |

Summer Wine's finely textured, bright, cranberry-red leaves are only slightly less spectacular than the pinkish white flowers. Attracts birds and butterflies.

Potentilla fruticosa 'Abbotswood'
Shrubby Cinquefoil

| ☀ | ↔ 80 cm | ↕ 80 cm | ✿ Summer/Autumn | ZONE 2 | ◠ | 🦋 |

The most floriferous white Potentilla. Its rounded, compact form is shrouded in innumerable, white flowers that provide an interesting visual interplay with the bluish-green foliage. Hardy, but prefers fertile, well-drained soil.

Potentilla fruticosa 'Goldfinger'
'Goldfinger' Cinquefoil

| ☀ | ⛅ | ↔ 1 m | ↕ 1 m | ✿ Summer/Autumn | ZONE 2 | ◠ |

With its full, mature height, covered in a profusion of yellow flowers that stand out against the green foliage, this plant works well in a free-form hedge, alone or in groups. Plant in full sun.

Potentilla fruticosa 'Mango Tango'
'Mango Tango' Cinquefoil

| ☀ | ⛅ | ↔ 60 cm | ↕ 60 cm | ✿ Summer/Autumn | ZONE 2 | ◠ | 🦋 |

This superb cultivar has distinctive, yellowish-orange bicolour flowers with a gradually reddening centre. Expect brighter colouration in semishade. The prolonged spectacle of the flowering amid the intensity of the shiny green foliage guarantees you'll love it in groups. Hardy and undemanding.

Potentilla fruticosa 'Pink Beauty'
'Pink Beauty' Cinquefoil

☀ ☁ ↔ 60 cm ↕ 80 cm ❀ Summer/Autumn **ZONE 3** ◯ 🦋

The double, bright pink flowers that swathe the dark green leaves are highly original. Grow in semishade to preserve the intensity of the flower colouring. Straightforward, but prefers fertile, well-drained soil.

Prunus cistena
Purpleleaf Sand Cherry

☀ ☁ ↔ 1.5 m ↕ 1.8 m ❀ Spring **ZONE 3** ☁ 🜨 ✂

Although it's quite hardy and resists pollution well, you'll also like it for its purple leaves that will stay dark if grown in full sun, and the contrasting, scented white flowers. To encourage flowers on the lower half of the bush, trim annually.

Rhus typhina 'Laciniata'
'Laciniata' Staghorn Sumac

☀ ↔ 2 m ↕ 2.5 m **ZONE 4** 🍄 🦋 🐦

This is a quick-growing Sumac with outreaching branches covered in finely dentated leaves that turn pumpkin-orange and scarlet in fall. When males and females are planted close together, you'll see dark red fruit that stays on the tree into winter. An elegant tree that indubitably makes a statement.

Rhus typhina 'Tiger Eyes'
'Tiger Eyes' Staghorn Sumac

☀ ☁ ↔ 2 m ↕ 2 m **ZONE 4** 🔰 🦋 🐦

The young, light-green shoots that turn bright yellow attract a lot of attention in a small garden. The deeply toothed, arching leaves stand out against the fuzzy pink branches. In autumn, the red fruit intermingles with ruddy orange foliage.

Salix integra 'Flamingo'
'Flamingo' Willow on stem

New

| ☀ | ⛅ | ↔ 1.25 m | ↕ 1.25 m | ZONE 4a | ◯ | ✂ |

If you're looking for a plant to stand out in your garden, you couldn't do better than this one, with its red branches and pink, green, and white foliage lasting through autumn. Frequent pruning throughout the season will accentuate foliage colour.

Salix integra 'Hakuro Nishiki'
Spotted Willow

| ☀ | ⛅ | ↔ 1.8 m | ↕ 1.5 m | ZONE 3 | ◯ |

When grown in semishade for intensified tonality, the beauty of the salmon-pink leaves that turn cream-spotted green are perhaps this cultivar's most popular feature. Will rapidly grow into an unusual hedge, but requires pruning and a rich, damp soil. Perfectly happy growing at the edge of a water feature.

Sambucus 'Black Lace'
'Black Lace' Elder

PW PROVEN WINNERS®

New

| ☀ | ⛅ | ↔ 2 m | ↕ 1.5 m | ✿ Summer | ZONE 4 | ◯ | ⬡ | 🐔 |

The finely dentated, dark purple foliage makes an ideal backdrop for the multitude of lightly perfumed, pink flowers that emerge in early summer. By autumn, the foliage begins to turn blood-red and its little berries attract birds.

Sambucus canadensis 'Aurea'
American Elder

| ☀ | ⛅ | ☁ | ↔ 2.5 m | ↕ 3 m | ✿ Summer | ZONE 3 | ⊎ | 🐔 |

The midsummer ivory flowers and the finely dentated golden-yellow foliage, which is brighter under the sun, will leave you satisfied. In fall and early winter, birds are attracted to the dark red fruit. A quick-grower that can be cut back occasionally.

Sorbaria sorbifolia
False Spirea

1.5 m | 1.5 m | Summer | ZONE 2

Sorbaria's extreme popularity is partly due to its extreme adaptability... its hardiness and ability to flourish while being ignored. The white flowers turn orange and will often still be on the plant the next spring. Spreads quickly in fertile soil, so use it as a standalone or in isolated groups.

Sorbaria sorbifolia 'Sem'
'Sem' False Spirea

1 m | 1 m | Summer | ZONE 3

A beautiful study in contrasts, with the new, reddish shoots revealing cream tints and translucent green leaves. More compact and less invasive than other Sorbarias, but equally tropical-looking. Hardy and tolerant of extreme conditions.

Spiraea arguta 'Grefsheim'
'Grefsheim' Spirea

1 m | 1.5 m | Spring | ZONE 4

Your neighbours will rave about your free-form hedge when they see this Spirea's elegantly arching branches, dense verdigris leaves and numerous bunches of white flowers emerging in the spring. To maintain its graceful beauty, do not prune.

Spiraea bumalda 'Anthony Waterer'
'Anthony Waterer' Bumalda Spirea

90 cm | 90 cm | Summer/ Autumn | ZONE 2b

Summer heralds a profusion of cranberry-red flowers that will still be on the plant when the foliage turns purple in fall. Tolerates all soil types and grows quickly. Deadhead faded flowers for abundant flowering.

Spiraea bumalda 'Flaming Mound'
'Flaming Mound' Bumalda Spirea

☀	↔ 60 cm	↕ 60 cm	❀ Summer/Autumn	ZONE 2b	◯	✄

This Spirea will bring light and colour to a green-leafed background. Its leaves start life bright red, then fade to orange, followed by light green, only to turn orange again in fall. Deadhead for abundant flowering of the dark pink blooms from July to September.

Spiraea bumalda 'Gold Mound'
'Gold Mound' Bumalda Spirea

☀	↔ 80 cm	↕ 70 cm	❀ Summer/Autumn	ZONE 4	◯

The golden yellow foliage of this aptly named cultivar turn lime-green in summer, when bunches of the pink flowers bloom. Will bring colour and light into your life, whether you plant it in a flower bed or in the middle of your yard.

Spiraea bumalda 'Goldflame'
'Goldflame' Bumalda Spirea

☀	↔ 70 cm	↕ 70 cm	❀ Summer/Autumn	ZONE 2b	◯

The young, copper-orange buds of this compact dwarf Spirea turn yellow over the summer before returning to their original colour in autumn. Makes a wonderful hedge, addition to your rockery, supplement to your flower bed or companion for your conifers, with its generous, pink flowers blooming over several months.

Spiraea japonica 'Magic Carpet'
'Magic Carpet' Japanese Spirea

☀	☁	↔ 60 cm	↕ 40 cm	❀ Summer/Autumn	ZONE 4	◯

This globular dwarf works marvellously as a groundcover or edging. The red leaf-buds turn yellow with bronze tips. In early summer, handfuls of dark pink flowers appear, to remain until the weather turns cold.

Spiraea japonica 'Shirobana'
'Shirobana' Japanese Spirea

☀	⛅	↔ 80 cm	↕ 80 cm	✿ Summer	ZONE 3	◯

Unique, as it has white, pale-pink and dark-pink flowers on the same plant. Adds a naturalistic touch to a country-style garden.

Spiraea japonica 'White Gold'
'White Gold' Japanese Spirea

New

☀	⛅	↔ 60 cm	↕ 80 cm	✿ Summer	ZONE 4	◯	🦋

The startling, golden-yellow foliage stands out under any conditions. A tiny mound of Spiraea that attracts butterflies with its diminutive white flowers.

Spiraea nipponica 'Snowmound'
'Snowmound' Japanese Spirea

☀	⛅	↔ 80 cm	↕ 80 cm	✿ Spring/Summer	ZONE 3	◯

'Snowmound' is a compact little bush with upright branches that support dark green foliage featuring brushed-denim blue undersides. A wealth of little white flowers appear at the end of spring. Appreciates rich soil.

Spiraea van houttei
Van Houtte Spirea

☀	⛅	↔ 2.5 m	↕ 1.8 m	✿ Spring/Summer	ZONE 3b	⊍

As popular as it is sensational, Van Houtte makes an unbeatable hedge for creating a cozy private garden. An avalanche of white flowers, contrasting against the bluish leaves, cascade in every direction. To conserve its graceful presence and generous flowering, do not prune.

Shrubs

Spiraea van houttei 'Gold Fountain'
Van Houtte 'Gold Fountain' Spirea

New

☀ ⛅ ↔ 2.5 to 3 m | ↕ 1 m | ✿ Spring | **ZONE 4** | ⌂

Typical of the species, with its plethora of flowers covering gracefully arching branches, but atypical for its golden foliage. The radiant colouring will add light to a semishade garden whether planted alone or as a freestyle hedge.

Stephanandra incisa 'Crispa'
'Crispa' Lace Shrub

☀ ⛅ ↔ 1.5 m | ↕ 50 cm | ✿ Summer | **ZONE 5** | 〜

The perfect rockery or low-wall plant, the Stephanandra is an elegant and unusual groundcover with the rambling stems that root easily, and an autumnal foliage that varies from orange to deep purple. This dwarf is a rapid grower.

Syringa 'Josée'
'Josée' Dwarf Lilac

☀ ↔ 1 m | ↕ 1 m | ✿ Spring/Autumn | **ZONE 3** | ⌂ | 🌱 | 🦋 | ✂

A lovely little Lilac that would fit nicely into a small garden. Because some of the dark pink flower buds are present at the same time as some of the single, bright-pink, odoriferous flowers, this shrub seems to have different coloured flowers. Blooms a second time at summer's end.

Syringa 'Tinkerbelle'
'Tinkerbelle' Lilac

☀ ⛅ ↔ 1.25 m | ↕ 1.5 m | ✿ Spring/Summer | **ZONE 3** | ⌂ | ✂

The cherry-red buds gradually open to pink flowers, giving this Lilac a sensational bicolour look. Hardy, resistant and perfect for small gardens.

Syringa meyeri 'Palibin'
Dwarf Korean Lilac

☀	☁	↔ 1 to 2 m	↕ 1 to 2 m	❀ Spring	ZONE 3			

This extremely hardy Lilac will beautify any little semi-shade garden with its abundance of violet-pink, highly perfumed flowers. Undemanding and tolerant of both dry spells and urban pollution.

Syringa patula 'Miss Kim'
'Miss Kim' Dwarf Lilac

☀	↔ 1.8 m	↕ 1.8 m	❀ Summer	ZONE 3				

A spectacular little Lilac in spring or autumn. It has a multitude of dark mauve buds that morph into paired panicles of perfumed flowers. Its leaves turn purple in autumn. A mound-shaped shrub that would do well in groups or as hedge.

Syringa prestoniae 'Miss Canada'
'Miss Canada' Lilac

☀	☁	↔ 3 m	↕ 2 m	❀ Summer	ZONE 2			

A really hardy Lilac that rapidly grows large and round, with hefty panicles of red buds that become magnificent pink flowers. Add sunlight for more flowers.

Syringa prestoniae 'Royalty'
'Royalty' Lilac

☀	☁	↔ 2.5 m	↕ 3 m	❀ Summer	ZONE 3			

In June, the single violet flowers emerge — in very large numbers, if exposed to full sun and pruned. This cultivar has the darkest flowers of any of the blue-flowering Lilacs.

Shrubs

Shrubs

Syringa vulgaris 'Belle de Nancy'
'Nancy' French Lilac

| ☀ | ↔ 3 m | ↕ 3 m | ✿ Spring/Summer | ZONE 3 | ⛰ | •⊐ᴱ | 🦋 | ✂ |

This French hybrid, which is hardy and resistant, will present purple buds that open to double, pinkish-mauve flowers in spring. Treat it like a Lilac, and prune to encourage subsequent blooms.

Syringa vulgaris 'Charles Joly'
'Charles Joly' French Lilac

| ☀ | ↔ 3 m | ↕ 2.5 m | ✿ Spring/Summer | ZONE 3 | ☁ | •⊐ᴱ | 🦋 | ✂ |

One of the first Lilacs to flower. To encourage more abundant blooming of its magnificent, perfumed, burgundy, double-flowers the next spring, deadhead the faded panicles.

Syringa vulgaris 'Mme Lemoine'
'Mme Lemoine' Lilac

| ☀ | ↔ 3 m | ↕ 3 m | ✿ Spring/Summer | ZONE 3 | ☁ | •⊐ᴱ | 🦋 | ✂ |

The rounded form of this ravishing Lilac is pleasing when it's planted alone, attractive when you see it in a group, and outstanding as a screen, especially in the spring when it's covered in elegant, double panicles of pure white, highly perfumed flowers. Deadhead them for maximized blooming the next spring.

Syringa vulgaris 'President Grevy'
'President Grevy' Lilac

| ☀ | ↔ 2.5 m | ↕ 3 m | ✿ Spring/Summer | ZONE 2b | ⛰ | •⊐ᴱ | 🦋 | ✂ |

An upgrade of the common Lilac that's very hardy and long lived. In spring, huge, double panicles of bluish-mauve flowers will assail your senses with their sweet perfume. It's a Lilac, so deadhead for good blooming the next year.

Syringa vulgaris 'Sensation'
'Sensation' Lilac

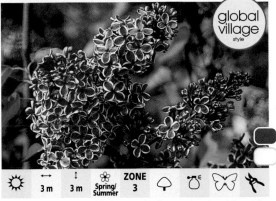

global village *style*

☀	↔	↕	❀	ZONE	⌂		🦋	✂
	3 m	3 m	Spring/Summer	3				

A real showstopper with its purple flowers bordered in white. Definitely unusual. It's a Lilac, so deadhead for good blooming the next year.

Syringa vulgaris 'Wedgwood Blue'
'Wedgwood Blue' Lilac

☀	↔	↕	❀	ZONE	☁		🦋	✂
	1.5 m	2 m	Spring/Summer	2				

'Wedgwood Blue' has flowers of that colour, rising out of pink buds to exquisitely perfume the surrounding air. It's a Lilac, so deadhead for good blooming the next year.

Tamarix ramosissima
Russian Tamarisk

☀	↔	↕	❀	ZONE	〗	✂
	2 m	2.5 m	Summer	3b		

What's not to love? An elegant shape, feathery arching foliage, spectacular pink flowers that resemble its leaves. A light pruning in early spring encourages flowering till the end of summer. Branch tips are sensitive to freezing.

Viburnum dentatum 'Autumn Jazz'
'Autumn Jazz' Viburnum

☀	☁	↔	↕	❀	ZONE		🦆
		2.5 m	2.5 m	Spring/Summer	3a		

The autumn spectacle alone justifies choosing this beauty – foliage sporting a range of impressive colours from yellow to orange, to red and burgundy. On top of that, creamy white spring flowers are followed by many bunches of indigo fruit that draws birds.

Viburnum dentatum 'Blue Muffin'
'Blue Muffin' Arrowwood Viburnum

☀	⛅	↔ 1 m	↕ 1.5 m	❀ Spring/Summer	ZONE 3	◯	🐦

A compact Viburnum with dense foliage and, at summer's end, deep blue fruits that attract birds until they're all eaten in autumn. Plant other varieties of Viburnum to foster fruiting.

Viburnum lantana 'Mohican'
'Mohican' Viburnum on stem

☀	⛅	☁	↔ 2.5 m	↕ 3 m	❀ Summer	ZONE 2b	◯	🐦

Hopefully not the last of the Mohicans, because you'll love the dimpled, green leaves with their downy undersides, the creamy white flowers in June, the bright red summer fruit that turns black over time, and the burgundy-red foliage in fall.

Viburnum sargentii 'Onondaga'
'Onondaga' Viburnum

☀	⛅	↔ 2 m	↕ 2.5 m	❀ Spring/Summer	ZONE 4a	🌿	🐦

A charming bush to fill out a flowerbed. Its sterile white flowers surround pink ones for an exceptional visual delight. In autumn, the leaves turn violet-red and an infinity of little red berries make an appearance.

Viburnum trilobum 'Alfredo'
'Alfredo' Viburnum

☀	⛅	↔ 1.5 m	↕ 1.5 m	❀ Spring/Summer	ZONE 2a	🌿	🐦

This one has all the qualities you're looking for: red-tipped new shoots interplay with numerous bunches of white flowers at the end of spring and the yellow and dark red autumnal foliage is interspersed with a plethora of scarlet berries. Resistant to the Leaf Beetle.

Viburnum trilobum 'Harvest Gold'
'Harvest Gold' viburnum

| ☀ | ⛅ | ↔ 1.5 m | ↕ 2 m | ❋ Spring/Summer | ZONE 3 | 〣 | 🐦 |

A hearty and undemanding bush that deserves a place of high visibility in your garden, due to its highly decorative white flowers, prolific fruits that last into winter, plus foliage that's golden in spring, yellowish-green in summer and ruby in fall.

Weigela florida 'Carnival'
'Carnival' Weigela

| ☀ | ⛅ | ↔ 1.2 m | ↕ 1.2 m | ❋ Spring/Autumn | ZONE 4 | ☁ | 🐦 | ✂ |

'Carnival' produces flowers in three shades to stand out among its lustrous green leaves: pink in early spring, then varying from red to white until late summer. Prune in early spring to stimulate flowering.

Weigela florida 'Fine Wine'
'Fine Wine' Weigela

PW PROVEN WINNERS

New

| ☀ | ↔ 80 cm | ↕ 60 cm | ❋ Summer/Autumn | ZONE 5 | ☁ | 🐦 |

A tiny bush that will contrast spectacularly with the other plants in your garden. Its bright amethyst foliage justifies its name. What's more, in spring it's smothered in a multitude of bright pink flowers.

Weigela florida 'Jean's Gold'
'Jean's Gold' Weigela

New

| ☀ | ↔ 1.5 m | ↕ 2.5 m | ❋ Summer/Autumn | ZONE 5 | 🐦 |

A Weigela that will brighten your garden with its intense red flowers standing out magnificently against the yellow summer leaves. Nor will birds complain when they fly in to taste the black berries of autumn.

Weigela florida 'Minuet'
'Minuet' Weigela

☀	☁	☁	↔ 50 cm	↕ 50 cm	❀ Summer	ZONE 3	☁	🐦

Watch the buds turn from purple to dark green with purple splotches. Lightly perfumed, pink flowers bloom copiously in early summer. This compact dwarf will add an elegant note to any small garden.

Weigela florida 'My Monet'
'My Monet' Weigela

New

☀	↔ 80 cm	↕ 40 cm	❀ Summer/ Autumn	ZONE 4	☁	🐦

The bright green foliage is speckled with cream and rose, creating a mind-blowing effect in small flower beds surrounded by dark green foliage. The colours are most intense in semi-shade.

Weigela florida 'Polka'
'Polka' Weigela

☀	☁	↔ 80 cm to 1.2 m	↕ 80 cm to 1 m	❀ Summer/ Autumn	ZONE 4	☁	🐦

This hybrid from the Dance series is hardy, long-flowering and compact. Its diminutive stature ironically features huge flowers in shades of pink amidst dark green foliage. A sure value.

Weigela florida 'Red Prince'
'Red Prince' Weigela

☀	☁	↔ 1.5 m	↕ 1.5 m	❀ Spring/ Summer	ZONE 4	⊔	🐦

A superb, erect shrub with gently arching branches that contribute to an unarguable elegance. Hardy and highly floriferous, producing two generations of red flowers; the first in May and the other in mid-to-late summer.

Weigela florida 'Rumba'
'Rumba' Weigela

☀	☁	↔ 1.2 m	↕ 1 m	✿ Summer/Autumn	ZONE 4	☁	🐦

Since it's a member of the Dance series, expect prolonged blooming from this compact bush. Plentiful, crimson-burgundy flowers with yellow throats complement the lime-green, purple-bordered leaves in early summer. Vigorous and spreading in form.

Weigela florida 'Samba'
'Samba' Weigela

☀	☁	↔ 80 cm	↕ 80 cm	✿ Summer/Autumn	ZONE 4	☁	🐦

Compact and rounded with near-purple foliage that provides a pleasing contrast with the profuse and prolonged flowering of dark pink blooms with yellow throats. A magnificent addition to any garden, there's no doubt.

Weigela florida 'White Knight'
'White Knight' Weigela

☀	☁	↔ 1.25 m	↕ 1.25 m	✿ Summer/Autumn	ZONE 5	🐦

'White Knight' will add a touch of originality to the most common of gardens, contributing a generous and long flowering of pale-pink buds that materialize as pure white, startling, small trumpets... and last all summer!

Weigela florida 'Wine & Roses'
'Wine & Roses' Weigela

PW PROVEN WINNERS

☀	☁	↔ 1.25 m	↕ 1.25 m	✿ Summer/Autumn	ZONE 4	⊍	🐦

This variety has purple foliage that shelters numerous, pink flowers into the fall, when its foliage becomes even brighter, it creates a startling contrast. Heighten this effect by planting it among green or yellow foliage. Creates an equally impressive effect on a patio or in the middle of your garden.

Shrubs

Andromeda polifolia 'Blue Ice'
'Blue Ice' Bog Rosemary

| ☀ | ☁ | ↔ 40 cm | ↕ 30 cm | ❀ Spring/Summer | ZONE 2 | ⌒ |

This creeping plant beautifies the forest floor all year with its lustrous, bluish-green foliage. It's frequently used to naturalize an area or as a border for large plantings. Give it a humid, acidic soil and it'll brighten your dark corners throughout the fall.

Arctostaphylos uva-ursi
Bearberry

global village style

| ☀ | ☁ | ↔ 70 to 100 cm | ↕ 20 cm | ❀ Spring | ZONE 2 | ⌒ | 🐦 |

Perfect for a natural style garden. With its whitish pink flowers that transform into bright red, edible berries, this beautiful groundcover will feed the birds and please your eye. You'll love the flamboyant, burgundy hue of this hardy plant's rustic leaves, as well.

Calluna vulgaris
Heather

| ☀ | ☁ | ↔ 40 cm | ↕ 25 cm | ❀ Summer/Autumn | ZONE 5 | ⌒ |

An acidophilic shrub that's particularly well-suited to flower beds, rock gardens or as a groundcover. Protect it with a good mulch and prepare to enjoy its flowers throughout most of the season – and its bronze-coloured foliage in fall.

Cotoneaster 'Hessei'
'Hessei' Cotoneaster

| ☀ | ↔ 1 m | ↕ 40 cm | ❀ Spring | ZONE 4 | ⌒ |

This cultivar has shiny, dark green foliage that turns burgundy in the fall, and dark pink flowers, followed – in autumn – by small red berries that attract birds. Use it as a groundcover or in flower beds.

Erica carnea 'Kramer's Red'
'Kramer's Red' Winter Heath

| ☀ | ⛅ | ↔ 40 cm | ↕ 25 cm | ❀ Spring | ZONE 5 | 〰 |

You'll love its dark green leaves, but you'll flip for its abundant, pinkish spring blooms that will light up the shadiest areas in your garden. This groundcover prefers acid soil and protection from strong winds.

Euonymus fortunei 'Canadale Gold'
'Canadale Gold' Wintercreeper

| ☀ | ⛅ | ↔ 1 m | ↕ 60 cm | ZONE 4 | 〰 |

A magnificent shrub featuring large, pale green leaves with golden-yellow margins. Use it as a groundcover under leafy trees or conifers where its thick, compact form will add light to normally sombre areas.

Euonymus fortunei 'Emerald Gaiety'
'Emerald Gaiety' Wintercreeper

| ☀ | ⛅ | ↔ 1.35 m | ↕ 60 cm | ZONE 4b | ☁ |

A lovely shrub with leaves sporting white borders that turn pink in fall. Hardy and easily grown, it never reacts negatively to a good trim. Its forgiving nature and decorative foliage, no doubt contribute largely to its popularity.

Euonymus fortunei 'Emerald'n Gold'
'Emerald'n Gold' Wintercreeper

global village style

| ☀ | ⛅ | ↔ 1.3 m | ↕ 90 cm | ZONE 4 | 〰 |

'Emerald'n Gold' is a jam-packed, creeping plant with brilliant, dark green leaves surrounded by yellow margins until autumn turns them into an equally brilliant dark pink. A coveted ornamental.

Evergreen Shrubs

Gaultheria procumbens
Wintergreen

				ZONE		
☁	30 cm	10 cm	Summer	**2**		

A magnificent, hardy, shade-loving groundcover that gives off a pleasing scent when disturbed. Its small, white-pinkish flowers turn into red fruit that provides a pleasant contrast with blankets of white snow all winter.

Ilex meserveae
Meserve Holly

					ZONE	
☀	☁	1.3 m	1.2 m	Spring	**5**	

An unusual shrub that will attract your attention all year with its brilliant, dentated foliage that varies from dark green to bluish depending on the variety. Protect it from wind and plant a male near one or more females to get the dark red berries that stand out all winter.

Pieris japonica 'Mountain Fire'
'Mountain Fire' Japanese Pieris

New

			ZONE	
☁	60 cm	50 cm	Spring	**5**

The dark red spring leaves of this evergreen Andromeda provide an interesting contrast with the previous year's dark green leaves. As if that were not attractive enough, prolific bouquets of gracefully arching, white flowers will also beautify this shade-loving bush.

Rhododendron 'Haaga'
'Haaga' Rhododendron

					ZONE	
☁	☁	1.5 m	1.5 m	Summer	**4**	🦋

Add a touch of elegance to your garden with these large, perfumed leaves. As is typical for Rhododendrons, its flower buds are resistant to cold and it prefers damp, well drained acidic soil and wind protection.

Rhododendron 'P.J.M.'
'P.J.M.' Rhododendron

☀ ☁ ☁ ↔ 1.2 m ↕ 1.5 m ❀ Spring/Summer **ZONE 4** ☁ 🦋

An extremely popular Rhododendron, due to its early flowering, extreme hardiness and aromatic foliage that takes on a mahogany tinge in winter. Tolerates dryness but requires an acidic, well drained soil.

Rhododendron catawbiense 'Boursault'
'Boursault' Catawba Rhododendron

☀ ☁ ☁ ↔ 1.2 m ↕ 1.5 m ❀ Spring/Summer **ZONE 5** ☁ 🦋

A compact, symmetrical, dense shrub with large leaves and a plenitude of lustrous, lilac flowers that are rather cold hardy. Protect from wind and give it an acidic, damp, but well drained soil.

Rhododendron catawbiense 'Nova Zembla'
'Nova Zembla' Catawba Rhododendron

☀ ☁ ☁ ↔ 1.2 m ↕ 1.2 m ❀ Spring/Summer **ZONE 5** ☁ 🦋

As its flower buds easily resist heat and cold, a pleasing mass of red flowers with darker centres appears late in spring. The lustrous leaves are dark green on top and pale green on bottom until autumn bids them change to bronze. A quickly growing acid-loving shrub.

Yucca filamentosa
Yucca, Adam's Needle

☀ ↔ 90 cm ↕ 1.2 m ❀ Summer **ZONE 4** 🌾

This Yucca has long, sword-like, fibrous, silver-green leaves with rough, filamentous borders. Its white flowers appear in the second or third year, and the plant dies afterwards, having procreated by side shoots that will soon take over. As befits a desert plant, it appreciates a hot, dry locale.

Buxus 'Green Mountain'
'Green Mountain' Boxwood

| ☀ | ⛅ | ↔ 80 cm | ↕ 1 m | ZONE 5 | △ | ◢ |

This beautiful addition to any English-style garden also works well as a medium-sized hedge that's easy to trim. Its dense, dark green foliage will persist, on the trimmed, uniformly pyramidal plant, into the winter months if protected from the coldest temperatures.

Buxus 'Green Velvet'
'Green Velvet' Boxwood

| ☀ | ⛅ | ☁ | ↔ 60 cm | ↕ 60 cm | ZONE 5 |

One of the best cultivars for a backdrop or low, dense hedge. In rich soil, it will spread well and will be easy to trim. Its little round, dark green leaves will overwinter.

Caragana arborescens
Siberian Peashrub

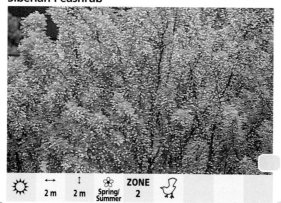

| ☀ | ↔ 2 m | ↕ 2 m | ❀ Spring/Summer | ZONE 2 | 🐦 |

An extremely hardy, undemanding Caragana that tolerates dryness to produce a high, free-form or sculpted hedge. Appreciated equally for its delicate, yellow spring flowers, bright yellow, autumn foliage and small bird-attracting berries.

Cotoneaster acutifolia
Peking Cotoneaster

| ☀ | ⛅ | ↔ 2 m | ↕ 2.5 m | ❀ Spring | ZONE 2 | 🐦 |

When used to create a hedge, this hardy Cotoneaster will create a dense screen with its green foliage and little pinkish white flowers in spring, leaves that turn yellow and red in the fall, and near-black fruit that will last into winter, if the birds so permit.

Lonicera xylosteoides 'Clavey's Dwarf'
'Clavey's Dwarf' Honeysuckle

☀ | ↔ 1.5 m | ↕ 1.25 m | ❀ Spring/Summer | ZONE 4 | 🐦

This hardy, diseases-resistant little bush's blue-green foliage and understated, creamy white flowers conspire to create a very pretty, compact and rounded hedge. At summer's end, expect flocks of birds attracted by the little red berries.

Physocarpus opulifolius nanus
Ninebark

☀ ☁ ☁ | ↔ 1 m | ↕ 1 m | ❀ Summer | ZONE 2 | 🐦

Makes an elegant, original hedge with its pinkish white flowers that precede red berries and their attendant hungry birds. The small leaves, which turn red in fall, are less dentated than is usual for a Physocarpus.

Ribes alpinum
Alpine Currant

☀ ☁ ☁ | ↔ 1.5 m | ↕ 1.5 m | ZONE 2 | 🐦

Dense and compact, this shrub's trilobate, dentated, dark green foliage will enhance any flower bed with its abundant scarlet red, edible fruit, thriving all summer long. Provide with rich, well drained soil and trim at will.

Rosa rubrifolia
Redleaf Rose

☀ | ↔ 1.25 m | ↕ 2 m | ❀ Summer | ZONE 4

This central European import is a study in contrasts with its small bouquets of pink flowers sprinkled among purple, emerald and bluish-grey foliage. Since it is so gracious, dense and colourful, it's perfect for a free-form hedge.

Salix purpurea 'Gracilis'
Dwarf Arctic Willow

☀	⛅	↔ 1.5 m	↕ 1.5 m	ZONE 2

You'll love its naturally rounded form and fine, arctic-blue foliage. Great for making a magnificent hedge as it grows rapidly, tolerating wind and dryness.

Sambucus canadensis
American Elderberry

☀	⛅	☁	↔ 2.5 m	↕ 3 m	❀ Spring/Summer	ZONE 3	🐦

The dense, quickly growing foliage will rapidly help you create an original, intimate garden. In summer the remarkable ivory flowers emerge. In autumn, birds are attracted to its numerous black fruit.

Spiraea japonica 'Golden Carpet'
'Golden Carpet' Spirea

☀	⛅	↔ 35 cm	↕ 20 cm	❀ Summer/Autumn	ZONE 4

This Spirea has yellowish spring foliage that turns green over the summer, as it hides behind numerous bunches of pink flowers that survive until autumn. Being a dwarf variety, it's great for creating a border or low hedge.

Spiraea japonica 'Green Carpet'
'Green Carpet' Spirea

☀	⛅	↔ 35 cm	↕ 15 cm	❀ Summer/Autumn	ZONE 4

One of the smallest 'Carpet' Spireas, making it ideal for mosaics, low hedges and flower beds. Its little bunches of pink flowers persist all summer, and the delicate, bright green foliage turns purple in autumn.

Spiraea japonica 'Sparkling Carpet'
'Sparkling Carpet' Spirea

☀	⛅		↔ 30 cm	↕ 20 cm	❀ Summer/ Autumn	ZONE 4

Its bronze leaves turn lime-green as they grow, and then mahogany in the fall. Throughout the summer months you'll be delighted by a carpet of flowers, whether you use it to form a low hedge, embellish your flower beds, or for foundation planting.

Symphoricarpos albus
Common Snowberry

☀	⛅	☁	↔ 1.5 m	↕ 1.25 m	❀ Summer/ Autumn	ZONE 2	☁	🐦

An indigenous, highly adaptive shrub that will eliminate any dark corner with its long-flowering white blooms, followed, in autumn, by a multitude of long-lasting white berries. Expect them to grace its arching stems into the first months of winter. Cut back in early spring.

Thuja occidentalis
Eastern White Cedar

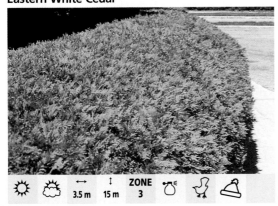

☀	⛅	↔ 3.5 m	↕ 15 m	ZONE 3	🌰	🦃	⌂

The ideal cedar for a very high, dense hedge. A perfect visual and conceptual border that also has the advantage of giving off a lovely woodsy odour, particularly when being trimmed. Likes constantly humid soil as much as it dislikes drying winds.

Thuja occidentalis 'Nigra'
Black Cedar

☀	⛅	↔ 2.5 m	↕ 6 m	ZONE 3	🌰

An extremely hardy cedar with an attractive conical form, a wide base and a tip that naturally points skywards. It's frequently used for hedges, but needs to be protected from strong winter winds, especially in the early years.

Stairway...

to heaven

Climbing plants are perfect for small gardens with very limited space. They will reward you with a lot of foliage on walls, trees and other vertical structures.

Create a vertical garden even in the smallest spaces. These luxuriant beauties will decorate your exterior throughout the spring and summer months with flamboyant fall colours and berries. Using winding stems or tendrils, they create a stairway to heaven by clinging to structures or other plants.

These practical and visually rewarding plants emphasize trellies, arbours or pergolas, and liven up old fences or mundane walls. So, to maximize the effect of a minimum of space, look up!

Clematis 'Carnaby'
'Carnaby' Clematis

Yours to Discover

Both annual and perennial climbing plants have a lot to offer, covering exterior structures with a magnificent verdant tapestry in very little time. The only problem? Too many to choose from!

You don't need extensive grounds to surround yourself with beauty. A small courtyard, roof-deck, tiny balcony or condo terrace can become that much coveted peaceful refuge. You simply need to use the surrounding structures as your props: either to hide them or to accentuate their appeal.

- Climbing plants attract the eye: their abundant foliage sometimes turns bright red, as it does with the Virginia Creeper. Most of them have small berries that, once the flowers have faded, attract birds. In fact, with some, the foliage is appealing enough to induce them to nest.

- There are so many places that seem custom-made for creeping vines: brick, cement or stone walls, metal or wood fences, pergolas, trellises, stair rails, and tree trunks. They'll grow in the ground or on a balcony, patio or window box. And nothing equals their ability to disguise an obtrusive, aesthetically unappealing element such as a hydro pole.

Types of climbing plants

In both the perennial and annual categories (see "Annuals and Tropical" section), there are climbing plants with winding stems such as the Kiwi, and those with soft stems that proliferate by underground rhizomes, such as Hops.

Climbing plants affix themselves in different ways. Winding stems, which as their name suggests, wind themselves around anything, tendrils, which wrap themselves around fine supports, and lastly, suckers – which allow the plant to hold onto vertical surfaces with their aerial roots.

The Ubiquitous Clematis

There is a reason why Clematises are seen nearly everywhere there are climbing plants. Their flowers, which offer a magnificent spectacle until autumn, are almost enough to decorate a garden by themselves. Their single, double or pendant, bell-shaped flowers are unequalled. What's more, Clematises are easy to grow. Place them in a well-drained soil rich in organic material and enjoy the spectacle.

Every year, new cultivars are added to the already wide range of Clematises. With so many too choose from, why not pick a few and distribute them throughout your garden?

Lonicera 'Mandarin'
'Mandarin' Climbing Honeysuckle

Tips and Tricks

- In order to create a magnificent duo of flowers – or simply to prolong the flowering period of climbing plants – it's possible to intertwine two plants of the same family for a beautiful effect.
- Clematises grow best when their base is shaded by other plants or obstacles, and their head is in the sun but protected from the most blazing sun rays of the day.

Actinidia kolomikta
Hardy Kiwi

| ☀ | ☁ | ↔ 2 to 3 m | ↕ 4 m | ✿ Summer | ZONE 4b | | |

The extraordinary leaves with cream and bright pink splashes are most remarkable in semishade. When male and female plants are interspersed, expect edible fruit that attracts birds. Requires well-drained soil.

Aristolochia durior 'Sipho'
Dutchman's Pipe

| ☀ | ☁ | ↔ 2 to 3 m | ↕ 10 m | ✿ Summer | ZONE 4 |

Its large, heart-shaped leaves spread quickly over walls and trellises, creating a luxuriant screen for an intimate garden. As spring breathes its last breath, tiny pipe-shaped flowers add a note of mystery. Give it damp soil and watch it climb!

Campsis radicans
Trumpet Vine, Trumpet Creeper

| ☀ | ↔ 2 m | ↕ 4 m | ✿ Summer/Autumn | ZONE 5 |

Like its fellow cultivars, this magnificent climber's abundance of trumpet-like flowers proliferate all summer among a dense thicket of emerald green leaves. Watch it turn your wall, arbour or pergola into a living work of art, where birds will love to nest. Spectacular!

Campsis radicans 'Indian Summer'
'Indian Summer' Trumpet Vine

| ☀ | ↔ 2 m | ↕ 4 m | ✿ Summer/Autumn | ZONE 5 |

A flamboyant plant that flowers profusely throughout the summer if kept in full sun. In shade, you'll see less of its ruby-throated, orange, trumpet-like flowers. Must be solidly anchored to a supporting structure, as it becomes rather heavy at maturity.

Celastrus scandens
American Bittersweet

☀ ⛅ | ↔ 1 to 2 m | ↕ 7 m | ❀ Summer | **ZONE 3b** | 🐦

A vigorous, native climbing plant that winds itself around the support structure. Plant a male and a female together so that in autumn, you can enjoy the abundant bird-magnet berries that vary from yellow to scarlet red.

Humulus lupulus 'Aureus'
Golden Hops

☀ ⛅ | ↔ 1.8 m | ↕ 5 m | ❀ Summer | **ZONE 3a** | ✂

Golden Hops' golden yellow leaves, which turn orange in autumn, are more striking in full sun. Its conical summer flowers will remind you of little artichokes. Plant at the foot of a pergola and cut right back to the soil in spring.

Hydrangea petiolaris
Climbing Hydrangea

☀ ⛅ | ↔ 2 to 3 m | ↕ 7 m | ❀ Summer | **ZONE 5** | 🐦

Looking to cover a wall? Here's the perfect choice. Its aerial roots cling to the surface where its dark green foliage contrasts beautifully with the delicate flowers that emerge in spring. Leave the flowers to dry on the vine and you'll enjoy them all winter.

Lonicera heckrottii 'Gold Flame'
'Gold Flame' Honeysuckle

☀ ⛅ | ↔ 2 m | ↕ 3 m | ❀ Summer/ Autumn | **ZONE 4** | 👜 🐦

A particularly pleasing variety due to its abundant, tubular, dark pink flowers with their butter-yellow highlights... and delicate perfume. Flowers abundantly until the first frosts.

Climbing plants

Lonicera 'Mandarin'
'Mandarin' Climbing Honeysuckle

| ☼ | ⛅ | ↔ 1 m | ↕ 2 to 3 m | ✿ Summer/Autumn | ZONE 3 | 🎕 | 🐦 |

Lonicera's popularity is spurred by its hardiness and extended flowering season. Its large, scented, tubular flowers stand out magnificently against the copper-tinged early summer foliage.

Lonicera periclymenum 'Harlequin'
'Harlequin' Honeysuckle

| ☼ | ↔ 1.25 m | ↕ 2.5 m | ✿ Spring/Summer | ZONE 4 | 🎕 |

Even without its elegant, scented, tubular flowers, this honeysuckle would supply an attractive surface-cover to walls or trellises, with its rose and cream speckled green leaves.

Parthenocissus quinquefolia 'Engelmanii'
'Engelmanii' Virginia Creeper

| ☼ | ⛅ | ↔ 2 m | ↕ 15 m | ZONE 3 | 🐦 |

The vigorous Virginia creeper will quickly cover whatever surface you offer it, including the ground! Its large, eponymous, five-lobed leaves are luminously red in autumn.

Parthenocissus tricuspidata 'Robusta'
'Robusta' Boston Ivy

| ☼ | ↔ 2 to 3 m | ↕ 10 m | ZONE 4 | 🐦 |

Boston ivy loves heights. This variety will grow up to 10 m on brick or stone walls, its trilobate leaves turning the entire surface bright red in the fall – at which time its contrasting blue fruit provides a feast for twittering birds.

Parthenocissus tricuspidata 'Veitchii'
'Veitchii' Boston Ivy

☀		↔ 2 to 3 m	↕ 10 m	ZONE 4	🦆

As befits the variety, this cultivar grabs onto surfaces with its tiny suckers. Adds Ivy-League charm to brick or stone walls — especially in autumn, when its lustrous leaves take on various red and copper tones.

Polygonum aubertii
Silver Flea Vine

☀	⛅	↔ 3 to 4 m	↕ 3 to 6 m	✿ Summer/Autumn	ZONE 5	🌿	✂

Copious sprays of fragrant, pendant white flowers make this the ideal plant for your pergola. Yes, you have to cut it back quite seriously every spring, but its delicate green leaves will quickly cover up the framework again.

Vitis riparia
Wild Grape

☀	⛅	☁	↔ 1 to 2 m	↕ 4 to 7 m	✿ Summer	ZONE 3	🌿	🦆

Though you might find them a little bitter, the acidic, purplish-blue grapes of this hardy native vine are a favourite delicacy of many birds. Plant it and forget it in sun or shade.

Wisteria macrostachya 'Blue Moon'
'Blue Moon' Wisteria

New

☀	⛅	↔ 1 m	↕ 4 m	✿ Summer/Autumn	ZONE 4	🌿	✂

Give it sun, a rich, well-drained soil, a solid support and annual pruning. This Wisteria will repay you abundantly with magnificent bunches of intoxicatingly, perfumed bluish-mauve flowers. Plus: it's hardy, insect-resistant and virtually disease-free!

Climbing plants

Clematis 'Joséphine'
'Joséphine' Clematis

| ☀ | ☁ | ↔ 1 to 2 m | ↕ 3 m | ❀ Summer/ Autumn | ZONE 4 |

You'll never regret planting this at the base of a trellis or a pergola: its magnificent lavender-coloured, double flowers proudly display central stripes. A cluster of pale pink petals comprise the heart of it all. Keep its roots cool and humid.

Clematis 'Marie-Louise Jensen'
'Marie-Louise Jensen' Clematis

New

| ☀ | ☁ | ↔ 2 to 2.5 m | ↕ | ❀ Summer/ Autumn | ZONE 4 |

Superb, double flowers with violet petals that lighten towards their centre. Makes a remarkable vertical mass when mixed with lavender or white flowers on a pergola or small tree.

Clematis 'Miss Bateman'
'Miss Bateman' Clematis

| ☀ | ☁ | ↔ 1 m | ↕ 2.5 m | ❀ Summer/ Autumn | ZONE 4 |

The pretty Miss Bateman's large white, red-centred flowers will add undeniable charm to any garden structure. A compact variety that flowers at the end of spring and then again at the end of summer.

Clematis 'Nelly Moser'
'Nelly Moser' Clematis

| ☀ | ☁ | ↔ 1 to 2 m | ↕ 3.5 m | ❀ Summer/ Autumn | ZONE 4 |

With its profusion of pale pink flowers and their striking, reddish central veins, you'll swear this is a bicolour Clematis. A vigorous climber that thrives in semishade and never needs to be cut back.

Clematis 'Niobe'
'Niobe' Clematis

☀	☁	↔ 1 m	↕ 2 m	✿ Summer/Autumn	ZONE 4	✂

These beautiful dark red flowers with their golden centres will add more than a touch of richness and colour to any fence, wall, metal or wood support. Equally striking when twining itself around the stem of a deciduous or conifer tree. Requires annual trimming til full maturity, .

Clematis 'Rouge Cardinale'
'Rouge Cardinale' Clematis

☀	☁	↔ 1 to 2 m	↕ 3 m	✿ Summer/Autumn	ZONE 4	✂

There's no doubt that this is one of the best Clematises on the market. Its huge, reddish purple flowers that lighten gradually throughout the season seem to be made of velvet. It's abundant flowering renders it perfect for not only climbing up structures and trees, but also trailing from a planter. Cut back in spring.

Clematis tangutica 'Golden Tiara'
'Golden Tiara' Tangutica Clematis

☀	☁	↔ 1 to 2 m	↕ 3 m	✿ Summer/Autumn	ZONE 3	

An extremely hardy Clematis with a plethora of suspended, bright yellow, star-like flowers, followed by feathery silver fruit that decorates the plant for the rest of the season. Plus, it never needs to be cut back!

Clematis 'Ville de Lyon'
'Ville de Lyon' Clematis

☀	☁	↔ 1 to 2 m	↕ 4 m	✿ Summer/Autumn	ZONE 4	✂

An abundance of blooms with scarlet borders surrounding carmine petals that contrast delightfully with butter-yellow stamens. Requires considerable pruning in spring.

Clematis

Another...

world

The Rose – which has been grown since ancient times – symbolizes romanticism and elegance, so it's no surprise writers, poets, painters and even architects have found inspiration in Roses for centuries. Its genealogy is complex, but it has long been intimately linked with mankind. To this day, hybrids are developed to defend a cause or celebrate a historic anniversary.

Thanks to its characteristic perfume and beauty, the Rose is as popular with gardeners as it is with interior decorators. Nor is there a shortage of choices: ancient and modern cultivars, miniature varieties, shrubs, climbers and the Rose also works well with many different landscape styles, whether it be the romantic garden, the country estate or a resolutely modern approach. Just select the Rose that inspires you.

The hybrids chosen for this guide are amongst the hardiest, most disease-resistant and easiest to grow. Easy? Yes, as long as you remember the basic rules summarized in the following pages. Because there are so many, one could get lost in the choices, so please don't hesitate to consult an advisor at your BOTANIX, who will be happy to help you pick out a Rose that matches your environment and tastes.

Rosa 'Blue Girl'
'Blue Girl' Rose

A flowering dynasty

The large Rose family offers various forms in several categories, including some cultivars categorized for a shared characteristics that form a lineage, such as the Explorer series.

- **Hybrid Tea and Grandiflora**: These, the most popular of all Roses, make magnificent cut flowers – they're the ones florists usually use. Semi-double or double, perfumed flowers; single flowers (Hybrid Tea) or several flowers (Grandiflora). They're fragile enough to require winter protection.

- **Floribunda**: Hardier than the Hybrid Tea or Grandiflora, with an abundance of scented, semi-double or double flowers. Repeat flowering.

- **Hardy Shrubs**: These bushes are the hardiest and least demanding. They are available with simple or double flowers in a vast choice of colours that may or may not be scented. Includes the Rugosa, is the most resistant to climatic extremes.

- **Rambling**: Climbing Roses that develop vigorously on such supports as trellises, arbours and pergolas. Depending on the cultivar, they may or may not be repeat flowering.

What are repeat-flowering Roses?

Roses usually flower spectacularly in early summer, staying on for about three weeks. Modern hybrids, however are often repeat flowering, meaning they'll keep flowering until October or even early November; abundantly at first and then rather more modestly until they stop.

Roses: I never promised you a Rose garden

Yes, Roses are getting easier to grow, but they still do need specific care. First of all, you want to maximize the sun they get, then you need to provide a well-drained soil that's rich in organic matter and nutritional elements, plus they need fertilization and, often, winter protection. The recommended pruning varies depending on flowering. Check out the information at **botanix.com** for advice on the most important aspects of growing Roses successfully.

Did you know?

- In temperate zones, the Rose is the most cultivated ornamental plant, and the one most used for cut flowers. Combine that with its usage in the perfume industry, and you'll understand why thousands of tons of Roses are produced every year.

A flowering dynasty

Rosa 'John Franklin'
'John Franklin' Rose

...a bouquet of Roses

Versatile

There are many types of Roses, so there are many ways you can use them in your garden. Here are but a few: in isolation or in a group, in a Rose garden, among other perennials in a flower bed, as a freestyle hedge, in pots on your patio or balcony, climbing elegantly over an arbour or pergola. And don't forget, the hardy Roses are just wild enough to help you create the slightly dishevelled ambience of a country garden.

Rosa rugosa
Rugosa Rose

...everything's looking rosy

...blooming beautifully

Rosa 'Flower Carpet Yellow'
'Flower Carpet Yellow' Rose

...Queen of flowers

Rosa 'Black Baccara'
'Black Baccara' Rose

New

☀	↔ 90 cm	↕ 90 cm to 1 m	❀ Spring/ Autumn	ZONE 5			

A definite plus in any garden, with its greyish green foliage providing a backdrop to the satin, dark red flowers that some-times – depending on the light – look like the elusive black Rose. Naturally, they make arresting cut flowers, too.

Rosa 'Blue Girl'
'Blue Girl' Rose

☀	↔ 60 cm	↕ 1 m	❀ Spring/ Autumn	ZONE 5			

The slightly lustrous, dark green foliage of this hybrid surrounds unusual, delicately perfumed, lavender-blue flowers that are the ideal table flower.

Rosa 'Chrysler Imperial'
'Chrysler Imperial' Rose

☀	↔ 60 cm	↕ 60 cm	❀ Spring/ Autumn	ZONE 5			

A classic Rose that has never lost its popularity thanks to its dark red, velvet-textured flowers that actually turn blue! Highly aromatic.

Rosa 'John F. Kennedy'
'John F. Kennedy' Rose

☀	↔ 60 to 90 cm	↕ 90 cm to 1 m	❀ Spring/ Autumn	ZONE 5			

From among the dark green foliage, the long, rugged stems of this cultivar produce contrasting, double white flowers with a strong scent, for a touch of elegant charm in your garden.

Rosa 'Lady Di'
'Lady Di' Rose

| ☀ | ↔ 1 m | ↕ 1.2 m | ✽ Spring/Autumn | ZONE 5 | | | |

Magnificent, subtle, coral-pink-tinted flowers burst out of the shiny green foliage. Intensely perfumed, and exceptional for indoor flower arrangements.

Rosa 'Prince Charles'
'Prince Charles' Rose

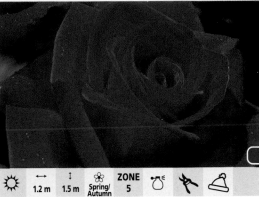

| ☀ | ↔ 1.2 m | ↕ 1.5 m | ✽ Spring/Autumn | ZONE 5 | | | |

The double, dark red, velour flowers of this Rose exhale a mild but captivating perfume. Combined with the dark green foliage, this will provide a spectacle all summer. An excellent addition to a Rose garden.

Rosa 'Queen Elizabeth'
'Queen Elizabeth' Rose

| ☀ | ↔ 80 cm | ↕ 1.2 m | ✽ Spring/Autumn | ZONE 5 | | | |

The long, vigorous stems of this popular Grandiflora provide cascades of double, pink flowers all summer. Magnificent in the garden. Magnificent in a flower vase.

Rosa 'Rio Samba'
'Rio Samba' Rose

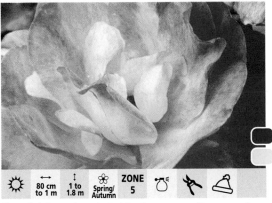

| ☀ | ↔ 80 cm to 1 m | ↕ 1 to 1.8 m | ✽ Spring/Autumn | ZONE 5 | | | |

The slightly perfumed double flowers usually grow alone, making it easier to appreciate the few yellow flower petals that turn pink as they age.

Rosa 'Abbotsford'
'Abbotsford' Rose

| ☼ | ↔ 60 cm | ↕ 40 cm | ❀ Spring/Autumn | ZONE 3 | ✂ | △ |

The double flowers of this compact, floriferous bush start out pale pink and turn fuchsia before becoming dark lavender. Sensational in groups or in a pot. Highly disease-resistant.

Rosa 'Cap-Diamant'
'Cap-Diamant' Rose

New

| ☼ | ↔ 1.2 m | ↕ 1 to 1.4 m | ❀ Spring/Autumn | ZONE 3 | ⚘ | ✂ |

This, the floral emblem of Québec City's 400th anniversary, was created to withstand our bitter winters. The spice-scented pink flowers last until the first frosts. An old-style Rose that's one of the most disease-resistant.

Rosa 'Champlain'
'Champlain' Rose

| ☼ | ↔ 80 cm | ↕ 1.2 m | ❀ Spring/Autumn | ZONE 4b | ⚘ | ✂ | △ |

This highly floriferous, Explorer-series Rose has spectacular bright red flowers. A hearty cultivar that would make a wonderful hedge or star attraction.

Rosa 'Emily Carr'
'Emily Carr' Rose

New

| ☼ | ↔ 1.5 m | ↕ 1 m | ❀ Summer/Autumn | ✂ | △ |

Created as a tribute to the B.C. painter, this hardy Rose flowers all summer long, requires little maintenance and rarely succumbs to disease. An elegant addition to your garden.

Rosa 'Félix Leclerc'
'Félix Leclerc' Rose

New

| ☀ | ↔ 1.25 m | ↕ 3 m | ❀ Summer/Autumn | ZONE 3 | ✂ | ⌂ |

A disease-resistant, winter-tolerant climber with splendid, bright pink flowers adding an aura of romance to your garden. Spring pruning required.

Rosa 'Frontenac'
'Frontenac' Rose

| ☀ | ↔ 1.2 m | ↕ 1.3 m | ❀ Spring/Autumn | ZONE 3 | ⟋ | ✂ |

This extremely hardy Explorer has numerous bunches of dark pink, semi-double flowers that give off an extremely pleasant scent. No winter protection required.

Rosa 'George Vancouver'
'George Vancouver' Rose

| ☀ | ↔ 1.2 m | ↕ 90 cm | ❀ Spring/Autumn | ZONE 4 | ⟋ | ✂ | ⌂ |

An extremely hardy Explorer with scented, semi-double, pink flowers in numerous bunches. No winter protection required.

Rosa 'Henry Kelsey'
'Henry Kelsey' Rose

| ☀ | ↔ 1 to 1.8 m | ↕ 1.5 to 2.5 m | ❀ Spring/Autumn | ZONE 3 | ⟋ | ✂ | ⌂ |

The dark-red, double lowers with their golden hearts emerge early in the season and continue blooming sporadically throughout the summer. A cultivar of the Explorer series, which is known for its hardiness.

Rosa 'Home Run'
'Home Run' Rose

New

☀	↔ 90 cm	↕ 90 cm	✿ Spring/Autumn	ZONE 5	⌂

You'll enjoy the superb, scarlet, simple flowers with their golden hearts all summer. Disease-resistant.

Rosa 'Hope for Humanity'
'Hope for Humanity' Rose

☀	↔ 60 cm to 1 m	↕ 40 to 70 cm	✿ Spring/Autumn	ZONE 3	⚬	✂	⌂

A bushy climbing Rose that, being part of the Parkland series, possesses all the qualities you need: performance, disease resistance and being highly ornamental. With its deep red flowers, this is assuredly an aesthetic asset in any garden.

Rosa 'John Cabot'
'John Cabot' Rose

spirit
style

☀	↔ 2.5 m	↕ 3 m	✿ Spring/Autumn	ZONE 3	⚬	✂	⌂

One of the most popular Roses, thanks to its generous flowering that lasts all summer, its intoxicating perfume and admirable disease resistance.

Rosa 'J.P. Connell'
'J.P. Connell' Rose

☀	↔ 1.25 m	↕ 1.5 m	✿ Spring/Summer	ZONE 3	⚬	✂

Another Explorer that flowers abundantly early in the season, and then continues offering up blooms more parsimoniously. The scented, double flowers are yellow when they emerge, and gradually turn to cream. Perfect for a free-form hedge or large flower bed.

Rosa 'John Franklin'
'John Franklin' Rose

| ☀ | ↔ 60 cm | ↕ 80 cm | ❁ Spring/Autumn | ZONE 4b | ⚘ | ✂ | △ |

Though it's an 'Explorer', this cultivar is unusually compact. You'll love its numerous bunches of pinkish-red, highly scented flowers.

Rosa 'Knock Out'
'Knock Out' Rose

| ☀ | ↔ 80 cm | ↕ 80 cm | ❁ Spring/Autumn | ZONE 4 | ⚘ | ✂ | △ |

The magnificent, cherry-red, simple flowers emerge from bright green foliage, for a long-lasting, classic display in your garden. Valued for its disease resistance and tolerance of dry spells.

Rosa 'Lambert Closse'
'Lambert Closse' Rose

| ☀ | ↔ 70 to 85 cm | ↕ 65 to 85 cm | ❁ Spring/Autumn | ZONE 4 | ⚘ | ✂ | △ |

This Explorer is a classic beauty, with its highly perfumed, bright pink, double flowers contrasting against the dark green foliage. Flowers until the first frosts.

Rosa 'Lady Elsie May'
'Lady Elsie May' Rose

New

| ☀ | ↔ 1 m | ↕ 1 m | ❁ Summer/Autumn | ZONE 4 | ⚘ | ✂ | △ |

Your garden will be beautiful all summer thanks to the delicate, pink flowers of this Rose and its lustrous foliage. Plant in groups or in containers to add ineffable charm to your yard.

Rosa 'Morden Blush'
'Morden Blush' Rose

☀	↔ 60 cm	↕ 70 cm	✿ Spring/ Autumn	ZONE 3b		

A Parkland with double, pink-tinted, white flowers blooming in embarrassing abundance. Undemanding, low-maintenance and hardy.

Rosa 'Morden Cardinette'
'Morden Cardinette' Rose

☀	↔ 30 to 50 cm	↕ 30 to 50 cm	✿ Spring/ Summer	ZONE 3		

A very elegant miniature Rose that's easy to grow in a pot or flower bed. The superb, red flowers of this Parkland will definitely please the eye.

Rosa 'Morden Centennial'
'Morden Centennial' Rose

☀	↔ 1.35 m	↕ 1 to 1.2 m	✿ Spring/ Autumn	ZONE 3b		

A Parkland Rose that produces very pretty, double, pink flowers with a subtle perfume from spring to the first frosts. Highly disease-resistant.

Rosa 'Morden Fireglow'
'Morden Fireglow' Rose

☀	↔ 60 cm	↕ 60 cm	✿ Spring/ Autumn	ZONE 3b			

A small Parkland that's coveted for its disease resistance and scented scarlet flowers that look like Hybrid Tea blooms.

Rosa 'Morden Snow Beauty'
'Morden Snow Beauty' Rose

☀	↔ 60 cm to 1.1 m	↕ 80 cm to 1.1 m	✿ Spring/ Autumn	ZONE 3		

This attractive Parkland generates magnificent, simple white flowers, from which a delicate perfume emanate. The whiteness of the blooms creates a luminous contrast with the dark green foliage.

Rosa 'Morden Sunrise'
'Morden Sunrise' Rose

☀	↔ 45 to 60 cm	↕ 45 to 60 cm	✿ Spring/ Autumn	ZONE 3			

A profusion of magnificent flowers with scintillating highlights flashing from yellow to pinkish orange. A highly unusual bush. Being a Parkland, diseases don't bother it.

Rosa 'Thérèse Bugnet'
'Thérèse Bugnet' Rose

☀	↔ 1.2 m	↕ 1.2 m	✿ Spring/ Autumn	ZONE 4a		

All summer, you'll enjoy the double flowers, and at the end of the season, you'll appreciate the violet colouring of its leaves. It's slightly dishevelled appearance makes it ideal for a country-garden atmosphere.

Rosa 'William Baffin'
'William Baffin' Rose

☀	↔ 2.5 m	↕ 2.5 m	✿ Spring/ Summer	ZONE 4		

This climbing Explorer is instantly recognizable when in bloom, as it has an unparalleled plethora of double, dark pink flowers with yellow hearts. Very resistant to fungus. Marvellously covers a wall or garden structure.

Hardy Shrub Roses

Rosa 'Winnipeg Parks'
'Winnipeg Parks' Rose

☀	↔ 30 to 70 cm	↕ 40 to 70 cm	✿ Spring/Autumn	ZONE 3			

Until autumn, an unbroken parade of bright pink flowers with golden stamens embellish the magnificent foliage of this Parkland.

Rosa cv.
Flower Carpet Series

☀	☁	↔ 90 cm	↕ 90 cm	✿ Spring/Autumn	ZONE 5		

Carpet series cultivars flower for long periods and tolerate slight shade. As they are highly disease-resistant, too, they are an excellent choice for a Rose garden.

Rosa rugosa 'Blanc Double de Coubert'
'Blanc Double de Coubert' Rugosa Rose

☀	↔ 1.8 m	↕ 1.5 m	✿ Spring/Summer	ZONE 3			

Highly abundant flowering even in poor soil. The double, pure white flowers with their yellow stamens exude a strong perfume. A hardy, undemanding bush that works equally well in a hedge or flower bed.

Rosa rugosa 'Hansa'
'Hansa' Rugosa Rose

☀	↔ 2 m	↕ 2 m	✿ Spring/Autumn	ZONE 3		

Your garden will be deliciously perfumed by the abundant violet-pink flowers of this undemanding and hardy Rose bush. Makes a wonderful hedge when pruned regularly.

Rosa 'Angel Face'
'Angel Face' Rose

☀	↔ 1.2 m	↕ 60 cm	✿ Spring/Autumn	ZONE 5			

This Rose bedecks itself in lavender-pink flowers with golden hearts and lustrous, dark green foliage. Like all Floribunda roses, it's very hardy. The strong perfume will waft through your garden, or pervade your living room if you put the flowers in a vase.

Rosa 'Iceberg'
'Iceberg' Rose

☀	↔ 80 cm to 1 m	↕ 60 to 90 cm	✿ Spring/Autumn	ZONE 5			

A key ingredient in a romantic garden with superb clusters of highly perfumed, double, white flowers. Very hardy.

Rosa 'Julia Child'
'Julia Child' Rose

New

☀	↔ 1 m	↕ 1 m	✿ Summer/Autumn	ZONE 4			

On any given day over the summer, you'll enjoy many golden yellow, classical Rose flowers that emanate a liquorice scent. Plant near perennials with white flowers or gold foliage. Very hardy.

Rosa 'Yvon Cléroux'
'Yvon Cléroux' Rose

☀	↔ 50 to 70 cm	↕ 40 to 70 cm	✿ Spring/Autumn	ZONE 5b			

A hybrid named in honour of the Québec horticultural pioneer and Botanix cofounder. Hardy and very floriferous with bright double, reddish-orange flowers that are slightly perfumed.

Perennials:

show us more!

When entering a garden, perennials are often what we notice first. A gathering of Sage, Daylilies, Astilbes, Echinaceas or Lavender is breathtaking. Colourful borders of Asters, Campanulas or Myosotis inevitably attract the eye.

Perennials are valued not only for their longevity and the fact that they grow back every year, but also for their virtually unlimited array of colours, shapes, textures and scents. Plus, their successive flowering allows you to prolong the beauty of your garden in an unbroken sequence right through the first frost, with one type of flower fading as another bursts into full bloom. Hostas and Heucheras are good examples of the many species that have highly decorative foliage. Create various forms of elegant flower beds by simply putting together interspersed perennials.

Perennials come in a wide variety of choices, choose them by soil type, sun exposure and location. Plant them anywhere and everywhere, including near high-traffic areas such as patios, decks, swimming pools and playgrounds – their range of colours, sizes and textures will bring rhythm and harmony to your outdoor life.

Without a doubt, perennials will be the central element in your garden, but if you want to make the most of their vast decorative potential, don't leap without looking. Enjoy the planning and dreaming stage first, and you'll find that your garden will also benefit in the long run!

Echinacea 'Vintage Wine'
'Vintage Wine' Coneflower

It's your move, go!

A good planting bed doesn't just happen. Don't hesitate to draw up a plan so you can preview the possibilities and create the best interrelationships. Be your own outdoor architect!

Save time and money by considering the following:

- Available ambient light and direct sunlight
- Soil-type
- Plant-size at maturity

Remember, the best gardens are the ones where each plant accentuates the appeal of its neighbours.

- Look for balance in your garden, placing the tallest plants behind and the smaller ones in front where they'll be appreciated.
- Create rhythm in your flower bed by integrating various forms, susch as upright, weeping and creeping. Also, exploit colour and foliage variations.
- Integrate several plants in the same species according to the size of your flower bed. The larger the flowerbed, the more plants of the same species it takes. This creates homogenous areas that have visual appeal from afar.
- Stagger flowering periods so you're never without blooms.

What about maintenance?

Most perennials demand little, but that doesn't mean none. At **botanix.com**, you'll find judicious planting and maintenance advice.

Ajuga reptans 'Black Scallop'
'Black Scallop' Bugleweed

Tips and Tricks

Add charm and character to your garden by grouping species, thematically. Allow your garden style to naturally harmonize with your house. Create a country-style garden by mixing Goldenrod, Echinacea, Achillea, or Fleabane. A Victorian garden would include traditional Poppies, Mallow, Digitalis, Yucca and Hollyhock. Create a wonderful underbrush garden with Hostas, Foamflowers, Violets, Solomon's Seal, and of course Trillium… and you'll soon imagine you're in a deep forest!

It's your move, go!

...*a rhythmic composition*

"Landscaping your garden is like interior decorating, but it's outside. Just like you have rooms in your house, your garden has sections you furnish after giving it some thought, using knowledge you've acquired. Every year, interesting new arrivals allow us to refresh areas that are getting a bit old."

Sylvie Picard, BOTANIX
Pépinière Lapointe, Mascouche

...restrained charm

...breaking waves

...life in the fast lane

...structural integrity

Acanthus spinosus
Spine Acanthus

| ☀ | ☁ | ↔ 40 cm | ↕ 1.5 m | ❀ Summer | ZONE 5 | ⛺ |

This rare and unusual plant features white and purple flowers on the same raceme and spiky foliage. Requires winter protection but survives dry spells easily.

Achillea clypeolata 'Moonshine'
'Moonshine' Yarrow

| ☀ | ↔ 40 cm | ↕ 60 cm | ❀ Summer/Autumn | ZONE 3 | 🌸 | 🦋 | 🐦 |

Ideal for a country garden and excellent for cut flowers, Moonshine has feathery, perfumed, silvery foliage and lemon-yellow flowers that bloom for an extended period. For maximum effect combine with violet or white flowers.

Achillea millefolium 'Red Beauty'
'Red Beauty' Common Yarrow

| ☀ | ↔ 40 cm | ↕ 60 cm to 1 m | ❀ Summer/Autumn | ZONE 3 | 🌸 | 🦋 | 🐦 |

Give this vigorous Yarrow a little time, and it will create a small corner of the prairies in your garden, with its delicate, bright reddish-purple flowers interspersed among other indigenous species.

Aconitum cammarum 'Bicolor'
'Bicolor' Monkshood

| ☀ | ☁ | ↔ 40 cm | ↕ 80 cm to 1.2 m | ❀ Summer/Autumn | ZONE 3 |

Let the long white and violet-blue floral spikes contribute a subtle elegance to your garden in the waning days of summer. Prefers fertile, well-drained soil. Note that certain parts of the plant are toxic.

Aconitum napellus
Common Monkshood

global village *style*

☀	☁	↔ 50 cm	↕ 1.15 m	✿ Summer/ Autumn	ZONE 4

At an impressive height, superb flower stalks reveal violet-blue blossoms among lustrous, dark green leaves. Plant in rich, damp, particulate soil. All parts are toxic.

Aegopodium podagraria 'Variegata'
Gout Weed

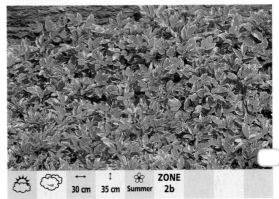

☁	☁	↔ 30 cm	↕ 35 cm	✿ Summer	ZONE 2b

A vigorous groundcover with variegated green and white foliage that takes to all soils and prefers shade. A highly invasive plant that requires a deep physical barrier to contain it.

Ajuga reptans 'Black Scallop'
'Black Scallop' Bugleweed

New

☀	☀	☁	↔ 80 cm	↕ 15 cm	✿ Spring/ Summer	ZONE 4

This is the darkest Bugleweed, with bright purple, persistent leaves that turn almost black in full sun. As a border, or in well-drained soil, will soon give character to your garden with its spreading habit.

Ajuga reptans 'Burgundy Glow'
'Burgundy Glow' Bugleweed

☀	☀	☁	↔ 20 cm	↕ 15 cm	✿ Spring/ Summer	ZONE 3

This tight groundcover is a great way to discourage weeds. Its colourful foliage will complement your other perennials. Likes rich, loose, well-drained soil.

Ajuga reptans 'Catlin's Giant'
'Catlin's Giant' Bugleweed

oasis style

| ☀ | ⛅ | ☁ | ↔ 30 cm | ↕ 30 cm | ❀ Spring/Summer | ZONE 3 |

The large, persistent, purple and dark green foliage of this cultivar will carpet your flower beds throughout the temperate months, as long as you provide it with rich, sandy and well-drained loam.

Alcea rosea
Hollyhock

| ☀ | ☁ | ↔ 40 cm | ↕ 1.5 to 2.25 m | ❀ Summer/Autumn | ZONE 3 |

Traditional Hollyhocks produce high floral stems with attractive, simple or double flowers with characteristic crumpled petal terminals. The seeds that falls on the ground give birth to new plants every year.

Alchemilla mollis
Lady's Mantle

global village style

| ☀ | ⛅ | ☁ | ↔ 30 cm | ↕ 30 to 40 cm | ❀ Summer | ZONE 3 |

The magnificent, soft and hairy foliage sports an umbel of small, yellow flowers that will bring light into undergrowth. Puts on a particularly delightful spectacle when raindrops or dew gather on its leaves.

Alyssum saxatile
Basket of Gold

| ☀ | ↔ 40 cm | ↕ 15 to 20 cm | ❀ Spring/Summer | ZONE 3 |

During springtime, while most of the spring-blooming plants are in blossom, a veritable floral explosion is released by the Basket of Gold. Works as well in a flower bed as in a rockery.

BOTANIX Experts by nature

Anemone hybrida 'Pamina'
Windflower

| ☀ | ☁ | ↔ 60 cm | ↕ 90 cm | ✿ Summer/Autumn | ZONE 4 |

Fill in the gap in your garden's blooming schedule with these late, dark pink blossoms. The trilobate, reticulate leaves are also interesting. In groups, they will bring light to undergrowth or a semishade area.

Anemone pulsatilla (syn. Pulsatilla vulgaris)
Pasque Flower

| ☀ | ↔ 30 cm | ↕ 20 to 30 cm | ✿ Spring | ZONE 4 |

An original cultivar with downy foliage and delicate flowers with well-separated, pointed petals, followed by filamentous fruit, like that of the Clematis. Likes friable, well-drained soil.

Anthemis tinctoria
Yellow Chamomile

| ☀ | ↔ 50 cm | ↕ 40 to 60 cm | ✿ Summer/Autumn | ZONE 3 | 🦋 |

This Chamomile brings a gold strike to your own garden. Even when they're dry, in autumn or early winter, the flowers will make a positive contribution to your garden's colour chart. Divide regularly to maintain vigour.

Aquilegia alpina
Alpine Columbine

| ☀ | ☁ | ↔ 25 cm | ↕ 35 to 40 cm | ✿ Summer | ZONE 3 | ✂ |

This diminutive Columbine forms a flat cushion with its delicate foliage and small scale, embellishing a rockery or small garden. Likes morning sun and late afternoon sun, but shies away from the afternoon heat. Remove flower-stalks after flowering.

Perennials

Aquilegia hybrida
Hybrid Columbine

☀️ ⛅ ↔️ 35 cm | ↕️ 40 to 80 cm | ❀ Spring/Summer | **ZONE 3** | 🐦 | ✂️

These hybrids feature single or double flowers available in a wide range of single colours or bicolour. It reseeds easily, and re-blooms easily if deadheaded. Attracts hummingbirds.

Aquilegia vulgaris 'Nora Barlow'
'Nora Barlow' Columbine

☀️ ⛅ ↔️ 40 cm | ↕️ 75 cm | ❀ Summer | **ZONE 3** | ✂️

The magnificent, reddish pink, double flowers with their white margins are tantalizingly suspended from the raceme, adding the dimension of movement to your garden. One of the more beautiful Columbine cultivars, that you won't regret having planted.

Arabis caucasica
Wall Rock-Cress

☀️ ↔️ 30 cm | ↕️ 15 cm | ❀ Spring/Summer | **ZONE 3**

A carpet of pink or white flowers adorn this groundcover in spring. Appreciated for its ability to withstand even the driest periods, you'll find it useful in a rockery are tumbling over a low wall.

Arenaria montana
Mountain Sandwort

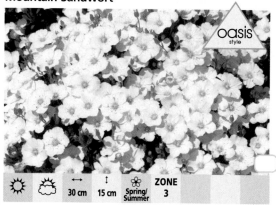

oasis style

☀️ ⛅ ↔️ 30 cm | ↕️ 15 cm | ❀ Spring/Summer | **ZONE 3**

Mountain Sandwort is a mass of chartreuse-throated, white flowers in spring. Its dark green foliage is persistent. Does well on a slope, as it likes well-drained soil.

Arenaria verna 'Aurea'
'Aurea' Sandwort

☀	⛅	↔ 25 cm	↕ 5 cm	❀ Summer	ZONE 3

You'd swear this string-like, brilliant foliage is moss, even when you see it covered in the pink or white flowers of spring. As it's highly tolerant of dryness, this is an appropriate plant to integrate into your rockery or leave hanging over a low stone wall.

Armeria maritima
Sea Pink Thrift

☀	⛅	↔ 25 cm	↕ 20 cm	❀ Summer	ZONE 3

The persistent, dark green foliage tufts are topped by ruffled flowers. Requires a fertile, sandy soil, making it ideal for rockeries. With its miniature size, it's also suitable for a small garden.

Artemisia schmidtiana 'Silver Mound'
'Silver Mound' Artemisia

☀	↔ 35 cm	↕ 30 cm	❀ Summer	ZONE 4

A classic with silky, silver-blue, aromatic foliage forming a globular mound. Likes poor, dry soil. When placed in a rich soil, it loses both form and vigour.

Artemisia stelleriana 'Silver Brocade'
'Silver Brocade' Artemisia

☀	↔ 45 cm	↕ 20 cm	ZONE 4	✂

The finely-toothed, silver foliage will bring a welcome contrast to your other garden plants. Cut back in spring to increase foliage density. Tolerates dry spells.

Perennials

Aruncus dioicus
Goat's Beard

☀ ⛅ ☁ ↔ 90 cm | ↕ 1 to 1.9 m | ❀ Summer | **ZONE 3** | ✂

Like the Astilbe, Arunculus clothes itself in numerous, long, cream panicles that need to be removed at the end of the season. Forms a spectacular little bush at maturity.

Asclepias incarnata
Swamp Milkweed/Silk Weed

☀ ↔ 60 cm | ↕ 1.2 m | ❀ Summer | **ZONE 3** | 🜹 🦋

The long leaves and dark green aromatic stems generate superb, vanilla-scented flower umbels that attract butterflies – monarchs especially love their nectar.

Asclepias tuberosa
Butterfly Weed

☀ ↔ 35 cm | ↕ 60 to 80 cm | ❀ Summer | **ZONE 3** | 🦋

All summer, this highly decorative variety brandishes clusters of little intensely coloured, star-shaped flowers that attract butterflies. Prefers well-drained soil and dislikes being transplanted.

Aster alpinus
Alpine Aster

☀ ↔ 40 cm | ↕ 30 cm | ❀ Spring/Summer | **ZONE 3**

The little, single or semi-double flowers are part of the joys of springtime. In order to avoid attacks of the fungus oidium, plant in an area with good air circulation and well-drained soil.

Aster dumosus
Michaelmas Daisy

☀	↔ 50 cm	↕ 30 to 60 cm	❁ Summer/ Autumn	ZONE 3b

Michaelmas Daisy blooms late with a superb palette of colours that seem to be competing for intensity. An agreeable way to prolong the season is to plant Wood's Pink at the edge of clumps of perennials with varied flower types and colours.

Aster novae-angliae
New England Aster

☀	↔ 70 cm	↕ 1 to 1.5 m	❁ Autumn	ZONE 3

An impressive, hardy plant with a plethora of brightly coloured flowers that close at night and on overcast days. To conserve its imposing beauty, plant near lower perennials to cover the stem, which loses its leaves over the season.

Astilbe arendsii 'Cattleya'
'Cattleya' Astilbe

☀	☁	↔ 60 cm	↕ 90 cm	❁ Summer	ZONE 3

The magnificent, starlet-pink of this Astilbe's long, feathery panicles attract the eye all summer. Requires very damp soil. Unsurpassed as a cut flower.

Astilbe arendsii 'Diamant'
'Diamant' Astilbe

☀	☁	↔ 50 cm	↕ 80 cm	❁ Summer	ZONE 3

Pristine white, pendant flowers adorn the panicles, in stark contrast to the dark foliage with its red reticulations. Prospers in rich, moist, crumbly soil. Creates a particularly felicitous tableau in front of Ligulariae.

Astilbe arendsii 'Fanal'
'Fanal' Astilbe

☀	☁	↔ 50 cm	↕ 45 cm	❀ Summer	ZONE 3

One of the most popular Astilbes, with long, blood-red spikes that jut out of bronze-tinted green foliage, and maintain their attractiveness throughout winter. Give it a rich soil and frequent watering.

Astilbe arendsii 'Red Sentinel'
'Red Sentinel' Astilbe

☀	☁	↔ 60 cm	↕ 70 cm	❀ Summer	ZONE 3

If the soil is kept moist, expect oversized, feathery red inflorescences for two full summer months. Looks great in a group and makes excellent cut flowers.

Astilbe arendsii 'Rock & Roll'
'Rock & Roll' Astilbe

New

☀	☁	↔ 60 cm	↕ 60 cm	❀ Summer	ZONE 3

Part of the Music series, with pretty, pinkish-white flowers all summer. Below, the ruby stems contrast with the green foliage. Do not deadhead, as the inflorescences will put on a show all winter.

Astilbe chinensis 'Vision in Red'
'Vision in Red' Astilbe

☀	☁	☁	↔ 25 cm	↕ 25 to 50 cm	❀ Summer	ZONE 3	

Water often for long, dense and feathery panicles that overhang the bronze-splattered green foliage and embellish sunny gardens or shady flower beds. An excellent cut flower.

Astilbe chinensis 'Vision in White'
'Vision in White' Astilbe

oasis style

| ☀ | ⛅ | ☁ | ↔ 25 cm | ↕ 25 to 50 cm | ✿ Summer | ZONE 3 | 💰 |

The long fluffy panicles and dark green foliage of the new 'Vision in White' will brighten your garden as much as the red variety. Do not let it dry out. A BOTANIX exclusive.

Astilbe simplicifolia 'Sprite'
'Sprite' Star Astilbe

| ⛅ | ☁ | ↔ 30 cm | ↕ 45 cm | ✿ Summer | ZONE 3 |

The delicate, pale pink inflorescences and lightly bronzed green leaves with their dainty serrations conspire to make this one of the most popular Astilbes. Prefers rich, damp soil.

Astilbe taquetii 'Superba'
'Superba' Astilbe

spirit style

| ☀ | ⛅ | ☁ | ↔ 50 cm | ↕ 1.1 m | ✿ Summer/Autumn | ZONE 3 |

Use this one in large groups or planted among other perennials to enjoy the long, pink panicles with purple highlights and the finely dentated foliage. Keep its soil moist.

Astilbe thunbergii 'Ostrich Plume'
Ostrich Plume

| ☀ | ⛅ | ☁ | ↔ 50 cm | ↕ 90 cm | ✿ Summer | ZONE 3 |

A vigorous cultivar that rapidly forms a colourful mass in your garden. Its fluffy pendant panicles, so popular with gardeners, will inject a certain je ne sais quoi into your leafy refuge. Likes deep, rich, moist soil.

Astilboides tabularis
Shieldleaf

| | | | ↔ 1.2 m | ↕ 80 cm to 1.3 m | ✿ Summer | ZONE 5 |

Tropics here we come: humongous circular, light green leaves and delicate, white summer flowers on tall shoots. Plant in rich soil in a spacious environment and water faithfully.

Astrantia major 'Ruby Wedding'
Ruby Masterwort

spirit
style

| | | ↔ 40 cm | ↕ 70 cm | ✿ Summer | ZONE 4 |

A vigorous Masterwort that produces magnificent ruby-coloured umbels with a touch of white. All summer, they overhang palmate foliage with toothed lobes. Will bring life to your flower bed in damp, well-drained soil.

Baptisia australis
False Indigo

| | | ↔ 50 cm | ↕ 1 m | ✿ Summer | ZONE 3 |

It takes a few years before the long, dusty violet spikes, with their white highlights, appear. The flamboyant flowering is worth the wait. Disease-resistant and dryness tolerant. Unbeatable cut flowers.

Belamcanda chinensis
Blackberry Lily

| | ↔ 25 cm | ↕ 60 to 80 cm | ✿ Summer | ZONE 4b |

Here's an exotic looking flower in shape and colour, plus, at the end of the season, it showcases little black decorative fruit (they last all winter because they're too hard for birds to eat) – whence the common name. Flowers all summer in well-drained soil. Do not deadhead or you'll never get the berry clusters.

Bellis perennis
English Daisy

| ☀ | ⛅ | ↔ 15 cm | ↕ 10 to 15 cm | ❀ Spring/ Autumn | ZONE 4 |

This little, round package generates adorable, small flowers that project over the leaf rosettes. A biannual that easily reseeds and makes a magnificent border for other plants as well as an ideal inhabitant of your rockery.

Bergenia cordifolia
Heart-Leaf Bergenia

| ☀ | ⛅ | ↔ 40 cm | ↕ 30 to 40 cm | ❀ Spring/ Summer | ZONE 4b |

In spring, stunning bunches of white, pink or red flowers cover the large round, lustrous leaves, which persist throughout winter. Best appreciated when planted in a group.

Brunnera macrophylla
Siberian Bugloss

global village style

| ⛅ | ⛅ | ↔ 35 to 45 cm | ↕ 20 to 35 cm | ❀ Spring/ Summer | ZONE 4 |

The large leaves at the heart of this Myositis are all that's really required for a successful flower bed, but when the diminutive, sky-blue flowers emerge from the delicate stalks, your shade garden will dazzle you with light. Likes deep particulate soil.

Brunnera macrophylla 'Looking Glass'
'Looking Glass' Siberian Bugloss

| ⛅ | ⛅ | ↔ 40 cm | ↕ 40 cm | ❀ Summer | ZONE 4 |

In spring, bunches of delicate, white flowers float above the large, silver leaves with their green veins. A genuine jewel that will make you feel like you really are Alice in Wonderland when you see it in a shady area of your garden. Keep its soil moist.

Campanula 'Samantha'
'Samantha' Campanula

☀ ☁ ↔ 35 cm ↕ 25 cm ✿ Summer **ZONE 3**

An original Campanula with large, luminous, tricolour flowers – yellow hearts, purple petal-margins and white in between – that stand out from the dark green foliage. Flowers all summer. An excellent choice to spill over a low wall.

Campanula carpatica 'Blue Chips'
'Blue Chips' Carpathian Bellflower

global village *style*

☀ ☁ ↔ 30 cm ↕ 25 cm ✿ Summer **ZONE 3**

This remarkable perennial with its dentated foliage will provide you with an abundance of wide yet little, blue or white bells all summer as long, as you remember to deadhead frequently. Grows easily in all soil types.

Campanula cochlearifolia
Fairy Thimbles

☀ ☁ ↔ 30 cm ↕ 10 cm ✿ Summer **ZONE 3**

An elfin Bellflower that's especially appropriate for alpine gardens and semishade. Plant in a cool spot that's well-drained, so it can flower abundantly all summer long.

Campanula glomerata
Cluster Bellflower

☀ ☁ ↔ 35 cm ↕ 35 to 60 cm ✿ Summer **ZONE 3**

This unusual Campanula has clusters of star-shaped, pastel-blue, white or mauve flowers growing cheek by jowl at the stalk terminals. Plant in groups to appreciate the contrast with the light green foliage, or highlight by interspersing with other flowering plants.

Campanula lactiflora
Milky Bellflower

☀ ⛅ ↔ 60 cm ↕ 1.2 to 1.5 m ❀ Summer **ZONE 5**

A large Bellflower with long panicles supporting five-petalled stars in pastel tones. In windy exposures, requires a tutor.

Campanula latifolia macrantha
Broad-Leaved Bellflower

☀ ⛅ ↔ 60 cm ↕ 1.2 m ❀ Summer **ZONE 3**

The large, narrow bells grow in groups of two or three on top of the long, upright stems, making excellent cut flowers. You'll find these lavender blue or white flowers to be even more striking when surrounded by their own kind.

Campanula persicifolia
Peachleaf Bellflower

☀ ⛅ ↔ 40 cm ↕ 50 to 80 cm ❀ Summer **ZONE 3b**

The ever-popular Peachleaf is coveted for its shiny foliage and wide-mouthed, mildly pendant flowers that top the tall stems. Easily grown.

Campanula portenschlagiana (Muralis)
Wall Bellflower

☀ ⛅ ↔ 30 to 40 cm ↕ 10 to 15 cm ❀ Spring/ Summer **ZONE 4**

A rampant spreader that gives life to a low wall with its prolonged, lavender flowering that will resonate with the grey stone over which it's spilling. Likes well-drained, impoverished soil.

Centaurea dealbata
Persian Cornflower

☀ | ↔ 50 cm | ↕ 50 to 80 cm | ❀ Summer | ZONE 4 | 🦋

The large, deeply serrated foliage and numerous, highly colourful bractated flowers will give your garden an original touch. Adapts to any soil as long as it's well-drained.

Centaurea montana
Mountain Blue

☀ ☁ | ↔ 40 cm | ↕ 45 to 60 cm | ❀ Spring/Summer | ZONE 4 | ✂

The stunning violet-blue flowers will not go unnoticed, but be sure to deadhead before they seed, as this is a highly invasive plant.

Cerastium tomentosum
Snow-in-Summer

☀ | ↔ 35 cm | ↕ 15 cm | ❀ Summer | ZONE 3

The fuzzy, silver foliage will highlight neighbouring plants, and in early summer, will provide a counterpart to its small white flowers. Tolerates poor, dry soils.

Chelone obliqua
Red Turtlehead

global village *style*

☀ ☁ ☁ | ↔ 50 cm | ↕ 60 to 80 cm | ❀ Summer/Autumn | ZONE 4

The lustrous dark green foliage and bright flowers form an elegant and luminous mass in semishade flower gardens, where its late flowering will prolong the beauty of your garden. Prefers damp soil.

Chrysanthemum 'Mammoth Autumn Red'
'Mammoth Autumn Red' Chrysanthemum

New

| ☀ | ↔ 70 cm | ↕ 90 cm | ❄ Autumn | ZONE 3 | 🦋 | ✂ | ⛑ |

The hardy Chrysanthemums are the perfect autumn plants. The Mammoth series are specifically designed for the hardships of our climate, so you can enjoy their striking colours until the first frosts. Mulch for winter and cut back in early spring.

Chrysanthemum 'Mammoth Star White'
'Mammoth Star White' Chrysanthemum

New

| ☀ | ↔ 70 cm | ↕ 90 cm | ❄ Autumn | ZONE 3 | 🦋 | ✂ | ⛑ |

A floriferous gardener's favourite and one of the last plants to bloom. Mulch for winter and cut back in early spring to combat sparse flowering.

Chrysanthemum 'Mammoth Twilight Pink'
'Mammoth Twilight Pink' Chrysanthemum

New

| ☀ | ↔ 70 cm | ↕ 90 cm | ❄ Autumn | ZONE 3 | 🦋 | ✂ | ⛑ |

You'll appreciate the profusion of colours of the Mammoth series chrysanthemums as the days grow shorter. This serie is perfectly adapted to our harsh climate. After flowering, cover in mulch. Cut back in early spring.

Chrysanthemum 'Mammoth Yellow Quill'
'Mammoth Yellow Quill' Chrysanthemum

New

| ☀ | ↔ 70 cm | ↕ 90 cm | ❄ Autumn | ZONE 3 | 🦋 | ✂ | ⛑ |

While your other flowering plants have gone to sleep, this hardy Mum will flower abundantly if mulched for winter and cut back in early spring.

Perennials

Chrysanthemum arcticum 'Red Chimo'
'Red Chimo' Arctic Chrysanthemum

| ☀ | ↔ 50 to 80 cm | ↕ 20 to 40 cm | ❀ Autumn | ZONE 2 |

A superb autumn plant that flowers late. Hardy, vigorous and rapid-growing with lustrous, rough leaves overgrown by pink, yellow-hearted flowers that will illuminate your garden.

Chrysanthemum coccineum
Painted Daisy

| ☀ | ↔ 45 cm | ↕ 60 to 80 cm | ❀ Summer | ZONE 3 | 🦋 |

A country-garden standard displaying brilliant, simple or double flowers that attract butterflies, though its foliage contains the natural insecticide pyrethrum. Likes dry, well-drained soils.

Cimicifuga ramosa 'Atropurpurea'
'Atropurpurea' Bugbane

| ☀ | ⛅ | ☁ | ↔ 90 to 1.2 cm | ↕ 2 m | ❀ Summer/ Autumn | ZONE 4 | 🌡 |

The slightly purple tone of this cultivar — even more remarkable in semishade — contrasts delightfully with the green foliage. Before autumn descends upon us, the long white floral spikes will lighten up your yard. Likes rich, damp soil.

Cimicifuga ramosa 'Brunette'
Black Snakeroot/Heartleaf Bugbane

| ☀ | ⛅ | ☁ | ↔ 80 cm | ↕ 1 to 1.5 m | ❀ Summer/ Autumn | ZONE 4 | 🌡 |

The perfumed, pinkish white flower-spikes and contrasting sombre foliage will make it difficult to notice anything else in your garden. In semishade, the leaf-colour is even more striking. Prefers rich, damp soil.

Convallaria majalis
Lily of the Valley

		↔ 20 cm	↕ 20 cm	✿ Spring	ZONE 3	

What could be better than Lily of the Valley to blanket your shade garden and perfume the spring air. One of the earliest plants to flower, with its typical, pearly white, bell-like, pendant flowers. Can become invasive, but is easy to control. The lovely red berries are toxic.

Coreopsis 'Crème Brûlée'
'Crème Brûlée' Coreopsis

global village style

☼	↔ 45 cm	↕ 50 cm	✿ Summer/ Autumn	ZONE 3

Resembles Moonbeam, but the flowers are larger, with more saturated colour. Well suited for planting in front of your ornamental grasses or throughout a country garden. Easy to grow.

Coreopsis 'Jethro Tull'
'Jethro Tull' Coreopsis

New

☼	↔ 45 cm	↕ 35 cm	✿ Spring/ Autumn	ZONE 5	✂

This cultivar is a compact Coreopsis. It generates a profusion of bright, golden yellow flowers with fluted petals (an inspiration for the name?). Likes well-drained soil and being deadheaded to stimulate flowering.

Coreopsis 'Tequila Sunrise'
'Tequila Sunrise' Coreopsis

☼	↔ 50 cm	↕ 45 cm	✿ Summer/ Autumn	ZONE 3

This Coreopsis has unique olive-green, cream-margined foliage that's splattered with pink in early summer and purple in the fall. In spring, the plant issues forth orange-yellow flowers that last until autumn.

Perennials

Coreopsis grandiflora 'Baby Sun'
'Baby Sun' Coreopsis

☀ | ↔ 30 cm | ↕ 40 cm | ❀ Summer/Autumn | **ZONE 4**

Spring heralds a mass of golden yellow flowers with red centres, evoking sunrays. Use with other country-style perennials or grasses to create a prairie look.

Coreopsis grandiflora 'Early Sunrise'
'Early Sunrise' Tickseed

☀ | ↔ 65 cm | ↕ 50 to 90 cm | ❀ Summer/Autumn | **ZONE 3** | 🦋

Many gardeners can't get enough of these abundant bright yellow flowers that bloom in all three gardening seasons. Well adapted to dry and impoverished soils.

Coreopsis verticillata 'Moonbeam'
'Moonbeam' Coreopsis

☀ | ↔ 35 to 45 cm | ↕ 35 to 55 cm | ❀ Summer/Autumn | **ZONE 3**

An infinity of little, pale-yellow flowers cover the delicate foliage from spring into the first frosts. You'll love to mix blue and white flowers with its indefatigable colours.

Crocosmia 'Lucifer'
Crocosmia

global village style

☀ | ⛅ | ↔ 30 cm | ↕ 90 cm | ❀ Summer | **ZONE 5**

A bulb that sends out vertical, Iris-like foliage and highly decorative paprika-red inflorescences that scream "tropical", in your garden or in a vase. Requires well-drained soil.

Delphinium 'King Arthur'
'King Arthur' Delphinium/Larkspur

☀	↔ 45 cm	↕ 1.3 m	❀ Summer	ZONE 4	🐥

The erect flower-heads will attract your eye with their dark blue, semi-double flowers. King Arthur's tall, so it works best behind other plants or in a vase. Likes fertile, well drained soil.

Delphinium elatum 'Dark Blue/White bee'
'Dark Blue/White bee' Delphinium/Larkspur

☀	↔ 45 cm	↕ 1 m	❀ Summer	ZONE 2	🦋	🐥

Magnificent flower spikes featuring sky-blue florets and white sepals that flower in early summer. Plant it in groups in rich, loose, well drained loam. Magic Fountain Series come in several colours.

Delphinium grandiflora 'Blue Butterfly'
'Blue Butterfly' Delphinium/Larkspur

☀	↔ 45 cm	↕ 50 cm	❀ Summer	ZONE 4	🐥

A compact dwarf with short stalks that sport a mass of deep blue flowers and forest-green foliage.

Dianthus 'Roshish One'
Cottage Pinks

New

☀	↔ 30 cm	↕ 25 cm	❀ Summer/ Autumn	ZONE 4	🌱

A floriferous cultivar with magnificent, velvet-textured dark pink flowers marked by traces of white and verdigris foliage. A great beauty that will dress up your rock garden, edging or flower bed. Requires a very well drained soil.

Perennials

Dianthus barbatus
Sweet William

☀	☁	↔ 20 cm	↕ 15 to 60 cm	❀ Summer/ Autumn	ZONE 4	⚘

A biannual with bunches of highly-coloured, fringed flowers overlooking narrow, persistent foliage all summer long. Some varieties are scented. Reseeds easily.

Dianthus deltoides 'Brilliant'
Maiden Pinks

☀	☁	↔ 45 cm	↕ 15 cm	❀ Summer/ Autumn	ZONE 3	🦋

This cultivar produces a glut of flowers that seem to float over the foliage. Ideal for any flower bed, edging or rockery. Requires friable, well drained loam.

Dianthus gracianopolitanus 'Firewitch'
'Firewitch' Cheddar Pinks

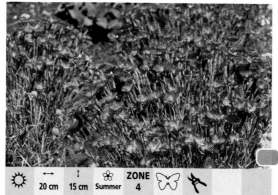

☀	↔ 20 cm	↕ 15 cm	❀ Summer	ZONE 4	🦋	✂

Butterflies are enamoured of the dark pink blooms, which also make excellent cut flowers. Being a dwarf variety, it's a good choice for a rockery. Remember to deadhead to prolong flowering, and give it a well-drained soil.

Dianthus gratianopolitanus 'Frosty Fire'
'Frosty Fire' Cheddar Pinks

☀	↔ 25 cm	↕ 15 to 20 cm	❀ Summer	ZONE 4	⚘	✂

Frosty Fire is a dwarf, so it works well for edging and rockeries. The shiny, greenish-blue foliage surrounds pretty, semi-double, bright red flowers that exude a sweet perfume.

Dianthus plumarius
Pinks

☀ | ↔ 30 cm | ↕ 20 to 30 cm | ❀ Summer | **ZONE 3** | 🝇

The subtly fringed, highly-scented flowers of this popular Dianthus – the original – jump out at you from the delicate, bluish foliage. Works well with purple-leafed plants in a rockery or flower bed.

Dicentra formosa 'Luxuriant'
'Luxuriant' Bleeding Heart

☀ | ☁ | ↕ 35 cm | ↕ 30 to 40 cm | ❀ Spring/Autumn | **ZONE 3**

A hardy little perennial with bluish, fern-like foliage. This undemanding plant looks great in groups, where it will illuminate a shade garden.

Dicentra spectabilis
Bleeding Heart

☀ | ☁ | ↔ 80 cm | ↕ 50 to 80 cm | ❀ Spring/Summer | **ZONE 3** | ✂

The shade garden lives for the ever-popular Dicentra, with groups of delicate, heart-shaped flowers dangling disarmingly from their stems. Looks wonderful against light green foliage. Likes cool, rich soil.

Dicentra spectabilis 'Goldheart'
'Goldheart' Common Bleeding Heart

☀ | ☀ | ☁ | ↔ 60 cm | ↕ 70 cm | ❀ Spring/Summer | **ZONE 4** | ✂

The little, pale-pink hearts fluttering under delicate stems, arching over the lime-green foliage will indubitably enliven the shadiest area of your garden. Protect from direct sun and cut back after a heat wave.

Digitalis purpurea 'Camelot White'
'Camelot White' Foxglove

spirit
style

☀ ⛅ ↔ 60 cm | ↕ 1.15 m | ❀ Summer | ZONE Bi-annual | 🦋 | 🐦

Purple stems support a mass of large tubular, white flowers with sage-green freckles in their throats. A floriferous biannual that resists frost but requires damp ground. Toxic if eaten. Camelot Series offer a large selection of colours.

Echinacea 'Art's Pride'
'Art's Pride' Coneflower

☀ ⛅ ↔ 90 cm | ↕ 90 cm | ❀ Summer | ZONE 3b | 🌸 | 🦋 | 🐦

Creates a flaming mass of orange and salmon in your garden. Attracts butterflies and birds. The perfumed flowers make a superior indoor bouquet.

Echinacea 'Fragrant Angel'
'Fragrant Angel' Coneflower

☀ ↔ 60 cm | ↕ 75 cm | ❀ Summer/Autumn | ZONE 4

Like Margaritas, Fragrant Angel's flowers have golden centres and white petals, making an interesting balance with dark green foliage. Brings the country look to your garden.

Echinacea 'Harvest Moon'
'Harvest Moon' Coneflower

☀ ⛅ ↔ 45 to 60 cm | ↕ 75 to 90 cm | ❀ Summer/Autumn | ZONE 4 | 🌸 | 🦋 | 🐦

This cultivar flowers continuously throughout the summer and into autumn, as do most Echinaceas. Its golden yellow flowers with their orange centres, mix well with other autumn-blooming perennials in red and violet.

BOTANIX Experts by nature

Echinacea 'Razzmatazz'
'Razzmatazz' Double Coneflower

| ☀ | ☁ | ↔ 60 cm | ↕ 75 cm | ✿ Summer | ZONE 4 | 🦋 |

A highly resistant, Dutch-developed beauty with many double, pinkish red floral pom-poms. There is no garden that wouldn't benefit from the presence of this cultivar.

Echinacea 'Summer Sky'
'Summer Sky' Coneflower

| ☀ | ↔ 60 cm | ↕ 90 cm | ✿ Summer | ZONE 4 |

A vibrant bicoloured version with superb, rose-tainted peach petals encircling the central cone. A future classic.

Echinacae 'Sundown'
'Sundown' Coneflower

| ☀ | ↔ 60 cm | ↕ 75 cm | ✿ Summer | ZONE 4 |

End the season on a joyous note with a multiplicity of sun-coloured flowers. Try planting a large quantity of them with purple or blue-coloured Echinaceas for an eye-pleasing show. Excellent cut flowers.

Echinacea 'Sunrise'
'Sunrise' Coneflower

| ☀ | ↔ 60 cm | ↕ 90 cm | ✿ Summer | ZONE 4 | 🦋 |

The lemon-yellow petals surround the brownish central cone, which turns gold as the season progresses. A vigorous Coneflower that's particularly satisfying when surrounded by Globe Thistles and White Yarrow.

Perennials

Echinacea 'Tiki Torch'
'Tiki Torch' Coneflower

New

☼	↔ 60 cm	↕ 60 cm	✿ Summer/Autumn	ZONE 4

A robust Echinacea with appealing upright foliage beneath numerous pink and orange flowers. Useful as a border, mixed in a flower bed or for cut flowers.

Echinacea 'Vintage Wine'
'Vintage Wine' Coneflower

New

☼	↔ 80 cm	↕ 25 cm	✿ Summer	ZONE 4	🌰

A Dutch cultivar featuring royal purple foliage accompanied by bright pink or white flowers. Its elongated flowering period makes it ideal for edging, flower beds and container planting.

Echinacea 'White Natalie'
'White Natalie' Coneflower

New

☼	↔ 45 cm	↕ 60 cm	✿ Summer/Autumn	ZONE 4	🌰

This compact variety has the largest white flowers of any Echinacea and a contrasting gold-flower centre. Plant near purple foliage and orange flowers for that country-garden look.

Echinacea purpurea 'Coconut Lime'
'Coconut Lime' Coneflower

New

☼	↔ 45 to 60 cm	↕ 45 to 60 cm	✿ Summer	ZONE 3	🦋	🐦

A compact plant that produces abundant, double, white flowers that are sensational in a garden or vase.

Echinacea purpurea 'Green Envy'
'Green Envy' Coneflower

New

☀ | ↔ 60 cm | ↕ 90 cm | ❀ Summer/Autumn | **ZONE 4** | 🦋 | 🐦

A unique cultivar with spectacular, season-long, jade-green petals and a dark green cone. Tolerates dry spells, as do most Echinaccas.

Echinacea purpurea 'Magnus'
'Magnus' Purple Coneflower

☀ | ↔ 50 cm | ↕ 80 cm to 1 m | ❀ Summer | **ZONE 3** | 🦋 | 🐦

With its hardy stems and unusually horizontal, long-lasting pink petals, this Magnum Opus makes great cut flowers.

Echinops ritro
Globe Thistle

spirit
style

☀ | ↔ 60 cm | ↕ 81 cm to 1.2 m | ❀ Summer | **ZONE 3** | 🦋 | 🐦

With "country-look" written all over them, these floral jewels do well in free-form flower beds, intermingled with Margaritas and Echinacea. Reseed easily, even in the driest of soil. The globular, blue flowers, which top tall with sturdy stems, turn mauve in time.

Erigeron hybridus 'Pink Jewel'
Dainty Daisy

☀ | ↔ 50 cm | ↕ 70 cm | ❀ Summer | **ZONE 3b**

An Aster-like, little perennial that will help you create the popular country-estate appearance. With its semi-double, yellow-centred pink flowers lasting all summer, it will add interest outdoors or as cut flowers. Likes dry, well-drained soil.

Eryngium planum
Sea Holly

☀ ↔ 60 cm | ↕ 50 to 90 cm | ❀ Summer | **ZONE 3b**

A Thistle-like plant that does well in poor, dry soil. Amethyst-blue flowers punctuate the spiny, silver foliage.

Eupatorium rugosum 'Chocolate'
'Chocolate' Joe-Pye Weed

☀ ☁ ↔ 50 cm | ↕ 80 cm | ❀ Autumn | **ZONE 4**

A large perennial that creates a magnificent contrast among the red or peach-coloured flowers. Its foliage goes from green to reddish-brown before the delicate, autumn flowers appear. Add mulch at season's end.

Euphorbia polychroma
Cushion/Common Spurge

☀ ↔ 45 cm | ↕ 30 to 40 cm | ❀ Spring/Summer | **ZONE 4**

The new, golden shoots stand out among the dark older branches. In autumn, its tough foliage turns a fascinating red. Likes dryness.

Filipendula rubra 'Venusta Magnifica'
Queen of the Prairie

spirit
style

☀ ☁ ↔ 80 cm | ↕ 1.8 m | ❀ Summer | **ZONE 3**

For a charming border, plant this impressively tall perennial in a semishade garden where its prolonged flowering – which seems to float magically over the palmate foliage – will add lustre.

Gaillardia grandiflora 'Fanfare'
'Fanfare' Blanket Flower

| ☀ | ↔ 35 cm | ↕ 20 to 35 cm | ❀ Summer/ Autumn | ZONE 3 | 🐦 | ✂ |

Earning its cultivar moniker, this hardy Blanket Flower, with its trumpet-shaped petals (yes, pctals!) will remain vigorous if cut back in fall. Will only grow in well-drained soil. Divide every two years.

Gaillardia grandiflora 'Goblin'
'Goblin' Blanket Flower

| ☀ | ↔ 35 cm | ↕ 20 to 35 cm | ❀ Summer/ Autumn | ZONE 3 | 🐦 | ✂ |

Bring sunlight itself to your garden by planting these in a group or intermingling with other species in a flower bed. Cut back at the end of summer to restore vigour. Divide every two years.

Gentiana dahurica
Gentian

| ☀ | ☁ | ↔ 30 to 40 cm | ↕ 30 cm | ❀ Summer/ Autumn | ZONE 3 |

This Gentian will stun you with its large, blue flowers and their tubular petals. In damp, well-drained soil, flowering will last a long time. An underused plant that's easy to grow.

Geranium 'Rozanne'
'Rozanne' Cranesbill Geranium

New

| ☀ | ☁ | ↔ 60 cm | ↕ 50 cm | ❀ Summer/ Autumn | ZONE 4 |

A hybrid to give your garden a visual lift: its luminous violet-blue, finely-toothed flowers with white hearts interact with deeply lobed foliage throughout the summer months. Heat tolerant in ground or in containers. Likes damp, well drained soil.

Geranium cinereum 'Ballerina'
'Ballerina' Geranium

| ☀ | ☁ | ↔ 20 to 30 cm | ↕ 15 to 20 cm | ✿ Summer/ Autumn | ZONE 4 |

A very low, spreading Geranium with abundant, fuchsia-veined, pink flowers encompassing dark hearts blooming all summer long, if given a well drained soil and lots of sunlight.

Geranium sanguineum
Bloody Cranesbill

| ☀ | ☁ | ↔ 45 cm | ↕ 30 cm | ✿ Summer/ Autumn | ZONE 3 |

After a few years, Bloody Geraniums will form a genuine cushion of foliage and flowers. Your garden will always be in bloom with these resistant, abundant pink flowers. Easily grown in any soil.

Geum borissii
Boris Avens

| ☀ | ☁ | ↔ 25 cm | ↕ 35 cm | ✿ Spring/ Autumn | ZONE 3 | ✂ |

Plant in borders for maximum effect, and deadhead in midsummer to induce the reappearance of a flamboyant wave of flowers. The attractive foliage lasts into winter.

Gypsophila paniculata
Baby's Breath

| ☀ | ↔ 50 to 70 cm | ↕ 45 to 90 cm | ✿ Summer | ZONE 3 |

The blue-tinted foliage underscores an infinite sea of miniscule white or pink flowers. Likes deep, dry, well-drained soil and detests being transplanted.

Gypsophila repens
Creeping Baby's Breath

| ☀ | ↔ 40 cm | ↕ 15 to 20 cm | ❁ Summer | ZONE 3 | ✂ |

Will carpet the ground with flowers, gracefully traipse over low walls, and add interest to the front of a crowded flower bed all summer. Give it a well-drained soil and deadhead to stimulate flowering.

Helenium 'Moerheim Beauty'
'Moerheim Beauty' Sneezeweed

| ☀ | ↔ 30 to 40 cm | ↕ 90 cm to 1 m | ❁ Summer/ Autumn | ZONE 3 |

The most popular Helenium, has a chocolate-brown cone surrounded by copper-red, velvet-textured petals. Makes excellent cut flowers in spring as it's an early bloomer.

Perennials

Helenium automnale 'Mardi Gras'
'Mardi Gras' Sneezeweed

global village style

| ☀ | ↔ 30 to 40 cm | ↕ 90 cm to 1 m | ❁ Summer | ZONE 3 |

Add interest to your water feature or flower bed with these relatively early-blooming flowers that range from bright yellow to orange with red highlights and brown centres.

Helianthemum hybrida
Golden Queen

| ☀ | ↔ 30 to 40 cm | ↕ 15 to 25 cm | ❁ Summer | ZONE 5 | ✂ |

An alpine plant that you'll appreciate in your rock garden or as a ground cover. The brightly-coloured petals encircle the contrasting centre. Tolerates dry soil and will provide a second flowering if the first is deadheaded on time.

Heliopsis helianthoides 'Loraine Sunshine'
'Loraine Sunshine' Heliopsis

| ☀ | ⛅ | ↔ 45 cm | ↕ 75 cm | ❀ Summer/Autumn | ZONE 3 | 🦋 | 🐦 |

A cultivar that stands out for its astonishing white and cream-coloured foliage with pronounced veins. Produces countless bright yellow flowers that last all summer. Likes rich, slightly acidic soil and tolerates dry spells rather well.

Heliopsis helianthoides var. scabra 'Summer Nights'
'Summer Nights' False Sunflower

| ☀ | ↔ 90 cm | ↕ 1.2 m | ❀ Summer/Autumn | ZONE 4 |

This compact cultivar is perfect for creating an uncultivated country-estate atmosphere. Green foliage with crimson highlights, and a plethora of orange-centred, yellow flowers. Plant in a group or interspersed with other perennials.

Heliopsis helianthoides var. scabra 'Summer Sun'
'Summer Sun' False Sunflower

| ☀ | ↔ 90 cm | ↕ 1.2 m | ❀ Summer/Autumn | ZONE 4 |

Features prolonged flowering of semi-double, golden yellow flowers that, like sunflowers, follow the sun. In the ground, they contribute to the bucolic atmosphere, and they are also enjoyable as cut flowers.

Hemerocallis 'Anzac'
'Anzac' Daylily

| ☀ | ⛅ | ↔ 60 cm | ↕ 70 cm | ❀ Summer | ZONE 3 |

As their name implies, Daylily flowers only last a day, but new blooms emerge at such a rapid rate that one never notices. This variety produces superb, edible, red flowers with yellow-green centres.

Hemerocallis 'Happy Returns'
'Happy Returns' Daylily

☀	☁	↔ 40 cm	↕ 30 to 40 cm	✿ Summer/Autumn	ZONE 3	🏺

An unlimited supply of edible, canary-yellow, trumpet flowers perfume the air all summer.

Hemerocallis 'Mose's Fire'
'Mose's Fire' Daylily

New

☀	☁	↔ 15 cm	↕ 55 cm	✿ Summer	ZONE 3

Don't expect any other plant to outshine these bright orange double-flowers with their golden margins. For a truly spectacular showing, mix with purple foliage and perennials that have bright yellow flowers.

Hemerocallis 'Orange Crush'
'Orange Crush' Daylily

global village style

☀	☁	↔ 45 to 60 cm	↕ 30 to 45 cm	✿ Summer/Autumn	ZONE 3	🏺

To really take advantage of the peach-coloured flowers with their yellow centres and red eyes, intersperse with plants that feature purple foliage or blue flowers. Edible and slightly scented. This new Daylily is a BOTANIX exclusive.

Hemerocallis 'Purple d'Oro'
'Purple d'Oro' Daylily

☀	☁	↔ 60 cm	↕ 50 cm	✿ Summer/Autumn	ZONE 3

Magnificent flowers! Every day, new edible blooms appear, gracing your garden with their restrained undulations and pink-violet petals. Attractive as cut flowers, too.

Perennials

Hemerocallis 'Rosy Returns'
'Rosy Returns' Daylily

☀	⛅	↔ 45 cm	↕ 45 cm	❀ Summer/Autumn	ZONE 3

An unending parade of pretty, edible, dark pink flowers with yellow throats. One of the smallest Daylilies, which provides a marvellous accompaniment for plants with pink or yellow flowers.

Hemerocallis 'Ruby d'Oro'
'Ruby d'Oro' Daylily

global village style

☀	⛅	↔ 60 cm	↕ 40 to 60 cm	❀ Summer/Autumn	ZONE 3	🌸

Ruby d'Oro stands out as soon as it starts flowering in early summer, thanks to its cherry-pink flowers with their yellow throats and delicate perfume. Easy to grow, tolerates dryness, and continuously produces edible flowers.

Hemerocallis 'Stella de Oro'
'Stella de Oro' Daylily

global village style

☀	⛅	↔ 60 to 80 cm	↕ 60 cm	❀ Summer/Autumn	ZONE 3

It's easy to understand the popularity of this abundant flower producer. It tolerates dryness and heat waves, produces edible blossoms, and looks particularly attractive in front of conifers such as cedar.

Hemerocallis 'Stella Ruby'
'Stella Ruby' Daylily

New

☀	⛅	↔ 60 to 80 cm	↕ 60 cm	❀ Summer/Autumn	ZONE 3	🌸

A red version of Stella de Oro, producing many edible, ruby-coloured flowers with chartreuse throats. A real eye-catcher.

Hemerocallis 'Stella Supreme'
'Stella Supreme' Daylily

Exclusive

☀ ⛅ ↔ 60 cm ↕ 50 cm ❀ Summer/Autumn **ZONE 3**

This cultivar grows appealing lemon-yellow flowers that emanate a light citrus odour. You'll love its long flowering period, low upkeep and general hardiness.

Heuchera 'Chocolate Ruffles'
'Chocolate Ruffles' Coral Bells

☀ ⛅ ↔ 45 cm ↕ 45 cm ❀ Summer **ZONE 4**

The dense foliage has ruffled leaf borders, and goes from burgundy at the base to chocolate brown at the edge, creating an interesting two-tone effect. The long, strong, arching, purple flower stems support a knot of tiny white flowers.

Heuchera 'Lime Rickey'
'Lime Rickey' Coral Bells

☀ ⛅ ↔ 45 to 60 cm ↕ 45 to 90 cm ❀ Summer **ZONE 3**

New shoots are chartreuse when they first appear, and sport striking, lime-green, undulating foliage that will bring a shot of light to a semishade garden or to the understory of a copse of trees. Hardy and rigorous, but requires a rich, well drained soil.

Heuchera 'Marmelade'
'Marmelade' Coral Bells

☀ ⛅ ↔ 40 cm ↕ 30 cm ❀ Summer **ZONE 4**

An exquisite mix of colours, including lime-green, golden yellow and salmon-pink. Plant near dark green foliage in damp, well drained soil.

Perennials

Heuchera 'Obsidian'
Fancy Leaf Coral Bells

New

| ☼ | ⛅ | ↔ 40 cm | ↕ 60 cm | ❀ Summer | ZONE 3 |

You'll definitely notice the lustrous, purple foliage – almost black, really – as soon as it appears in early spring. Near the beginning of summer, the preternaturally large leaves are counterbalanced by miniature white flowers that look like shooting stars on the elegant, arching flower stems.

Heuchera 'Peach Flambe'
'Peach Flambe' Coral Bells

New

| ☼ | ⛅ | ↔ 45 cm | ↕ 45 cm | ❀ Summer | ZONE 4 |

It's here: rich autumnal colours in midsummer! A superb variety with large, flamboyant foliage that mixes peach, red and bronze. In spring, the long stems support loose spikes of white flowers.

Heuchera 'Tiramisu'
'Tiramisu' Coral Bells

New

| ☼ | ⛅ | ↔ 35 cm | ↕ 40 cm | ❀ Summer | ZONE 4 |

Another Heuchera named after a delectable dessert, and another Heuchera that lives up to its name, with magnificent, light green foliage highlighted with tones of red, purple and bronze. Wonderful in borders. Wonderful in large groups.

Heuchera micrantha 'Palace Purple'
'Palace Purple' Coral Bells

| ☼ | ⛅ | ↔ 35 cm | ↕ 35 to 50 cm | ❀ Summer | ZONE 3 |

An ever-popular classic with deep purple foliage that easily contrasts with bright, neighbouring flowers and forms a particularly felicitous partnership with Astilbes and Hostas.

Heuchera villosa 'Caramel'
'Caramel' Coral Bells

☁️	↔️ 45 cm	↕️ 40 cm	❄️ Summer	ZONE 4

The warm golden tones of this cultivar gradually turn orange as summer progresses. Highly resistant to heat waves, but requires rich, damp soil.

Heucherella 'Stoplight'
'Stoplight' Foamy Bells

☁️	↔️ 30 cm	↕️ 15 cm	❄️ Summer	ZONE 4

Luminous, lime-yellow foliage with a dark red central splotch that leaks out along the veins. An elegant groundcover in semi-shade, it thrives in cool, damp, well-drained soil.

Hibiscus moscheutos cv.
Hibiscuses/Mallows

☀️	↔️ 45 to 60 cm	↕️ 90 cm to 1.2 m	❄️ Summer	ZONE 5	🦋	🔔

Any Hibiscus brings a touch of the tropics to a sunny spot in your garden. The *Disco* series – with its colours that range from white to red – are the first to flower. Require winter protection.

Hibiscus moscheutos cv.
Hibiscuses

☀️	↔️ 60 to 90 cm	↕️ 60 to 90 cm	❄️ Summer/Autumn	ZONE 5	🦋	🔔

The *Luna* series is composed of compact, bushy and highly floriferous Hibiscuses. The large white, red or pink flowers tolerate heat well, but the plant requires winter protection.

Perennials

Hosta 'Big Daddy'
'Big Daddy' Hosta

| ☁ | ☁ | ↔ 90 cm | ↕ 60 cm | ✿ Summer | ZONE 3 |

This Hosta will eventually grow into a dark, greenish-blue cushion featuring thick, rippling, cup-shaped leaves. At some point in the summer, several white floral bells on waving stalks will pierce the atmosphere above.

Hosta 'Blue Angel'
'Blue Angel' Hosta

| ☁ | ☁ | ↔ 1.5 m | ↕ 80 cm | ✿ Summer | ZONE 3 |

You'll need a lot of space in the shade for Blue Angel — it forms a sizable mound with its exotically large leaves. Understandably, a classic.

Hosta 'Fire & Ice'
'Fire & Ice' Hosta

| ☀ | ☁ | ↔ 25 cm | ↕ 45 cm | ✿ Summer | ZONE 3 |

The dark green leaves and their cream centres provide relief from the monochrome foliage so prevalent in shade gardens. This cultivar has two other distinct advantages: mauve flowers... and it's one of the few Hostas that slugs simply don't fancy!

Hosta 'Gold Standard'
'Gold Standard' Hosta

| ☀ | ☀ | ☁ | ↔ 90 cm | ↕ 50 cm | ✿ Summer | ZONE 3 |

The more sun this cultivar gets, the more its leaves will turn cream-coloured, instead of the bright green with dark green borders you'll see in the shade. A pleasant sight when planted in groups, but not without its merits among the rich foliage of some other species.

BOTANIX Experts by nature

Hosta 'Halcyon'
'Halcyon' Hosta

☀		↔ 80 to 90 cm	↕ 35 to 45 cm	❀ Summer	ZONE 3

Oval, bluish-green foliage and white, tubular, overhanging flowers characterize this variety. It's a versatile candidate that's easily integrated into any shade garden.

Hosta 'Inniswood'
'Inniswood' Hosta

☀	☁	↔ 90 cm	↕ 50 cm	❀ Spring/ Summer	ZONE 3

At maturity, expect a full square-metre of area to be occupied by the large, heart-shaped, bright green leaves with their dark green margins.

Hosta 'Royal Standard'
'Royal Standard' Hosta

spirit
style

☀	☀	☁	↔ 95 cm	↕ 60 cm	❀ Summer	ZONE 3	⚘

This Hosta sets a royal standard indeed, with its unusual rippled leaf margins, and its delicately perfumed, white summer flowers contrasting with the dark green foliage. Especially rewarding when planted near dappled foliage.

Hosta 'Sum and Substance'
'Sum and Substance' Hosta

☀	☀	☁	↔ 2 m	↕ 75 cm	❀ Summer	ZONE 3

One of the largest Hostas on the market – and that's saying something! It's so big, you really have to plant it alone. Tolerates sunlight, resists slugs, and features chartreuse, strongly veined leaves that turn yellow in semishade.

Hosta 'Wide Brim'
'Wide Brim' Hosta

| ☁ ☁ | ↔ 90 cm | ↕ 55 cm | ❀ Summer | ZONE 3 |

The bright green, bumpy leaves with their cream margins will add a dash of artlessness to your garden. A quick grower that soon fits in with its associates in the underbrush.

Hosta fortunei 'Patriot'
'Patriot' Hosta

| ☀ ☁ ☁ | ↔ 60 cm | ↕ 45 cm | ❀ Summer | ZONE 3 |

Rather unusual for a Hosta, as the foliage is green at the centre and cream-coloured elsewhere. In summer, even if exposed to the sun, it provides many suspended, mauve flowers. A former Grower's-Hosta-of-the-year that's still a classic.

Hosta plantagina 'August Moon'
'August Moon' Hosta

| ☀ ☁ | ↔ 1 m | ↕ 50 cm | ❀ Summer | ZONE 3 |

An outstanding Hosta with textured foliage that's green with gold highlights in spring and a more uniform, golden yellow in summer. Ideal for creating contrast in your garden. The white flowers are a favourite for creating indoor bouquets.

Hosta sieboldiana 'Elegans'
Siebold Hosta

| ☁ ☁ | ↔ 90 cm | ↕ 55 cm | ❀ Summer | ZONE 3 |

The superbly luxurious, verdigris foliage of this Hosta under-scores the vertical stems with their floral bells. A slow grower that resists slug-damage.

Hosta sieboldiana 'Frances Williams'
'Frances Williams' Siebold Hosta

| ☀ | ☁ | ↔ 1 m | ↕ 80 cm | ❀ Summer | ZONE 3 |

Another Hosta that needs a lot of space, and best used as a stand-alone. The thick, dark green leaves ringed in light green do not attract slugs.

Houttuyana cordata 'Tricolor' (syn. 'Chameleon')
'Tricolor' Chameleon Plant

| ☀ | ☁ | ↔ 30 to 60 cm | ↕ 25 to 30 cm | ❀ Summer | ZONE 4 |

Highly original and stunningly beautiful, combining green, yellow and red foliage on ruddy stalks. Can be invasive in damp areas.

Iberis sempervirens
Candytuft

| ☀ | ↔ 30 cm | ↕ 20 to 30 cm | ❀ Spring/Summer | ZONE 3 |

In spring, when Candytuft is decked out in a full mantle of tiny, white or pink flowers, it forms a floral carpet. The green foliage does not drop off in winter. Likes fertile, well-drained soil.

Iris germanica
Bearded Iris, German Iris

| ☀ | ↔ 60 cm | ↕ 60 to 95 cm | ❀ Summer/Autumn | ZONE 3 |

A well-liked German Iris that boasts blue-highlighted foliage from which purple flowers emerge. Uncannily appropriate near a water feature or dappled grasses.

Perennials

Iris kaempferi
Japanese Iris

☀	↔ 40 to 60 cm	↕ 60 to 90 cm	✿ Summer	ZONE 4

With midsummer comes the magnificent, single or double flowers that are ringed or marbled. Starting in spring, gracefully arching foliage erects from below when planted in damp soil.

Iris pallida 'Aureo-variegata'
'Aureo-variegata' Sweet Iris

☀	↔ 40 cm	↕ 70 cm to 1 m	✿ Summer	ZONE 4	👜

Its rhizomes are used to make perfume, and the towering stalks bear violet-blue flowers that some claim smell like grapes. The foliage, mottled with bright green and butter-yellow is a unique feature. A showstopper.

Iris pumila
Dwarf Bearded Iris

☀	↔ 12 cm	↕ 15 to 25 cm	✿ Spring/ Summer	ZONE 4

An early-flowering dwarf Iris that blooms at the same time as Lilacs and other spring bulbs. Doesn't like much dampness. The perfumed flowers are available in many colours.

Iris sibirica
Siberian Iris

☀	↔ 35 cm	↕ 50 to 80 cm	✿ Summer	ZONE 3

The bluish-green foliage and striking, bicolour flowers are particularly suitable for water features. They will add interest to your garden when planted in large groups. Tolerates spring flooding.

Iris versicolor
Blue Flag

| ☀ | ⛅ | ↔ 35 cm | ↕ 40 to 80 cm | ❁ Spring/ Summer | ZONE 3b |

This indigenous woodland plant, with its delicate, violet-blue flowers that reveal flashes of white and gold, is Quebec's national flower. As it likes damp soil, Blue Flag works well with water features.

Kniphofia uvaria
Torch Lilly

| ☀ | ↔ 40 cm | ↕ 60 cm to 1 m | ❁ Summer | ZONE 5 | 🐦 | 🎩 |

A highly unusual plant, also referred to as Red Hot Poker. It produces thick spikes of brightly-coloured, tubular flowers that delight hummingbirds. Requires winter protection and very well-drained soil.

Lamiastrum galeobdolon 'Herman's Pride'
'Herman's Pride' Golden Nettle

| ⛅ | ☁ | ↔ 35 to 50 cm | ↕ 20 to 25 cm | ❁ Spring/ Summer | ZONE 3 |

A delightful groundcover featuring delicate, yellow spring flowers topping dentated, silver leaves with green veins. Add a ray of sunlight to your shade garden with this vigorous plant that requires so little maintenance, some consider it invasive.

Lamium maculatum 'Pink Pewter'
'Pink Pewter' Dead Nettle

| ⛅ | ☁ | ↔ 25 to 40 cm | ↕ 15 to 20 cm | ❁ Spring/ Summer | ZONE 3 |

Much liked for their glistening, silver-spotted green leaves and the continuous flowering of bright pink blooms on short spikes. Use as a groundcover or in a shady border.

Perennials

Lavandula angustifolia 'Grosso'
'Grosso' English Lavender

☀	↔	↕	❀	ZONE			✂
	60 cm	60 cm	Summer	4b			

Lavender forms an attractive, low bush that — particularly when flowering — fairly screams «Provence». This cultivar produces dusty green foliage and a profusion of aromatic, violet flower spikes that attract butterflies. Tolerates dryness, but must be cut back in spring to maintain its vigour.

Lavandula angustifolia 'Munstead'
'Munstead' English Lavender

spirit style

☀	↔	↕	❀	ZONE			✂
	60 cm	40 cm	Summer	4b			

The impressive spikes of highly perfumed, blue flowers attract butterflies. Tolerates dryness, but needs a well-drained soil and must be cut back in spring to maintain its vigour.

Lavatera thuringiaca
Tree Mallow

☀	☁	↔	↕	❀	ZONE	✂
		70 cm	80 cm to 1 m	Summer	4b	

The pretty, pink flowers with their dentated petals are an appropriate addition to a country garden. Easily reseeds, though it doesn't like being transplanted. Cut back within 15 cm of the ground in spring.

Leontopodium alpinum
Edelweiss

☀	↔	↕	❀	ZONE
	25 cm	15 to 20 cm	Summer	4

Austria's floral emblem has downy foliage and short, star-shaped flowers. This alpine flower is suited to rockeries and container-planting. Likes well drained soil.

Leucanthemum superbum 'Becky'
'Becky' Shasta Daisy

| ☀ | ☁ | ↔ 90 cm | ↕ 90 cm | ✿ Summer/Autumn | ZONE 4 | ✂ |

The flowers of the hardy and prolific 'Becky' thrive all summer, particularly if you remember to deadhead the fading blossoms. Very popular as cut flowers, and an important ingredient in the creation of a country-style garden.

Leucanthemum superbum 'Goldraush'
'Goldrausch' Shasta Daisy

New

| ☀ | ↔ 30 to 35 cm | ↕ 35 to 40 cm | ✿ Summer/Autumn | ZONE 4 - 9 | ✂ |

A compact plant that looks like it's having a bad hair day – with its haywire, thin, fringed, almost ciliate petals. Easy to grow in pots, and plays well with other plants. Extended flowering period.

Liatris spicata 'Kobold'
Spike Gayfeather

| ☀ | ↔ 40 cm | ↕ 40 to 70 cm | ✿ Summer | ZONE 3 | 🦋 |

The long spikes are garnished with deep purple flowers that bloom in series from top to bottom. Virtually the only care required is a division every three years to maintain plant-vigour.

Ligularia 'Osiris Fantaisie'
'Osiris Fantaisie' Ligularia

New

| ☀ | ☁ | ↔ 30 to 60 cm | ↕ 60 cm | ✿ Summer | ZONE 3 |

The characteristic yellow flower spikes are borne on purple stalks that rise out of unusual crenulated, dark green leaves with even darker undersides.

Perennials

Ligularia dentata 'Britt-Marie Crawford'
'Britt-Marie Crawford' Ligularia

| ☀ | ☁ | ↔ 90 cm to 1.2 m | ↕ 90 cm to 1.2 m | ✿ Summer | ZONE 4 | 🦋 |

Features lustrous, purple leaves, and near-black shoots from which numerous little bunches of golden-yellow flowers materialize. Ligulariae love semishade and constantly damp soil.

Ligularia przewalskyii
Ligularia

| ☀ | ☁ | ↔ 90 cm to 1.2 m | ↕ 1.3 to 1.6 m | ✿ Summer | ZONE 3 | 🦋 |

The long spikes of golden-yellow flowers contrast uncannily well with the black stems. The magnificent dark green, highly dentated foliage completes the charm. Likes morning sun and semishade.

Ligularia stenocephala 'Little Rocket'
'Little Rocket' Narrow-Spiked Ligularia

New

| ☀ | ☁ | ↔ 60 cm | ↕ 60 cm | ✿ Summer | ZONE 4 |

A miniature version of 'The Rocket' with all the strengths of the larger inspiration. In a semishade garden, the bright yellow flowers compete with the green, strongly dentated foliage, for your attention.

Ligularia stenocephala 'The Rocket'
Rocket Ligularia

| ☀ | ☁ | ↔ 80 cm | ↕ 90 cm to 1.5 m | ✿ Summer/ Autumn | ZONE 3 | 🦋 |

The superb, bright green, crenulated foliage is punctuated by long, conical spikes of golden flowers. Under hot, noonday sun-rays, the flowers become slightly limp, but towards evening, regain their vigour. Requires rich, cool soil.

Lilium 'Crimson Pixie'
'Crimson Pixie' Asiatic Lily

☀ ☁ ↔ 45 cm ↕ 40 cm ❀ Spring **ZONE 3**

Like the other members of the Pixie series, its flowers are bright. In this case, their scarlet tint will add colour to your garden because they're so bright and because there are so many of them. Whether grown in-ground or in pots, requires a rich, well-drained soil.

Lilium 'Orange Pixie'
'Orange Pixie' Asiatic Lily

☀ ☁ ↔ 45 cm ↕ 40 cm ❀ Spring **ZONE 3**

The large, orange trumpets exhale the exquisite perfume distinctive of that of the Lilies. Makes a pleasing scene with white and blue flowered species as well as those with golden leaves. Give it fertile, well-drained soil.

Lilium asiatic 'Butter Pixie'
'Butter Pixie' Asiatic Lily

☀ ☁ ↔ 30 cm ↕ 45 cm ❀ Summer **ZONE 3**

The large, flower trumpets that are typical of the Asiatic Lilies *Pixie* Series come in white, yellow, orange or red. A prolific bloomer that's equally rewarding in the garden or in a container on your patio. Likes rich, well-drained soil.

Lilium orientale 'Stargazer'
'Stargazer' Oriental Lily

☀ ☁ ↔ 60 cm ↕ 60 cm to 1 m ❀ Summer **ZONE 4**

A strikingly beautiful Lily with large, dark pink flowers featuring ruby blotches, pale pink borders and a delicate green heart. Spectacular in a regulated garden and as cut flowers.

Linum perenne
Blue Flax

| ☀ | ☁ | ↔ 50 to 70 cm | ↕ 40 to 60 cm | ❀ Summer | **ZONE 4** | 🐦 |

Plant it in a well-drained soil and your Blue Flax will reward you with a mass of delicate, white or blue flowers towering over supple, curved foliage. Tolerates dry spells.

Lobelia cardinalis
Cardinal Flower

| ☁ | ↔ 30 cm | ↕ 80 cm to 1.2 m | ❀ Summer | **ZONE 4** | 🐦 | 🚿 |

This plant loves damp soil, and its scarlet flowers attract hummingbirds. Protect it from wind and, if you don't have much snow on the ground, cover in winter.

Lunaria annua
Money Plant

| ☀ | ☁ | ↔ 45 cm | ↕ 70 to 90 cm | ❀ Summer | **ZONE 4** | 🏺 |

The pretty flowers give way to its fruit: flat, silvered, translucent discs that look like coins. It's a biannual that's frequently cut while fruiting for indoor flower arrangements. Reseeds abundantly.

Lupinus 'Manhattan Lights'
'Manhattan Lights' Lupin

New

| ☀ | ↔ 60 cm | ↕ 60 to 90 cm | ❀ Summer | **ZONE 4** | 🦋 | 🐦 |

In spring, the dark mauve buds are found intermingled with the yellow, fully opened flowers – creating a bicolour affect. Will attract attention whether placed in the middle or at the back of a flower bed. A BOTANIX exclusive.

Lupinus hybridus
Hybrid Lupin

☀		↔ 60 cm	↕ 60 to 90 cm	✿ Summer	ZONE 4

The long, brightly-coloured flower spikes overlook the palmate, light green foliage. Requires constantly humid but well-drained soil that's slightly acidic. Mulch to protect the roots, or plant in the middle of other perennials.

Lychnis arkwrightii 'Orange Gnome'
Arkwright's Campion

☀	⛅	↔ 25 cm	↕ 30 cm	✿ Summer	ZONE 4	✂

The reddish-orange flowers of this dwarf emerge from bronze-green foliage, producing an interesting interplay of colours. Give it a well-drained soil and deadhead after flowering.

Lysimachia clethroides
Gooseneck Loosestrife

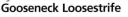

☀	⛅	↔ 40 to 60 cm	↕ 60 to 90 cm	✿ Summer	ZONE 3

This Lysimachia is easily recognized thanks to its hooked, white inflorescences that all point in the same direction, looking like a gaggle of geese from the neck up. Can be invasive.

Lysimachia nummularia
Creeping Jenny

☀	⛅	☁	↔ 30 to 40 cm	↕ 10 cm	✿ Spring/ Summer	ZONE 3	

Quickly creates an eye-catching carpet of round, paired foliage and yellow flowers. The flowers of 'Aurea' are scintillating gold. Can be invasive.

Lysimachia punctata
Yellow Loosestrife

| ☀ | ☁ | ↔ 40 cm | ↕ 60 to 80 cm | ❀ Spring/ Summer | ZONE 3 |

Spectacular flowering of long, floral spikes that grow right out of the foliage. A potentially invasive plant that will soon form an impenetrable mass. Likes loose, well-drained soil.

Lythrum salicaria 'Robert'
'Robert' Purple Loosestrife

| ☀ | ☁ | ↔ 45 cm | ↕ 70 cm to 1.1 m | ❀ Summer/ Autumn | ZONE 3 | 🦋 |

Unlike other Lythrums, 'Robert' is not very invasive. Its long spikes of pink flowers last all summer if grown in damp soil. Adds a natural look to any water feature.

Lythrum salicaria 'Terra Nova'
'Terra Nova' Loosestrife

| ☀ | ☁ | ↔ 40 cm | ↕ 55 cm | ❀ Summer/ Autumn | ZONE 3 | 🦋 |

A completely sterile Lythrum that won't invade your garden, but will grow into a superb clump near a water feature. Below the bright pink flowers, the delicate, narrow foliage will rustle in light winds throughout the summer.

Malva moschata
Musk Mallow

| ☀ | ☁ | ↔ 40 cm | ↕ 50 to 80 cm | ❀ Summer | ZONE 3 |

The romantic country-cottage perennial par excellence, featuring aromatic foliage and large, mauve flowers with striated petals. Only lives a few years, but reseeds easily. Tolerates all soil types.

Monarda 'Petite Delight'
'Petite Delight' Bee Balm/Bergamot

| ☀ | ☁ | ↔ 45 cm | ↕ 40 cm | ✿ Summer | ZONE 4 | 🦋 | 🐦 |

A compact dwarf variety with mildew-resistant foliage. The magnificent, long-flowering, dark pink flowers attract birds and butterflies.

Monarda hybrida
Hybrid Bee Balm/Bergamot

| ☀ | ↔ 35 cm | ↕ 50 to 90 cm | ✿ Summer | ZONE 4 | 🦋 | 🐦 |

This vigorous perennial that generates flowers so exotic they look like they come from outer space. It has brightly-coloured bracts, and aromatic foliage when rubbed. Likes rich, damp soil and can become invasive.

Myosotis scorpioides 'Semperflorens'
Forget-me-not

| ☀ | ☁ | ↔ 25 cm | ↕ 20 cm | ✿ Summer/Autumn | ZONE 4 |

With its clear blue flowers that last all year and miniature foliage, this plant looks almost like a mist. Frequently used as a ground cover, eventually forming a large blue carpet.

Oenothera fruticosa 'Fyrverkeri' (Fireworks)
'Fyrverkeri' (Fireworks) Common Sundrops

| ☀ | ↔ 60 cm | ↕ 45 cm | ✿ Spring/Summer | ZONE 4 | | 🐦 |

The red buds develop into bunches of bright yellow flowers topping crimson stems that overlook the burgundy foliage. Smaller than other Oenotherae, it creates a compact mound.

Perennials

Oenothera missouriensis
Ozark Sundrops

| | 40 cm | 15 to 20 cm | Summer/ Autumn | ZONE 4 | | |

Produces an abundance of striking, lemon-yellow flowers that last all summer, opening at night to be colonized by nocturnal insects. Adapts to all soils and tolerates dry spells.

Oenothera speciosa 'Rosea'
'Rosea' Sundrops

| | 50 cm | 40 cm | Spring/ Autumn | ZONE 4 | | |

A highly floriferous cultivar that boasts a light perfume given off by its dainty, pink flowers. Its creeping habit combined with its ability to reseed enthusiastically in damp soil will soon give you a wild and colourful mound.

Opuntia humifusa
Opuntia

| | 30 to 60 cm | 20 to 30 cm | Summer/ Autumn | ZONE 4 |

Pure exoticism. Its frail – almost dead-looking – winter character is taken over by vigorous health in spring, and magnificent, yellow flowers in summer. A hearty cactus that likes dry, sandy, well-drained soil.

Pachysandra terminalis 'Variegata'
Variegated Japanese Spurge

| | | 30 cm | 20 cm | Spring | ZONE 3 |

Here is the ideal groundcover for shade gardens. Its lustrous, yellow-margined foliage will cover a lot of ground in a relatively short time. An undemanding plant that requires rich, acidic, well-drained soil.

Paeonia lactiflora 'Bowl of Beauty'
'Bowl of Beauty' Garden Poppy

| ☀ | ↔ 65 to 80 cm | ↕ 80 cm | ✿ Spring/Summer | ZONE 3 | ⚘ |

Bowl of Beauty produces exceptionally beautiful large, pink flowers with white hearts. An undemanding plant that requires rich, acidic, well-drained soil.

Paeonia lactiflora 'Karl Rosenfield'
'Karl Rosenfield' Peony

| ☀ | ↔ 65 cm | ↕ 90 cm | ✿ Summer | ZONE 3 | ⚘ |

In early summer, the superb, dark red, double flowers appear. An undemanding plant that, like other members of the Poppy family, requires rich, friable, well-drained soil. Fantastic cut flowers.

Paeonia lactiflora 'Krinkled White'
'Krinkled White' Peony

New

| ☀ | ↔ 65 to 80 cm | ↕ 80 cm | ✿ Spring/Summer | ZONE 3 | ⚘ |

A sumptuous variety featuring blue or satin-white flowers with yellow centres. For a traditional garden, to accompany Roses, blue or pink flowered perennials and vines.

Paeonia lactiflora 'Sarah Bernhardt'
'Sarah Bernhardt' Peony

| ☀ | ↔ 65 cm | ↕ 90 cm | ✿ Summer | ZONE 3 | ⚘ |

The dark pink, double flowers will lend a charming, elegant air to a sunny garden... and provide excellent cut flowers. Requires a well-drained soil, a tutor, and frequent watering in spring.

Perennials

Papaver nudicaule
Island Poppy

☀	↔ 20 cm	↕ 25 to 35 cm	❀ Summer/ Autumn	ZONE 2	

The single, intense-coloured flowers of this hardy Poppy, bloom all summer. It produces less flowers on warm days, as it's adapted to a cooler climate. Likes dry, well-drained soil.

Papaver orientale
Oriental Poppy

☀	↔ 40 cm	↕ 60 to 80 cm	❀ Summer	ZONE 4

The richly-coloured flowers, with their slightly undulating, black-speckled petals create a true display of fireworks in your garden. After flowering, the foliage yellows, the perfect time to cut back to a few centimetres of the ground. Likes well-drained soil.

Penstemon digitalis 'Husker Red'
'Husker Red' Beard Tongue

☀	☁	↔ 30 cm	↕ 85 cm	❀ Summer	ZONE 4	🐦

This perennial contributes sophistication to your garden: pinkish-white flowers resembling upright bells on long spikes like a Digitalis, with persistent, burgundy foliage. Resists dry spells.

Perovskia atriplicifolia 'Little Spire'
'Little Spire' Russian Sage

☀	↔ 60 cm	↕ 60 cm	❀ Summer/ Autumn	ZONE 5

A dwarf version of Russian Sage. All summer long, the lavender-blue flower spikes will cover the finely dentated, silvered foliage. Its ideal destiny is to be grown in a group in a small garden.

Phlox paniculata 'David'
'David' Phlox

☀	↔ 60 cm	↕ 1.1 m	❀ Summer/Autumn	ZONE 3			

With height like this, David is superlative for the back row in your flower bed, where its Hydrangea-like flowers can accompany Echinacea, Sage or any other contrasting perennial. Mildew resistant. Prefers rich, sandy, well-drained soil.

Phlox paniculata 'Laura'
'Laura' Phlox

☀	↔ 60 cm	↕ 90 cm	❀ Summer/Autumn	ZONE 3	

Large bunches of white-hearted, purple flowers adorn this plant all summer. For maximum effect, plant near white-flowered perennials. Mildew resistant.

Phlox subulata
Moss Pink

☀	☁	↔ 35 cm	↕ 10 to 15 cm	❀ Spring/Summer	ZONE 3

The foliage is so dense, it actually looks like moss, even when the dazzling flowers cover the entire plant. Cut back after flowering to limit growth.

Physostegia virginiana
Obedience

☀	☁	↔ 40 cm	↕ 80 cm	❀ Summer/Autumn	ZONE 3

Tiny tubular flowers emerge in rows around the flower-spike. An indigenous plants that makes good, long-lasting cut flowers. Potentially invasive.

Platycodon grandiflorus 'Fuji White'
'Fuji White' Balloon Flower

spirit
style

| ☀ | ↔ 30 to 50 cm | ↕ 45 to 60 cm | ❀ Summer | ZONE 3 |

A floriferous little perennial that takes its time peeking out of the ground in spring, but soon makes up for it by producing large, white bell-shaped flowers. Excellent for flower bed edging or as cut flowers. Be careful not to overwater.

Polemonium reptans 'Stairway to Heaven'
'Stairway to Heaven' Greek Valerian/Jacob's Ladder

| ☁ | ☁ | ↔ 40 cm | ↕ 40 cm | ❀ Spring | ZONE 3 |

A charming groundcover with green, cream-mottled foliage that's joined, in spring, by diminutive blue flowers. A nice mix with classic shade plants such as Hostas and Ferns.

Polemonium reptans 'Touch of Class'
'Touch of Class' Greek Valerian/Jacob's Ladder

New

| ☀ | ☁ | ↔ 45 cm | ↕ 60 cm | ❀ Summer | ZONE 3 |

A plethora of pink buds turn into tiny, bluish flowers that complement the magnificent verdigris, white-margined foliage. This improved cultivar will certainly attract attention in a shade garden.

Polygonatum odoratum 'Variegatum'
'Variegatum' Solomon's Seal

| ☁ | ☁ | ↔ 30 cm | ↕ 60 to 80 cm | ❀ Summer | ZONE 3 | ⚘ |

In a shady area, a clump of Solomon's Seal is nothing short of sensational. In spring, a row of highly scented, little, white bells dangle from bowed stems that also support bright green foliage. Amazing with Ferns.

Polygonum affine
Knotweed/Himalayan Fleeceflower

☀	⛅	↔ 35 cm	↕ 20 cm	❁ Summer/Autumn	ZONE 3

Looking for a highly-coloured carpet to front your borders? Try Knotweed: the pink or red floral spikes last all summer and the foliage reddens in autumn.

Potentilla atrosanguinea
Himalayan Cinquefoil

☀	⛅	↔ 45 to 60 cm	↕ 15 to 60 cm	❁ Summer	ZONE 4

The large Potentilla family comprises erect and spreading varieties in a wide range of colours. The flowers, which resemble wild roses, are easy to grow and will blossom continuously throughout the summer in dry, well-drained soil.

Primula denticulata
Drumstick Primrose

⛅	↔ 15 cm	↕ 20 to 25 cm	❁ Spring/Summer	ZONE 4

In spring, the stems produce compact bunches of tiny, white flowers before the leaves come out. Plant in rich, friable soil at the front of a flower bed and welcome spring in style.

Primula polyantha
Polyanthus Primrose

⛅	↔ 20 cm	↕ 15 to 25 cm	❁ Spring/Summer	ZONE 4	⚬	⌂

This pretty Primula presages spring in an impressive assortment of colours. Though it prefers cool temperatures, it's advised to wrap your Primula in mulch in autumn if you have insufficient snow cover.

Perennials

Rodgersia aesculifolia
Fingerleaf Rodgersia

☀ ☁ ↔ 60 to 90 cm | ↕ 60 cm to 1.35 m | ❀ Summer | **ZONE 4**

When fully grown, this plant is of an impressive dimension. After giving it a few years to settle in, beautiful, creamy-white panicles shade the palmate leaves in summer.

Rudbeckia fulgida 'Goldsturm'
'Goldsturm' Coneflower

global village style

☀ ↔ 45 cm | ↕ 60 to 80 cm | ❀ Summer/Autumn | **ZONE 3** 🦋 🐦

This popular Rudbeckia has a very attractive effect when planted in groups, where the golden yellow flowers, with their brown hearts please the eye of humans, birds and butterflies. An undemanding plant that adds a winsome country-garden touch to any layout.

Rudbeckia nitida 'Herbstsonne'
Autumn Sun Coneflower

☀ ↔ 80 cm | ↕ 1.2 to 2 m | ❀ Summer/Autumn | **ZONE 3** 🦋 🐦

An extremely tall Coneflower that makes an attractive backdrop. Plant in well-drained soil and take pleasure in the green cone encircled by its yellow petals beckoning to you from the back of the flower bed.

Salvia nemorosa 'Blue Queen'
Dwarf 'Blue Queen' Sage

global village style

☀ ↔ 40 cm | ↕ 30 cm | ❀ Summer/Autumn | **ZONE 4**

The upright clusters of violet-blue flowers resonate with the cerulean foliage, below. Blue Queen is a compact Sage that forms a marvellous mass of country comfort in your garden.

Salvia nemorosa 'Caradonna'
Perennial Sage

☀	↔ 60 cm	↕ 45 cm	✿ Summer/Autumn	ZONE 4

The long black stems of this cultivar culminate in violet floral spikes that contrast pleasantly with the verdigris foliage, forming an attractive counterpoint with yellow or orange-flowered perennials.

Salvia superba 'May Night'
'May Night' Sage

global village style

☀	↔ 45 cm	↕ 50 cm	✿ Summer	ZONE 4	

A magnificent, generously flowering cultivar with elevated violet blooms towering over the attractive narrow foliage. Looks best planted near silver foliage and yellow flowers. Deadhead to encourage flowering.

Saponaria ocymoides
Rock Soapwort

☀	↔ 30 cm	↕ 15 cm	✿ Spring/Summer	ZONE 3

A small plant that provides an elegant groundcover with its many clusters of pink flowers covering the leaves. Plant in well-drained soil, in a rockery or cascading over a low wall.

Scabiosa columbaria 'Butterfly Blue'
Pincushion Flower

☀	↔ 30 cm	↕ 45 cm	✿ Summer/Summer	ZONE 5		🦋

The delicate, mauve-blue, perfumed blossoms appear at the tips of the tall stems. The precisely but deeply dentated leaves lie below. Planted in a group, they contribute a gentle, welcoming tone to your garden. Also make excellent cut flowers.

Sedum 'Carl'
'Carl' Orpine

| ☀ | ↔ 45 cm | ↕ 45 cm | ✿ Autumn | ZONE 4 | 🦋 |

An autumn succulent that's coveted for its late blooming, bright pink flower-clusters – and the pulpy, dense, cactus-like foliage for which Sedums are generally known. A slow spreader that's best planted in groups near grasses, Asters or Sage.

Sedum reflexum 'Angelina'
Stone Orpine

| ☀ | ☁ | ↔ 40 cm | ↕ 15 cm | ✿ Summer | ZONE 3 |

Eerily conifer-like, with bright yellow summer flowers that brilliantly carpet the ground before turning amber in autumn. Also good in a rockery, a low wall or between stones.

Sedum spectabile 'Autumn Joy'
Showy Stonecrop

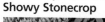

spirit
style

| ☀ | ↔ 60 cm | ↕ 60 cm | ✿ Autumn | ZONE 3 |

A classic perennial that will never go out of style, with its bunched buds that resemble broccoli, opening to pink flowers that darken as they age, until they attain their final bronze colour in the fall. Adapts to dryness but requires well-drained soil.

Sedum spurium
Dragon's Blood Stonecrop

| ☀ | ↔ 30 cm | ↕ 10 to 15 cm | ✿ Summer | ZONE 3 |

A hardy little plant whose fleshy leaves tell you it does well in dry areas. Its plentiful flowers – purple or pink depending on the cultivar – will delight you in a rock garden or planted between patio stones.

BOTANIX Experts by nature

Sempervivum hybridum
Hens and Chickens

☼	↔ 15 cm	↕ 10 to 15 cm	✽ Summer/ Autumn	ZONE 3

The large, fleshy, green leaves with their violet tips are arranged in a characteristic flower-petal format. Prefers poor, well-drained, sunny and dry locations.

Sidalcea malviflora 'Little Princess'
'Little Princess' Prairie Mallow

☼	↔ 30 cm	↕ 40 cm	✽ Summer	ZONE 4

Little Princess boasts many bright pink flowers and light green, lobed foliage. Plant in bunches, in friable, well-drained soil and wonder why this beauty isn't more popular.

Solidago 'Golden Wings'
'Golden Wings' Goldenrod

☼	↔ 80 cm	↕ 1.5 m	✽ Summer/ Autumn	ZONE 3

In summertime, this field plant becomes a mass of golden yellow spikes that look best near purple foliage and violet flowers. With time, forms an imposing bush. Divide every three or four years. Likes damp, well-drained soil.

Solidago hybrida
Goldenrod

☼	↔ 45 cm	↕ 35 to 70 cm	✽ Summer/ Autumn	ZONE 3

When planted in a group, this ubiquitous woodland plant re-creates the wilds with its prodigiously tall, striking gold panicles that turn into cotton balls in autumn. Great for cut flowers, too!

Stachys byzantina
Lamb's Ears

☀ ↔ 40 cm | ↕ 40 cm | ❀ Summer | **ZONE 3**

The distinctive, soft and furry leaves of this perennial look terrific when spreading their greyish-green colour all over the ground at the foot of trees. Add red, pink or blue flowers and you've created a brief rest for tired eyes.

Stokesia laevis
Stoke's Aster

☀ ☁ ↔ 25 cm | ↕ 30 to 40 cm | ❀ Summer | **ZONE 4**

This monotypic genus has lustrous, dark green, evergreen leaves from which the flowers emerge until late autumn, if deadheaded. Requires well-drained soil and winter protection.

Thalictrum aquilegifolium
Columbine Meadow Rue

☀ ☁ ↔ 50 cm | ↕ 1 to 1.2 m | ❀ Summer | **ZONE 4**

An excellent backdrop: pink or white flowers rise high over the blue-tinted foliage. Undaunted by other tall perennial neighbours – such as red Bergamot – if planted in a loose, well-drained and acidic soil. Nice dried flowers.

Thymus pseudolanuginosus
Woolly Thyme

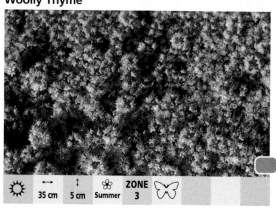

☀ ↔ 35 cm | ↕ 5 cm | ❀ Summer | **ZONE 3** 🦋

In summer, this tiny plant with its miniature, woolly, verdigris leaves becomes a blanket of pink flower-clusters. Requires a well-drained soil. Tolerates light traffic, but also works well spilling over low walls or filling the gaps in your patio stones.

Thymus serpyllum
Creeping/Wild Thyme

| ☀ | | ↔ 25 cm | ↕ 10 cm | ✿ Summer | ZONE 3 | 🦋 |

The quintessential groundcover, exuding a mild perfume, spreading well without requiring water and completely covering itself in flowers during the summer. Supports light traffic and tolerates poor soil.

Tiarella cordifolia
Foamflower

| ⛅ | ☁ | ↔ 35 cm | ↕ 20 to 30 cm | ✿ Spring/Summer | ZONE 3 |

Plant in groups under your trees for a spectacular carpet that's punctuated by countless spikes of tiny star-shaped flowers in spring. In fertile, friable and slightly acidic soil, it will thrive and the foliage will turn copper in autumn.

Tradescantia andersoniana 'Blue & Gold'
'Blue & Gold' Spiderwort

| ☀ | ⛅ | ↔ 45 cm | ↕ 60 cm | ✿ Summer/Autumn | ZONE 3 |

This Tradescantia produces long, arching, yellowish leaves and superb, short-lived, bright flowers that are ceaselessly replenished. Requires a rich, damp soil. The cultivar name highlights the petals that contrast with the yellow anthers.

Tricyrtis hirta 'Miyazaki'
Hairy Toad Lily

| ⛅ | ☁ | ↔ 40 to 70 cm | ↕ 40 to 70 cm | ✿ Summer/Autumn | ZONE 4 |

As summer ends shop, unusual, star-shaped flowers emerge. You'll love their curled stamens and violet freckles. Repay it with damp soil in a shady spot and mulch liberally.

Perennials

Trollius culturum
Orange Princess Trollius/Hybrid Globeflower

| ☀ | ☁ | ↔ 35 cm | ↕ 50 to 90 cm | ❀ Spring/ Summer | ZONE 3 |

Spring will delight you with scintillating yellow or orange, globular flowers that thrust themselves above the dark green, trilobate foliage. Likes damp, fertile soil.

Veronica 'Sunny Border Blue'
Sunny Speedwell

| ☀ | ☁ | ↔ 30 cm | ↕ 55 cm | ❀ Summer | ZONE 3 | 🦋 | 🐦 |

Especially when the numerous, upright spikes of blue-violet flowers make their appearance, you'll be pleased with this perennial. Plant in well-drained, fertile soil near gold foliage or bright flowers.

Veronica prostata 'Aztek Gold'
'Aztek Gold' Speedwell

| ☀ | ☁ | ↔ 35 cm | ↕ 15 cm | ❀ Spring | ZONE 4 | 🦋 |

In semishade, the foliage is green everyday, but in full sun you'll appreciate the golden leaves. Early summer sees the arrival of contrasting, short, blue flower-spikes. In fertile, well-drained soil will rapidly carpet the ground.

Veronica spicata 'Red Fox'
Spiked Red Speedwell

| ☀ | ☁ | ↔ 30 to 50 cm | ↕ 30 to 50 cm | ❀ Summer | ZONE 3 | 🦋 | 🐦 |

One of the most floriferous cultivars, constantly producing a profusion of pink spikes throughout the summer months. Particularly attractive when accompanying silvery leaves and pale pink flowers. Requires well-drained soil.

Veronica spicata 'Royal Candles'
Dwarf Spike Speedwell

| ☀ | ⛅ | ↔ 30 to 50 cm | ↕ 40 cm | ❀ Summer | ZONE 3 | 🦋 |

The spike-racemes of blue florets stand upright over the lustrous, clustered, basal foliage, for a delightful contrast that lasts all summer. Being a Speedwell, it appreciates well-drained soil and looks best in groups or interspersed with other plants.

Vinca minor 'Bowles'
'Bowles' White Common Periwinkle

| ⛅ | ☁ | ↔ 30 cm | ↕ 20 cm | ❀ Spring | ZONE 4 |

A lustrous, evergreen foliage that's typical of the Vincas, but somewhat larger than usual in this case. The delicate, blue flowers appear sporadically until the first frost. Slowly forms a dense floor in a shaded environment provided it has a rich, well-drained soil.

Viola 'Etain'
'Etain' Violet

New

| ☀ | ⛅ | ↔ 20 cm | ↕ 25 cm | ❀ Spring/Autumn | ZONE 5b |

The bright yellow panels, with their mauve margins will illuminate a woodland understory or shady spot in your garden. Plant many together for a naturalistic groundcover that will spread quickly if regularly watered.

Viola corsica
Corsican Pansy

| ☀ | ⛅ | ☁ | ↔ 20 cm | ↕ 20 cm | ❀ Spring/Autumn | ZONE 5 |

Flowers abundantly all summer, making it ideal for planting in groups or scattered over the lawn in studied nonchalance. Thrives in fertile, crumbly, well-drained soil.

Perennials

Garden lace

Ferns may date back to prehistoric times, but that doesn't stop them from being the latest trend in gardening. Their indigenous character coupled with the delicacy of their fronds make them ideal ornamentals for any garden.

Ferns require very little maintenance as long as they're in rich, damp soil. They offer a startling range of textures and foliage that inevitably provides a remarkable background or luxurious duvet under trees. Planted in large groups, they form a spectacular vegetal mass that contributes an ineffable air of freshness to any garden... and nothing offsets a pot of annuals better than a fern or two in their midst.

How delectable!
One species (the Ostrich Fern or *matteucia*) produces the famous fiddleheads which can be eaten as green vegetable. These incipient fronds, which are still rolled up like a snail shell when best eaten – at 10 to 15 cm – are inedible when unrolled. The tastiest ones are flat, green and crunchy. Don't forget to wash them well, and boil them for eight to 10 minutes before savouring.

Osmunda cinnamomea
Cinnamon Fern

Adiantum pedatum
Common Maidenhair Fern

global village *style*

☁ ☁ ↔ 40 cm ↕ 40 to 60 cm **ZONE 2**

One of the most beautiful indigenous ferns, featuring delicate, bright green, lacy foliage and slightly curved black petioles. Its creeping rhizomes produce dense, compact masses of foliage that provide an elegant understory for your trees.

Athyrium filix-femina
Lady Fern

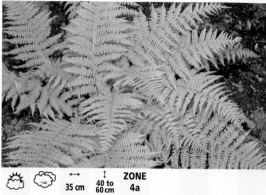

☁ ☁ ↔ 35 cm ↕ 40 to 60 cm **ZONE 4a**

This little native fern lends a note of elegance to your underbrush, with its large tufts of bright green foliage quickly filling up your semishade garden. Requires constant humid soil.

Athyrium nipponicum 'Pictum'
Japanese Painted Fern

global village *style*

☁ ☁ ↔ 35 cm ↕ 25 to 40 cm **ZONE 4b**

Athyrie's bright silver foliage, burgundy veins and purple shoots will surely attract attention. Give it rich, humid soil and enjoy its slow growth.

Dryopteris spinulosa
Toothed Wood Fern

☼ ☁ ☁ ↔ 50 cm ↕ 60 to 90 cm **ZONE 2**

Florists can't get enough of these long, strong fronds for filling up their bouquets. In your garden, they'll look marvellous planted among your hostas and other shade loving plants. Likes rich, cool soil.

Matteucia struthiopteris
Ostrich Fern

☀️ ☁️ ↔️ 60 cm ↕️ 70 cm to 1.2 m **ZONE 4a**

The dark green fronds of this native species form a narrow, elegant funnel. The only species that gives us edible fiddleheads. Try eating them between the time they poke their heads out of the soil and the time they reach 10 to 15 cm in height. The more water you give it, the more it will grow.

Onoclea sensibilis
Bead Fern, Sensitive Fern

☀️ ☀️ ☁️ ↔️ 50 cm ↕️ 40 to 70 cm **ZONE 3b**

A highly fertile North American species that produces rough, brown fronds containing the reproductive spores and bright-green sterile fronds with finely toothed leaves. Foliage turns copper coloured in fall. Prefers very damp soil.

Osmunda cinnamomea
Cinnamon Fern

☀️ ☁️ ↔️ 60 cm ↕️ 60 cm to 1.5 m **ZONE 3**

The young, woolly sprouts grow into long, outreaching fronds that turn cinnamon coloured in spring. Ideal at the water's edge or to carpet an underbrush.

Osmunda regalis
Royal Fern

☀️ ☁️ ☁️ ↔️ 80 cm ↕️ 80 cm to 1.8 m **ZONE 4**

Delicate green fronds emerge from the reddish petioles in spring, and in early autumn take on a flamboyant pumpkin-orange colour. An excellent choice for a shady, damp garden.

The wind

that blows the barley...

Resistant, vigorous and undemanding are just three of the many seductive characteristics of grasses. A little corner of the prairies in your own garden. Thanks to their end-of-season flowering and their seemingly-delighted mass movement in the slightest breeze, giving off flashes of gold, silver or copper, they provide a respite for the eye and a corner of beauty up until the snow falls... and sometimes beyond, when a few inches of fluffy snow amidst the pale tufts incite the heart to poetry.

With their natural look and considerable ornamental value, grasses quickly turn into a country field or form a natural border for water features. Their characteristic vertical and linear, ribbon-like foliage provides a welcome contrast in a flowerbed, while their volume can be used to add discernible structure to your garden. Their feathery floral spikes, meanwhile, bring movement, softness and delicacy to the fore. Annuals such as Pennisetum Setaseum attractively fill empty spaces on your land or harmonize with potted annuals on your patio.

With their increasing popularity, we have to say, grasses are being swept forward by the winds of change!

Did you know?
- Many grasses make excellent dried plants, while their inflorescences – particularly Chasmanthium and Miscanthus – add a Feng-Shui-like charm to fresh or dried flower arrangements.

Miscanthus sinensis 'Strictus'
'Strictus' Miscanthus

Calamagrostis acutiflora 'Karl Fœrster'
'Karl Fœrster' Calamagrostis

| ☀ | ⛅ | ↔ 50 cm | ↕ 1.5 to 2 m | ❀ Summer | ZONE 4a | ⦀ | 🐦 |

Thanks to its golden summer florets, a bed of Calamagrostis is reminiscent of a wheat field. It tolerates semishade, but prefers sun and requires a constantly damp soil. A striking grass with golden-yellow foliage in autumn.

Calamagrostis acutiflora 'Overdam'
'Overdam' Calamagrostis

| ☀ | ⛅ | ↔ 40 cm | ↕ 1.2 to 1.5 m | ❀ Spring/ Summer | ZONE 4b | ⦀ | 🐦 |

Come autumn, this silver grass' foliage turns pink, and its narrow, golden-green panicles will remind you of cumulo-cirrus clouds in a pink sunset. Even the strongest winds won't bend the robust stalks supporting these elegant seedheads.

Chasmanthium latifolium
Northern Sea Oat

| ☀ | ⛅ | ↔ 50 cm | ↕ 1.5 to 1.8 m | ❀ Summer | ZONE 5 | 🌾 |

Drooping golden spikes top the slender, slightly arching culms. Plant in a rich soil – where it will be protected from wind – and Latifolium should do well enough to form a charming woodland bush.

Festuca glauca
Blue Fescue

| ☀ | ↔ 30 cm | ↕ 15 to 45 cm | ❀ Summer | ZONE 4 | 🌾 |

The excessively thin spikes provide a highly decorative, silver-blue clump that's well scaled for a small garden, bestowing a graceful colour variation on your rock garden and blanketing the ground. Likes dry, sandy soil.

Hakonechloa macra 'Aureola'
Japanese Forest Grass

☁	↔ 40 cm	↕ 25 to 45 cm	✿ Summ./ Autumn	ZONE 5	〰

Make a fine border for a row of shrubs or illuminate a shady spot in your garden with this combination of green midribs and magnificent yellow blades. Looks like gently curling ribbons layered in successive cascades.

Helictotrichon sempervirens
Blue Oat Grass

☀	↔ 50 cm	↕ 40 to 90 cm	✿ Summer	ZONE 3b	〰

With its symmetrically spreading form and the silver and verdigris stalks supporting blue oats, this plant resembles a coloured fountain shooting out of the ground. Its unusual foliage looks best when grown in well-drained soil.

Imperata cylindrica 'Red Baron'
'Red Baron' Grass

global village style

☀	↔ 45 cm	↕ 40 to 60 cm	ZONE 5	⫼

Red Baron's rigidly upright foliage will never go unnoticed at the edge of your pond or even in the middle of a well-stocked flowerbed. The leaves starts out a soft green colour, but redden as the hot days tick by, finishing up the summer in various shades of bright copper. Requires winter protection.

Miscanthus sinensis 'Malepartus'
'Malepartus' Miscanthus

global village style

☀	↔ 1 m	↕ 2 m	✿ Autumn	ZONE 4	〰

Due to its extraordinary height, this grass works well as a screen or focal centre with its white florets overshooting the foliage – green in spring and summer, then unmistakably copper-coloured in fall. Likes humid, fertile soil.

Ornamental Grasses

Miscanthus sinensis 'Purpurascens'
Purple Silver Grass

spirit style

| ☀ | ↔ 90 cm to 1.1 m | ↕ 1.75 m | ✿ Autumn | ZONE 4b | 〜 |

The long, slim tufts of this grass first turns purple, then orange in autumn. It is topped with silver-panicle, feathery seedheads that last well into winter. Flame Grass is a sure-fire way to create that natural, bucolic garden look.

Miscanthus sinensis 'Sarabande'
'Sarabande' Miscanthus

| ☀ | ↔ 1.20 m | ↕ 2 m | ✿ Autumn | ZONE 4a | 〜 |

The golden inflorescences and fine, silver-green foliage of this Miscanthus allow it to star in many situations: alone, as a screen or border, at the water's edge, as a backdrop for other plants, in a thick clump, or indoors when dried.

Miscanthus sinensis 'Silberfeder'
'Silberfeder' Miscanthus

global village style

| ☀ | ↔ 1 m | ↕ 1.4 to 2 m | ✿ Autumn | ZONE 4 | 〜 |

The highly decorative 'Silberfeder' produces silver feathers that last into winter and linear, white-lined foliage that turns ochre at summer's end. Provide lots of space, as it grows larger over the years.

Miscanthus sinensis 'Strictus'
'Strictus' Miscanthus

| ☀ | ↔ 1.2 m | ↕ 2 m | ✿ Autumn | ZONE 4 | 〜 |

The very unusual, horizontal yellow bands on the green blades stand out even more when grown in full sun. Create a magnificent winter garden by planting it among shrubs with winter-bearing berries and conifers, where you'll appreciate the persistent golden fall colour.

Miscanthus sinensis 'Variegatus'
'Variegatus' Miscanthus

☀ ↔ 80 cm to 1.2 m ↕ 1.2 to 1.8 m **ZONE 5**

An elegant species that will brighten your garden with its creamy white leaf borders that turn straw yellow in mid-autumn. Rarely flowers in northern latitudes, but will nevertheless stand out all year round.

Panicum virgatum 'Heavy Metal'
'Heavy Metal' Switch Grass

☀ ↔ 90 cm ↕ 90 cm ✿ Summ./Autumn **ZONE 4**

The dark pink feathers sported by the metallic blue foliage create an impressive border. Equally appealing in autumn, with its yellowish, red-tipped foliage towered by ecru seedheads. Requires well-drained soil.

Panicum virgatum 'Rotstrahlbusch'
'Rotstrahlbusch' Switch Grass

☀ ↔ 1 m ↕ 1 to 1.5 m ✿ Summ./Autumn **ZONE 4**

Its verdigris foliage with scarlet and gold highlights will embrace your garden like sunlight. As autumn winds begin to blow, purple inflorescences contrast with the reddening spikes. Requires a loose, rich soil.

Panicum virgatum 'Shenandoah'
'Shenandoah' Switch Grass

☀ ↔ 90 cm ↕ 1.2 m ✿ Summ./Autumn **ZONE 4**

This German cultivar brings a Heraclitean fire to your garden when its tips turn crimson in midsummer, and all the foliage turns burgundy in the fall. Tolerates all soil types.

Panicum virgatum 'Squaw'
'Squaw' Switch Grass

| ☀ | ↔ 90 cm | ↕ 1.2 m | ❋ Summer/ Autumn | ZONE 4 | 〜 |

At maturity, you'll have a very impressive clump of primarily green foliage surveyed from on high by exceptional feathery bracts. The red-spattered leaf-tips spread their colour to all the foliage in the fall. In a mixed border or planted in isolation, Squaw is sure to add interest to your garden.

Pennisetum setaseum
Fountain Grass

| ☀ | ☁ | ↔ 20 cm | ↕ 75 cm | ❋ Summer/ Autumn | ZONE annual | 〜 |

A highly floriferous annual grass that's simply sensational, due to its vaporous, intriguingly soft, nodding purple-tinged spikes that wave gently in the wind. Will grow rapidly in friable, well-drained soil.

Pennisetum setaseum 'Rubrum'
'Rubrum' Fountain Grass

| ☀ | ↔ 20 cm | ↕ 75 cm | ❋ Summer/ Autumn | ZONE annual | 〜 |

A royal purple version of Fountain Grass with slim, arching foliage. This annual also produces an abundance of delicately feathery, reddish purple seed spikes. Plant it in the ground or in pots.

Phalaris arundinacea 'Picta'
Ribbon Grass

| ☀ | ☁ | ↔ 50 to 60 cm | ↕ 35 to 45 cm | ❋ Spring/ Summer | ZONE 3b | 〜 |

Its white-striped, bright green foliage makes a great groundcover. In summer, self-effacing pinkish white bracts rise among the leaf tips. Give it lots of space as it is invasive.

botanix.com

Discover a world of information and ideas at botanix.com :

- New arrivals and Favorites
- Hints and Tips
- Plant Selector
- Flyers

... and much more!

BOTANIX
Experts by nature

Those irreplaceable...

annuals

Annuals have long been dear to homeowners' hearts. A cushion of flowers cascading from a flower box under a windowsill always attracts the eye and seduces the soul, and a few pots and urns overflowing with flowers instantly transform a patio into a paradise!

It's not difficult to understand why annuals are so popular: they have so many uses and they just don't stop flowering. Let's face it, they practically monopolize flower boxes, pots and hanging baskets, plus they have the following qualities:

- Already flowering in early spring, they continue to do so into late fall;
- Annuals can go anywhere in your garden: on your patio, at the foot of trees or shrubs, in hanging baskets and pots, near the pool, in the vegetable garden, on your balcony railing and at windowsills;
- They allow you to create a new décor every year, changing the whole look of a flower bed and permitting experimentation with various compositions and styles from one year to the next;
- As soon as they're planted, you can start enjoying them;
- They're not invasive and they form borders that will stay clean and orderly throughout the season;
- Some of them make very attractive cut flowers.

Nicotiana
Nicotine

With their enormous ornamental potential and many other advantages, annuals deserve every gardener's attention. Be imaginative and experiment with them a little bit; annuals won't let you down.

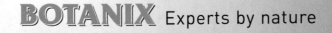

Renewing your garden

Generally speaking, the lifecycle of your annuals is no longer than one season. As they come from warm countries, they can't survive our winters so they need replacing every year. It means more planting time, but the reward is that they enable us to create variations on our floral composition, or make an entirely new garden décor every year!

Planting

Growing your own seedlings or making your own cuttings has two distinct advantages: you save money and you have access to a greater variety of choices. Buying annuals has an advantage too: transferring them to your garden doesn't stress them as much, since they're sold in small pots or multicellular containers. Annuals can be planted at any time there's no risk of frost.

Good Earth

Usually annuals require fertile, well structured soil that drains easily. After planting, add compost or a slow-release granular fertilizer. Fertilize regularly to maintain vigour and encourage flowering.

So many types of pots

A variety of pots and flower baskets is available to satisfy any taste, style or budget. Fired-Clay and concrete pots are stylish and less likely to tip over in the wind. Plastic, metal or resin pots generally look more modern, though they are often made to imitate older containers. The most expensive ones are usually made of concrete and of fibreglass.

Maintenance

Deadheading, which is the removal of faded flowers, encourages continuous, abundant flowering. Towards midseason, it's often advisable to fertilize, and cut back the foliage of some plants as they begin to show signs of fatigue. Some of the taller and more fragile annuals may need tutors.

Rudbeckia hirta 'Capuccino'
'Cappucino' Rudbeckia

The 2008 Exceptionals

The Exceptionals Program is a top-10 of new annual cultivars selected according to specific criteria. See the complete list on page 263.

Did you know?

Having annuals doesn't always mean discarding them at the end of the season. Many are perennials in their country of origin, but they're simply not able to live through our harsh winters. Many species such as Coleus, Begonias, Fuchsias, Lantanas, Heliotropes and Pelargonium winter happily indoors. They'll continue to develop and can be brought out again the next spring. If you don't have much place in front of sunny windows in your house, think about taking cuttings from your annuals at the end of the summer, potting them for their winter indoors, and bringing them out the following year.

Golden rules for the successful integration of annuals

- Group together varieties that have the same light and fertilizing requirements.
- Choose a dominant colour and two or three other tints that go with it.
- Vary textures and set off flowers with decorative foliage.
- For a gentle, peaceful vista that rests the eye, try juxtaposing similar colours or shades of the same colour. For a more vibrant, invigorating effect, go for contrasts, rich tones and colour-saturation.
- For more abundant flowering in your pots, place tall plants at the back or centre, surrounded by lower plants, with trailing leaves or flowers spilling over the edge.
- Plant some annuals among your perennials so that area has flowers throughout the season. For more visual impact, limit the color palette and plant in groups.

Bringing the tropics home

Tropical plants offer gardeners the advantage that they flower more continuously and their unusual forms are striking and exotic. Often, they can be treated as annuals that are brought inside at the end of the season where they continue to develop and often flower. BOTANIX garden centres have an enormous array of Hibiscuses, Palms, Banana Plants and many species grafted onto standards. Our selection of tropicals is presented on page 266.

Cestrum elegans
Red Cestrum

Eugenia paniculata
Eugenia Standard

... unusual inflorescences

...colour harmony

...exotic effect ensured

Alyssum maritima
Sweet Alyssum

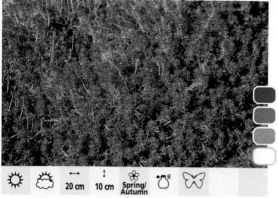

☀ ☁ ↔ 20 cm ↕ 10 cm ❀ Spring/Autumn ⚘ 🦋

Alyssum forms a dense, pretty border that attracts helpful insects, so it's good to plant near or in your vegetable garden. Likes a medium-rich soil that's well-drained.

Angelonia angustifolia 'AngelMist Purple'
Angelonia

☀ ↔ 25 to 30 cm ↕ 45 to 60 cm ❀ Spring/Autumn

The erect stems of this annual add a touch of elegance to pots and flower boxes throughout the season. Likes full sun and heat.

Anigozanthos 'Kanga Red'
Kangaroo Paw

☀ ↔ 60 cm ↕ 60 cm ❀ Spring/Autumn

The fine, erect foliage and velvety, tubular flowers of this Australian immigrant are natural-looking enough, but they will add a touch of the exotic to your rockery or water feature. The flowers also make interesting bouquets.

Argyranthemum frutescens 'Vanilla Butterfly'
Summer Daisy

☀ ↔ 30 cm ↕ 45 to 90 cm ❀ Spring/Autumn

A very attractive annual with creamy yellow flowers that last until the first frosts. Grow either in the ground or in pots with other plants. Likes rather rich, particulate, well-drained soil.

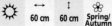

Bacopa 'Abunda Giant White'
Giant White Bacopa

☀ ☁ ↔ 60 cm ↕ 5 to 10 cm ❁ Spring/Autumn

This Bacopa's myriad white flowers all add beauty to your hanging baskets. If given sufficient water in a rich, well-drained soil, will thrive throughout the gardening season.

Begonia 'Dragon Wing'
'Dragon Wing' Begonia

☁ ↔ 45 cm ↕ 30 to 40 cm ❁ Spring/Autumn

The pending pink or red flowers are gracefully suspended from arching branches. Thrives in the ground or containers.

Begonia semperflorens
Begonia

☀ ☁ ☁ ↔ 20 cm ↕ 20 cm ❁ Spring/Autumn

A popular Begonia that grows pretty much anywhere, in any light. Quickly forms a pretty mass. Particularly agreeable with other annuals in a flower bed or pot.

Brassica oleracea 'Nagoya'
'Nagoya' Ornamental Cabbage

New

☀ ↔ 20 to 30 cm ↕ 20 to 30 cm

Has an unusual form, and foliage that stays completely green all summer, with the central leaves turning dark pink in autumn. The leaves immediately surrounding the heart gradually turn pale until they become cream coloured.

Annuals

Calibrachoa 'Million Bells Tangerine'
'Million Bells' Calibrachoa

☀ ↔ 20 cm ↕ 20 cm ✿ Spring/Autumn

This plant looks like a miniature Petunia, with spectacular flowers blooming all season. Very resistant to dry spells, so it's a shoo-in for hanging baskets.

Canna 'African Sunset'
'African Sunset' Canna Lily

New

☀ ↔ 40 to 50 cm ↕ 60 cm to 1.75 m ✿ Summer/Autumn

With its banana-like foliage, this large plant will decorate your garden by itself. The bright orange flowers stand out against the large leaves. An impressive, vigorous plant that loves heat and tolerates wind.

Celosia argentea 'Fresh Look Gold'
Feather Cockscomb

☀ ↔ 35 cm ↕ 45 cm ✿ Spring/Autumn

A tropical that's highly tolerant of heat waves and dry spells. The striking inflorescences of this series will brighten up any flower bed and look fabulous in a vase.

Celosia venezuela 'Caracas'
Plume Flower

☀ ↔ 35 cm ↕ 45 cm ✿ Spring/Autumn

With its abundant violet plumes, this one makes a spectacular border, potted plant or mass planting. Like all Celosia, it's tolerant of heat and dryness. An ideal annual.

Cleome 'Senorita Rosalita'
'Senorita Rosalita' Cleome

☀ | ↔ 50 cm | ↕ 80 cm | ✿ Summer/Autumn | 🦋

This unusually small cultivar stands out when planted in masse, and is particularly well suited to a country-style garden. Though the flowers make superb bouquets, you may well prefer to leave them on the plant as long as possible, as they attract butterflies.

Cosmos bipinnatus 'Sonata Pink'
'Sonata Pink' Cosmos

☀ | ↔ 30 to 40 cm | ↕ 45 to 60 cm | ✿ Spring/Autumn

Compact and highly floriferous, with huge flowers available in many colours. It's hard to decide whether it's better in a pot with other annuals or in the ground, turning your yard into a country garden. Tolerates poor, dry soils.

Dahlia 'Gallery Art Deco'
Deco Dwarf Dahlia

☀ | ↔ 60 to 90 cm | ↕ 30 to 45 cm | ✿ Spring/Autumn | 🦋

The Gallery series comprises dwarf cultivars that work well in borders or pots, and planted in groups. Superb, compact flowers that last until the frosts take them out.

Dahlia 'Melody Lisa'
'Melody Lisa' Dahlia

☀ | ↔ 25 to 30 cm | ↕ 45 cm | ✿ Spring/Autumn | 🦋

This Dahlia produces large, magnificent, pink flowers with subtle golden highlights. Easy to grow almost anywhere in the garden as long as the soil is rich and deep. Good cut flowers.

Annuals

Diascia barberae 'Wink'
'Wink' Diascia

☀ ⛅ ↔ 20 cm | ↕ 15 to 30 cm | ❀ Spring/Autumn

A delicate annual that prospers throughout the season as long as it has a friable, well drained soil. The pink or mauve flowers emerge in little bunches to embellish the smallest garden.

Euphorbia hypericifolia 'Diamond Frost'
'Diamond Frost' Euphorbia

☀ ↔ 40 cm | ↕ 30 cm | Spring/Autumn

An exceptional, bushy plant with white flowers that grow from early spring to late autumn, making it look like a bright fog. Indoors, may flower until January.

Gazania splendens 'Kiss Mahogany'
'Kiss Mahogany' Treasure Flower

☀ ↔ 25 to 30 cm | ↕ 15 to 20 cm | ❀ Spring/Autumn

Throughout the growing season, this rigorous plant produces bright red flowers on short stems. Prefers well-drained soil and, like most Gazanias, tolerates short dry spells.

Hedera helix
English Ivy

☀ ⛅ ☁ ↔ 80 cm | ↕ 15 cm

English Ivy is the perfect green leaf for container planting, tumbling over a low wall or covering the ground. Likes a moderately rich, crumbly, well-drained soil. No flowers.

Impatiens wallerana 'Dazzler Cranberry'
'Dazzler Cranberry' Impatiens

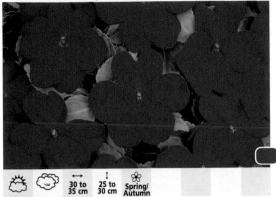

☀ ☁ | ↔ 30 to 35 cm | ↕ 25 to 30 cm | ❀ Spring/Autumn

This Impatiens' generous and continuous flowering makes it ideal for planting in groups. Dazzler also grows well in hanging baskets or large containers. Be careful not to over fertilize.

Ipomoea tricolor 'Heavenly Blue'
'Heavenly Blue' Moonflower

☀ ☁ | ↔ 90 cm to 1.8 m | ↕ 2.5 to 3 m | ❀ Spring/Autumn

The spectacular, 10-cm, sky-blue flowers with their mauve stripes will cover a trellis in no time, opening in the mornings until autumn if grown in well-drained soil. Don't eat the seeds, as they're toxic and will start many new plants for you in the spring.

Lantana camara 'Lucky Red Hot'
'Lucky Red Hot' Verbena

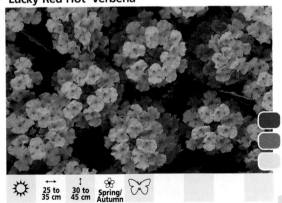

☀ | ↔ 25 to 35 cm | ↕ 30 to 45 cm | ❀ Spring/Autumn | 🦋

This Lantana's brightly coloured flowers emerge from dark green foliage. A bushy show-stopper that likes well-drained loam.

Lophospermum 'Great Cascade'
'Great Cascade' Lophospermum

☀ ☁ | ↔ 30 cm | ↕ 2.1 m | ❀ Spring/Autumn

The numerous bright red, trumpet-like flowers dangle graciously from hanging baskets or elegantly climb a trellis. Flowers all season in damp, well-drained soil if regularly fertilized.

Lysimachia 'Lyssi'
'Lyssi' Lysimachia

☀ ☁ ↔ 30 cm ↕ 15 cm ✿ Spring/Autumn

The pretty bunches of yellow flowers against the dark green foliage will provide visual delight all summer. A good potted accompaniment to other annuals.

Nicotiana sylvestris
Nicotine

☀ ☁ ↔ 60 cm ↕ 1.5 m ✿ Summer/Autumn ⚠

This Argentinean import is a large plant with large leaves and a multitude of white, trumpet-like flowers that exude an intense perfume. All parts are toxic.

Osteospermum
Cape Daisy

☀ ☁ ↔ 60 to 90 cm ↕ 30 to 45 cm ✿ Summer

This Daisy-like South African native looks good in containers or as a groundcover. Either way, these flowers will add colour to your life all summer.

Pelargonium hortorum 'Kim'
'Kim' Geranium

☀ ☁ ↔ 30 cm ↕ 60 cm ✿ Spring/Autumn

An upright variety that will add colour to your flower pots, flower boxes or flower beds. Like its fellow cultivars, flowers more prolifically when deadheaded and can be brought indoors in autumn.

Pelargonium hortorum 'PopCorn'
'PopCorn' Geranium

☀ ☁ ↔ 30 to 40 cm ↕ 25 to 30 cm ✿ Spring/Autumn

It's pretty, disease-resistant, quick growing, and has large round, simple or double flowers that resemble popcorn. One wonders why it's not more popular. Deadhead to stimulate flowering and bring indoors at season's end.

Penstemon 'Phoenix Red'
'Phoenix Red' Bearded Tongue

☀ ↔ 30 cm ↕ 60 cm ✿ Spring/Autumn

Unusual, with numerous, red, trumpet-shaped flowers. Plant in bare spots among perennials or annuals where the long flowering period will soon fill the space sensationally.

Annuals

Perilla 'Magilla'
Beefsteak Plant

☀ ☁ ☁ ↔ 40 cm ↕ 90 cm

The magnificent, plum coloured foliage with the pink central nerves will add beauty and brightness to your potted annuals. A vigorous grower that likes hot weather.

Petunia 'Wave Blue'
'Wave Blue' Petunia

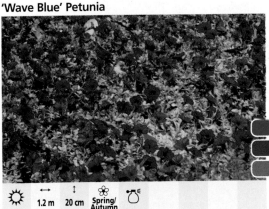

☀ ↔ 1.2 m ↕ 20 cm ✿ Spring/Autumn 🏺

A spreading Petunia that flowers abundantly from the beginning of the season to the end. Likes well-drained, loose soil.

Plectranthus forsteri 'Variegatus'
Mintleaf

☀ ☁ ↔ 80 cm ↕ 20 cm

The magnificent, odoriferous green foliage with cream spots will bring out the best in other container plants. Likes rich, slightly sandy soil.

Ricinus communis
Castor Oil Plant

☀ ↔ 1 m ↕ 1 to 1.5 m ✿ Spring/Summer

The height of these plants, coupled with the size of the leaves and their unusual shape, contribute an air of the tropical to any garden. The fabulous spiked, pink seedpods grow in groups surrounded by the dark green and purple foliage. Plant in a rich, moderately damp soil accompanying pink and red flowering plants.

Rudbeckia hirta
Black-Eyed Susan

☀ ☁ ↔ 35 to 45 cm ↕ 80 cm to 1 m ✿ Summer/Autumn 🦋 🐦

Did someone say country garden? The profuse, large flowers with their narrow, yellow petals and domed, dark brown centres top solid stems... and they look great in a vase, too.

Scaevola aemula 'Saphira Blue'
'Saphira Blue' Fairy Fan-Flower

☀ ☁ ↔ 45 cm ↕ 20 cm ✿ Spring/Autumn

A charming annual that will drape elegantly from hanging planters, when grown alone or with other delicate-flowered annuals. In rich, well-drained soil, will flower generously all summer.

Senecio mikanioides
German Ivy

An excellent consort for annual flowers in flower boxes or hanging baskets. Thrives all season in loose, well-drained soil.

Solenostemon scutellarioides 'KingWood Torch'
'KingWood Torch' Coleus

This vigorous cultivar can be grown alone to spectacular effect in containers or flower beds, where it's flamboyant, crenulated, magenta foliage with lime-green margins reveals orange or burgundy centres, depending on the light. Also grows well indoors.

Solenostemon scutellarioides 'Kiwi Fern'
'Kiwi Fern' Coleus

An original, elongated, burgundy foliage with yellow-green margins. Its height makes it ideal for pot or large-container growing. Does very well indoors.

Solenostemon scutellarioides 'Pineapple'
'Pineapple' Coleus

Huge, magnificent, exotic-looking leaves that combine chartreuse borders with purplish red interiors. This beauty can be grown alone or as a consort to flowering plants indoors or out.

 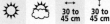

Tropaeolum majus
Garden Nasturtium

☼ ☁ ↔ 30 cm ↕ 25 to 40 cm ✿ Spring/Autumn

The Nasturtium's typically round leaves and flowers are edible, which is suitable, since they do so well in vegetable gardens. The dwarf varieties work well in flower beds while you can grow the larger ones like vines. They tolerate poor but friable and well-drained soil.

Verbena 'Temari Violet'
'Temari Violet' Verbena

☼ ↔ 40 cm ↕ 10 cm ✿ Spring/Autumn 🌡

A trailing plant that lends itself naturally to hanging baskets, but when planted in the ground will make a superb border, enhance your rockery and start new plants where stems touch the ground. Water frequently.

Verbena 'Tapiens Blue Violet'
'Tapiens Blue Violet' Verbena

☼ ↔ 75 cm to 90 cm ↕ 10 cm ✿ Spring/Autumn 🌡

Thanks to its arching branches, the many blooms, which give off a delicate scent, flower freely in hanging baskets or pots. A disease-resistant annual that likes frequent watering.

Vinca major 'Wojo's Gem'
'Wojo's Gem' Vinca/Periwinkle

☼ ☁ ↔ 35 to 45 cm ↕ 15 to 30 cm ✿ Spring

Bring light into your garden with these dark green leaves and their generous cream spots. Plant on the outside edge of a pot that holds flowering annuals, where its trailing leaves will add to the scenery. Delicate blue flowers appear in spring.

Vinca minor 'Illumination'
'Illumination' Vinca/Periwinkle

☀ ☁ ↔ 30 to 50 cm ↕ 10 cm ❀ Spring

The green-margined leaves start out chartreuse, and then turn gold before becoming cream coloured. All these colours look particularly good on the end of the reddish stems. The delicate, blue, spring flowering also contrasts nicely with the foliage. Disease and insect resistant.

Viola wittrockiana 'Delta Fire'
'Delta Fire' Pansy

☀ ☁ ☁ ↔ 15 to 20 cm ↕ 15 to 20 cm ❀ Spring/ Autumn

The abundant, yellowish-orange flowers with their red centres will be a welcome addition to your garden, all season. Grow in pots with other annuals or use as a groundcover. The flowers are edible.

Viola wittrockiana 'Karma Deep Blue Blotch'
'Karma Deep Blue Blotch' Pansy

☀ ☁ ☁ ↔ 20 cm ↕ 20 cm ❀ Spring/ Autumn

The popularity of this annual is attributed to its long flowering, which creates a luminous groundcover all season, or provides a good consort for other annuals in containers. If planted in the ground, may reappear. Edible flowers.

Zinnia 'Profusion White'
Bedding Zinnia

☀ ↔ 25 to 40 cm ↕ 30 to 40 cm ❀ Spring/ Autumn

Profusion Zinnias flower abundantly until the first frosts without undue maintenance. They are also highly disease-resistant, tolerate heat waves and don't mind dry soil. Furthermore, they look great edging a flower bed or planted in groups.

Instant inspiration!

BOTANIX's *Living Spaces* brochure is overflowing with garden accessories and exclusive arrangements of annuals, plus great ideas for making the most of the latest landscaping trends. Everything you need to create a garden that reflects your unique style.

Coming out in April 2008.
Don't miss it.
It's free!

The 2008 Exceptionals

The only such program in North America!

Every year, the Exceptionals create a top-10 of new cultivars in order to guide you in your choice of annuals. These plants, which are listed below, are available in all BOTANIX garden centres starting in the spring.

For 2007, the annuals were tested in **Daniel A. Séguin's Saint-Hyacinthe horticultural demonstration and testing garden**. Throughout the testing period, no pesticides were used. Using special flags, visitors first picked the plants they found most attractive when they visited the garden, then a group of horticulturalists went over that list to create the top-of 10 using these criteria:

- Performance
- Hardiness and adaptation to the Nordic climate of Quebec and Ontario
- Disease and insect resistance
- Ability to thrive with little maintenance
- Popularity with visitors

As usual, the public is invited to visit the garden in Saint-Hyacinthe, where they can vote for the 2009 Exceptionals.

Begonia boliviensis 'Bonfire'
Bonfire

☀ ☁ ↔ 40 cm ↕ 20 cm ✿ Summer/Autumn

This Begonia, which produces superb, graciously pendant, orange flowers on arching branches can be easily grown in pots or hanging baskets. Water thoroughly and let dry out before watering again.

Begonia tuberhybrida 'Nonstop Deep Salmon'
Nonstop Deep Salmon Tuberous Begonia

☀ ☁ ↔ 40 cm ↕ 30 cm ✿ Spring/Autumn

All season, you'll enjoy a profusion of large, double, Salmon-orange flowers. Like all tuberous Begonias, grows as well in pots as in the ground as long as it's provided with a rich, damp and well drained soil.

Calibrachoa 'Superbells Dreamsicle'
Superbells

☀ ☁ ↔ 60 cm ↕ 10 cm ✿ Spring/Autumn

Superbells looks like a miniature weeping Petunia with flowers that start out orange in the spring and gradually turn apricot-coloured. Will bloom until the first frosts whether grown in a pot or as a ground cover. Requires light, rich, friable, cool and well drained soil.

Lobelia erinus 'Purple Star'
'Purple Star' Lobelia

☀ ☁ ↔ 30 cm ↕ 15 cm ✿ Spring/Autumn

This weeping Lobelia features unusual and magnificent mauve-tinted flowers. An annual that's neither withered by heat nor scorched by full sun. It prefers a rather rich, crumbly and well drained soil.

Nemesia strumosa 'Angelart Pear'
'Angelart Pear' Nemesia

☀ ☁ ↔ 25 cm ↕ 10 cm ✿ Spring/Autumn 🌸

Throughout the summer, hundreds of perfumed yellow flowers entirely cover the foliage of this floriferous beauty. Spectacular in a container or flowerbed. Grows well in the sun, but prefers a cool, semishade environment.

Pennisetum 'Prince'
Pennisetum Grass

☀ ↔ 1 m ↕ 1.5 m

This purple annual grass darkens as summer temperatures climb. A strong, fast grower that will thrive in rich, cool and well drained soil. No flowers.

BOTANIX Experts by nature

Pennisetum setaceum 'Rubrum Dwarf'
Burgundy Blaze

☀ ☁   ↔ 45 cm   ↕ 35 cm   ❀ Summer/Autumn

Rubrum Dwarf is simply a dwarf version of the grass, Rubrum. You'll love its compact habit, purple foliage and abundant ecru inflorescences with pink and purple highlights.

Petunia 'Supertunia Raspberry Blast'
'Raspberry Blast' Petunia

☀   ↔ 45 cm   ↕ 20 cm   ❀ Spring/Autumn

What's amazing about this Petunia is its robustness, compactness and the innumerable pale pink flowers with magenta highlights that last throughout the season. Also, the faded blooms disappear quickly. Requires a light, well drained soil.

Rudbeckia hirta 'Capuccino'
'Cappucino' Rudbeckia

☀ ☁   ↔ 40 cm   ↕ 50 cm   ❀ Summer/Autumn

The abundant, large yellow flowers of this magnificent, late-blooming annual have coffee-coloured brown centres. Adapts to almost any soil that's moderately rich, slightly sandy and well drained. Flowers until the first frosts.

Verbena 'Tukana Raspberry'
'Tukana Raspberry' Verbena

☀   ↔ 35 cm   ↕ 15 cm   ❀ Summer/Autumn

A magenta-pink floral carpet to edge your flowerbed. Tolerates dryness, but prefers a damp, friable soil and lots of sunlight to ward off powdery mildew, though it is the most resistant Verbena to that pathogen.

Bougainvillea buttiana
Bougainvillea Standard

☀ ↔ 1 m | ↕ 1.5 m | ❀ Summer/Autumn | ZONE Tropical | ✂

The bright red bracts surround little flowers that contrast with the yellow-splotched green leaves. Requires constantly damp soil. Cut back radically and bring inside at the end of the season. Let the soil dry out by two thirds before watering again.

Brugmansia hybrida
Brugmansia

☀ ↔ 1 to 1.5 m | ↕ 1 to 1.5 m | ❀ Summer/Autumn | ZONE Tropical | 🧪

This gorgeous tree is ideal for a balcony or patio, with its large, deep, pendant trumpet-shaped flowers that exude an intoxicating scent after nightfall. Treat with insecticide and bring indoors when the cool weather sets in.

Cestrum elegans
Red Cestrum

New

☀ ☁ | ↔ 2.4 m | ↕ 3 m | ZONE Tropical | 🧪 🦋

The bunches of perfumed, purplish-red, tubular flowers attract butterflies before transforming into small reddish-black berries. All parts are toxic. Bring inside at the first sign of frost.

Dipladenia sanderi
Mandevilla Standard

☀ ↔ 1.25 m | ↕ 1.2 m | ❀ Summer/Autumn | ZONE Tropical | ✂

Elegantly sensational with its large, yellow-throated flowers emerging from supple stems that last all summer. An excellent patio plant. Like most tropical plants, it likes warmth, so – at the end of the season – prune and bring indoors.

BOTANIX Experts by nature

Duranta repens (erecta)
Golden Dewdrop

New

☀ ☁ ↔ 2.4 m ↕ 4.5 m **ZONE** Tropical

After the white, lavender or violet spikes with their vanilla perfume fade, they're replaced by bunches of yellow berries that cause the branches to droop gracefully. Due to its shape and tolerance of dryness, this is a good candidate for container growing.

Dypsis elegans
Dypsis Palm

New

☀ ☁ ↔ 1 m ↕ 2 m **ZONE** Tropical

This Madagascar native will add a tropical accent to your patio. Thrives in dry soil, but must be brought inside in fall.

Tropicals

Eugenia paniculata
Eugenia on stem

oasis
style

☀ ☁ ↔ 60 cm ↕ 1.2 m ✿ Spring/ Autumn **ZONE** Tropical

An Australian plant with shoots that emerge copper-brown only to turn shiny, dark green over the season. This small shrub produces pretty, white flowers before bearing small purple fruit.

Fuchsia hybrida
Fuchsia Standard

☁ ↔ 90 cm ↕ 1 to 1.5 m ✿ Summer/ Autumn **ZONE** Tropical

The bright colours of the pending, tubular flowers form an alluring contrast with the dark green, almost purple foliage. Treat it like an annual, placing it on your porch or patio where it won't be subjected to strong winds. Deadhead for abundant flowering.

Hibiscus rosa-sinensis 'Comet Halo'
'Comet Halo' Hibiscus

New

| ☀ | ↔ 30 to 45 cm | ↕ 30 to 45 cm | ✽ Summer/ Autumn | ZONE Tropical |

The large, dark pink flowers with their orange borders can last up to four days. A tropical that requires fertile soil and regular watering. Winter indoors.

Hibiscus rosa-sinensis 'Moonlight'
'Moonlight' Hibiscus

New

| ☀ | ↔ 30 to 45 cm | ↕ 30 to 45 cm | ✽ Summer/ Autumn | ZONE Tropical |

An aptly named variety as it's strongly reminiscent of a tropical full moon. The red-hearted, white flowers can bloom all year if it's transferred inside at the end of summer and placed in a sunny window.

Hibiscus rosa-sinensis 'Sunlight'
'Sunlight' Hibiscus

New

| ☀ | ↔ 30 to 45 cm | ↕ 30 to 45 cm | ✽ Summer/ Autumn | ZONE Tropical |

All summer, this Hibiscus will treat you with its magnificent white-hearted, yellow flowers. Grows well in a pot, but should be brought inside for winter and placed in a sunny spot.

Howea forsteriana
Kentia Palm

New

| ☀ | ☁ | ↔ 1 m | ↕ 2 m | ZONE Tropical |

This Tasmanian devil prefers dry soil and thrives indoors, where it's vertical fronds will remind you of southern seas. Requires a rich, well-drained soil.

Lilium 'Buff Pixie'
Oriental Lily

☀ ☁ | ↔ 20 cm | ↕ 1 m | ❁ Summer | **ZONE** Tropical | ⚱

Plant this beautiful perennial in a pot and watch it turn your patio into a foreign locale, then transfer to the ground in autumn. Available in a superb palette of colours, some with scented flowers.

Musa basjoo
Banana

New

☀ | ↔ 2 m | ↕ 3 m | ❁ Spring | **ZONE** Tropical

Nothing says "exotic" better than a banana plant. These delicious little bananas emerge from the burgundy flowers at the centre of the plant. The leaves are also edible. Requires maximum sunlight and damp soil. Bring inside for winter.

Tropicals

Nerium oleander
Oleander

☀ | ↔ 1 m | ↕ 2 m | ❁ Summer/ Autumn | **ZONE** Tropical | ⚱

Evocative of the European Mediterranean countries, where it's extremely popular. The single or double, aromatic flowers are interspersed with the species' typical narrow leaves. Can easily live indoors if there's enough light.

Tibouchina urvilleana
Glory Bush Standard

New

☀ | ↔ 3 m | ↕ 4 m | ❁ Summer/ Autumn | **ZONE** Tropical

The magnificent, velvet-textured, verdigris foliage and a profusion of violet flowers in summer come to us from the rainforests of South America. In autumn, bring it indoors and keep it in a humid area.

Effortless...

beauty

Whether annual or perennial, your bulbs are fleshy, subterranean roots that store nutritional elements for the annual reconstitution of the above-ground part of the plant. Annual bulbs, also known as 'tender bulbs', can't survive in the ground in winter. They must therefore be dug up and kept inside until they are replanted early the following spring. Perennial bulbs, also referred to as 'hardy bulbs' and 'spring bulbs', can tough it out through our winters. They are planted in fall, from the end of September to the beginning of November, and flower early or late the following spring.

Perennial bulbs complement your decor all over the garden: under trees and bushes, popping up through the ground cover, in the rockery or between other plants. When the bulbs have finished flowering, other perennials take their place above soil, so your garden can have successive flowerings, and you, successive joy. Some species, such as Crocuses and Scillia, can be planted directly in your lawn, at the foot of trees, or in the underbrush, for a natural look. Many annual bulbs, including Dahlias, have spectacular, sunbathing flowers, whereas Begonias have attractive, pretty flowers that will happily embellish a shady area of your garden.

Bulbs are the gardeners delight: beautiful and undemanding. Thanks to magnificent perennial bulbs like Snowdrops, Crocuses, Glory-of-the-Snow and Scillia, your garden will explode with enchanting flowers in early spring. Not to be outdone, annual bulbs surprise us in the summertime with their awesome, original blooms.

Looking for tips and advice on planting and maintaining bulbs? Visit **botanix.com**

Tulipa hybrida
Tulip

A world of possibilities

Discover a wide selection of annual and perennial bulbs with the Plant Selector at **botanix.com** or visit a BOTANIX garden centre.

Canna hybrida
Canna

☀	↔ 40 cm to 50 cm	↕ 60 cm to 1.75 m	❀ Summer/Autumn

With foliage resembling a banana and asymmetric flowers in hot shades, this impressive, rapidly growing plant loves heat and tolerates the wind. Fertilize and water regularly.

Gladiolus hybridus
Gladiolus

☀	↔ 15 cm	↕ 60 cm to 1.2 m	❀ Summer/Autumn

A charming annual that has never lost its popularity. It flowers from the bottom to the top on long individual stems, which make it excellent for cut flowers. All like a rich, well drained soil and the tallest ones need to be staked.

Hippeastrum hybridum
Amaryllis

☀	↔ 30 cm	↕ 60 cm	❀ Variable

The large, funnel-shaped flowers grow in bunches, if you keep the soil well drained. Adventurous gardeners may want to try growing it in a well-lit room, but must remember to keep it cool and dry from October to December.

Allium azureum, syn. A. caeruleum
Allium Azureum

☼☁	↔ 10 cm	↕ 20 to 40 cm	✿ Summer	ZONE 5

The ice blue, spherical flowers appear on the ends of solid stocks in early summer, at which time they immediately begin to discourage many bothersome insects. Use in group plantings for a spectacular effect. Prefers warmth and well drained soil.

Crocus hybridus
Crocus

☼	☼☁	↔ 10 cm	↕ 15 cm	✿ Spring	ZONE 3

Its luminous flowers open and close with the light. Being small, they're ideal in rock gardens or sprinkled throughout the lawn. Their leaves look like blades of grass, so simply postpone your first mowing by a few weeks.

Perennial Bulbs

Hyacinthus orientalis
Hyacinth (Large-Flowered)

☁	☼☁	↔ 15 cm	↕ 25 cm	✿ Spring	ZONE 4

Everyone loves its sophisticated perfume. Plant under windows or near footpaths, but always in loose soil. This bulb can be forced indoors.

Tulipa hybrida
Parrot Tulip

☼	☼☁	↔ 8 to 10 cm	↕ 30 to 50 cm	✿ Summer	ZONE 4

A spectacular flower with original colours. The tall stalks, which often arch, bear large, fringed and twisted petals that are irregularly dentated. Cut bearing stalks at the base in order to maintain the bulb's vigour.

Vivacity...

in serenity

Nothing quite matches the power of a water feature with plants to induce calm and serenity. Can anything be more restful and inspiring than contemplating a pond where flora and fauna interact peacefully? What a relaxing and inspiring refuge, punctuated only by the music of falling water, the whir of a soaring dragonfly and the ever-so-subtle waves created by its gentle descent on the pond surface!

Belying this outward tranquility, your pond is teaming with dynamic life: the autonomous world of our distant ancestral cradle reuniting the vegetable animal and mineral spheres.

Creating a water garden involves reproducing a complex, natural environment of interdependent life forms wherein plants play a life-giving role and an aesthetic one. They must, therefore, be judiciously selected. They can help maintain your water's ability to support fish and discourage algae because they are, in fact, natural aeration and filtration plants.

By following expert advice in creating this fascinating world, you'll build an ecosystem you'll not only be proud of, but also that you and your family will seek out for its peaceful vibrations.

Nelumbo nucifera
Lotus

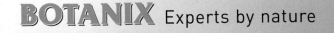

Perfect Balance

Your water feature should include plants from the four aquatic groups and respect the recommended ratios. Each group plays an essential role in your pond, and their presence contributes to a healthy equilibrium.

- **Floating plants** don't touch the bottom, they float freely on the water surface. Most are tropical and should be treated like annuals. They provide shade for your garden. **Ratio: 2 per 1.5 m².**

- **Oxygenating** plants are also called **'submerged'**, because that's exactly what they are. Some varieties float between the surface and the ground, others take root in the latter. Either way, they oxygenate and purify your water as well as providing food and shelter for both microscopic organisms and fish. **Ratio: 4 per m².**

- **Emergent vegetation**, also called **'moist area plants'**, **'littoral plants'** and **'marginal plants'**, can be rooted in either the soil or submerged containers. Most of the plant (stems, leaves, flowers) is above the surface of the water. These plants not only give your aquatic garden a magnificent, natural look, but also, they attract birds, frogs, toads and insects. **Ratio: variable depending on the desired arrangement.**

- **Water Lilies**, also known as 'floating-leaf plants' root in the earth at the pond's edge or in pots at the bottom. The leaves floating to the surface creates a shade that's much appreciated by fish, and that will embellish your garden spectacularly with their incomparable blossoms. **Ratio: 1 per 2 m².**

Know-how

Developing an aquatic garden demands the respect of certain planting, fertilizing and management rules to avoid having recourse to chemical water clarifiers. Fish, being highly sensitive to water quality, also require attention. At **botanix.com**, you can find out more about these rules.

Juncus effusus 'Spiralis'
Corkscrew Rush

Tips and Tricks

- The Golden rule: in order to attain the biological equilibrium required for a healthy water-feature, it's important to cover 1/3 of the water surface with plants and leave 2/3 open.

- To accompany emergent plants, place flat stones around the pond for a natural look. In order to camouflage unappealing clutter at the bottom of your pond, place some stones or pebbles there, too.

Acorus calamus 'Variegatus'
Variegated Sweet Scented Rush

| | | 60 to 90 cm | 60 cm to 1.2 m | ZONE 4 | | Emergent |

The rugged, scented, cream-striped green leaves are like the Iris'. A naturalistic focal point for your water feature with roots that purify the water they grow out of.

Alocasia esculanta 'Imperial'
'Imperial' Elephant Ear

global village style

| | 15 to 60 cm | 60 cm to 1.2 m | ZONE annual | Emergent |

The huge, bumpy, dark green and purple leaves of this annual add a tropical touch to your pond. Prefers being in damp soil rather than being immersed. Can be brought indoors at season's end.

Caltha palustris
Marsh Marigold

| | | 40 cm | 30 cm | Spring | ZONE 3 | | Emergent |

In spring, this plant forms an attractive mass of shiny foliage punctuated by cupolas of little golden yellow flowers. Thrives at the edge of a water feature.

Ceratophyllum demersum
Common Hornwort

| | 10 to 20 cm | 60 cm to 2 m | ZONE 3 | Oxygenating |

The extremely thin and graceful foliage of this plant adds a naturalistic aspect to your pond. It floats almost at the water's surface, supplying oxygen, encouraging fish reproduction and reducing the proliferation of algae.

Cyperus alternifolius
Umbrella Plant

global village style

| ☀ | ☁ | ↔ 30 to 60 cm | ↕ 45 cm to 1.2 m | ZONE annual | | Emergent |

This plant will add a hint of the Nile to your water basin when planted at the edge or in a pot at the bottom. Bring indoors for winter.

Cyperus isocladus (haspans)
Dwarf Papyrus

global village style

| ☀ | ↔ 40 cm | ↕ 45 cm | ZONE annual | | Emergent |

Looks very much like a small version of the giant Papyrus. Has small tufts of long, slim foliage at the top of its narrow stems. Unusual and appealing.

Cyperus papyrus
Papyrus/Paper Reed

| ☀ | ↔ 40 cm | ↕ 3 m | ZONE annual | | Emergent |

A human-sized plant with very long and fine stems that sprout star-shaped narrow, arching leaves. Needs wind protection to prevent stem breakage.

Eichhornia crassipes
Water Hyacinth

| ☀ | ☁ | ↔ 20 to 40 cm | ↕ 10 to 15 cm | ✿ Summer | ZONE annual | ⚘ | Floating |

If your water is warm enough, the magnificent flowers will stay open most of the summer. And thanks to its textured and ballooned foliage, it floats on the surface. The secret to its thriving and flowering can be summed up in three words: warm, warm, warm.

Aquatic Plants

Elodea canadensis
Canadian Waterpest

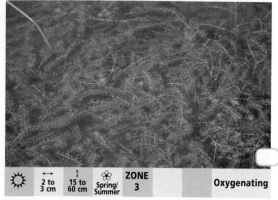

☀	↔ 2 to 3 cm	↕ 15 to 60 cm	❀ Spring/ Summer	ZONE 3	Oxygenating

This dark green, filiform native plant moves with the waves as it cleans the water. Because Koi love it, it's recommended you cover it with a net for protection. However, if you don't have a high ratio of Koi, this is not a worry, since it reproduces prolifically.

Eriophorum angustifolium
Common Cottongrass

☀	↔ 30 cm	↕ 30 to 60 cm	❀ Summer	ZONE 4	Emergent

The white spikes of fluffy, cotton-like flowers are highly unusual, and the long, narrow foliage criss-crossing the centre is an additional attraction. Plant at the edge of the water or no more than 10 cm from the surface.

Hyménocallis caribaea 'Variegata'
Variegated Spider Lily

global village *style*

☀	↔ 20 cm	↕ 60 cm	❀ Spring	ZONE annual		Emergent

Easily recognized, the Spider Lily has fascinating, white flowers that look like albino spiders. The greyish green foliage has cream margins. Plant at water's edge or in a pot under 15 cm of water.

Iris laevigata 'Variegata'
Striped Water Iris

☀	☁	↔ 20 cm	↕ 80 cm	❀ Spring/ Summer	ZONE 4	Emergent

An Asian import that you can plant in groups at the edge of your pond for a blush of narrow, bluish green foliage with white highlights. Sports violet flowers in early summer.

Iris pseudacorus
Yellow Flag

| ☀ | ⛅ | ↔ 60 cm | ↕ 90 cm to 1.5 m | ✿ Spring/Summer | ZONE 4 | | Emergent |

You will certainly notice the bright yellow flowers, especially if planted in a group. As long as they are planted in rich soil from 5 to 60 cm underwater, they'll thrive with little care.

Juncus effusus
Common Rush

global village style

| ☀ | ↔ 50 cm | ↕ 45 cm | ZONE 3 | | Emergent |

The slender, strong and erect leaves will stand out from any other foliage you may have in your pond. Many people like to plant it nearby, but it also flourishes in a pot under a dozen centimetres of water.

Juncus effusus 'Spiralis'
Corkscrew Rush

global village style

| ☀ | ↔ 50 cm | ↕ 45 cm | ZONE 3 | | Emergent |

You'll never mistake the tufts of slim, spiralling, bad-hair-day foliage for any other plant. Prosperous both in damp soil and in containers 10 cm or so beneath the water surface.

Nelumbo hybridum
Lotus

| ☀ | ↔ 1.5 to 2 m | ↕ 1 to 2 m | ✿ Spring/Autumn | ZONE 5 | ⚜ | | Emergent |

This is what water features are all about! The magnificent, single white, pink or yellow flowers are long-lasting – all summer, if it's really warm.

Nymphaea 'Attraction'
'Attraction' Waterlily

| ☀ | ↔ 1.2 to 1.8 m | ✿ Spring/ Autumn | ZONE 3 | ⚱ | | Waterlily |

If it's colour you're after, this Waterlily is for you. When young, they're bright red with irregular spots of white, and dark red at maturity. Throughout this evolution, they're highly perfumed.

Nymphaea 'Marliacea Chromatella'
'Marliacea Chromatella' Waterlily

| ☀ | ☁ | ↔ 1 to 1.5 m | ✿ Spring/ Autumn | ZONE 5 | | Waterlily |

This superb Waterlily, with its butter-yellow petals surrounding the dark yellow centre stay open to illuminate the surroundings long after the sun has set. One of the few Waterlilys to tolerate light shade. The large, lustrous foliage floats on the water surface.

Nymphaea 'Mme Wilfron Gonnère'
'Mme Wilfron Gonnère' Waterlily

| ☀ | ↔ 1 to 1.5 m | ✿ Spring/ Autumn | ZONE 5 | ⚱ | | Waterlily |

The little, floating, round leaves of this Waterlily surround attractive, double, pink flowers with yellow centres. The sweet perfume of its flowers will pervade the surrounding atmosphere.

Petasites hybridus
Butterbur

global village *style*

| ☀ | ↔ 1 m | ↕ 1 m | ✿ Spring | ZONE 5 | | Emergent |

Appreciated for its large, oval leaves that grow up to 70 cm in diameter. Bunches of pale pink flowers precede the leaves.

Pistia stratiotes
Water Lettuce

☀	☁	↔ 15 to 20 cm	↕ 6 to 10 cm	ZONE annual		Floating

The lime green rosettes of foliage will stand out in your pond. Unless your water is really cold or shaded, it's best to put your Water Lettuce in a floating bowl or hoop to limit their spread.

Sagittaria latifolia
Japanese Arrowhead

☀	☁	↔ 30 to 60 cm	↕ 80 cm to 1 m	✿ Summer/ Autumn	ZONE 3	Emergent

The little, arrow-shaped leaves topping the lean stalks, point skyward. This plant, which is highly resistant to insects and disease, will provide you with white flowers all summer.

Salvinia natans
Floating Fern

☀	↔ 3 to 5 cm	↕ 3 to 10 cm	ZONE annual		Floating

With time, this little floating Fern creates a green water-top carpet that purifies and oxygenates your pond. It's an easily-grown annual that requires calm water.

Typha minima
Dwarf Reedmace/Bullrush

☀	☁	↔ 20 to 30 cm	↕ 30 to 60 cm	✿ Summer/ Autumn	ZONE 4	Emergent

The delicate, linear foliage ends in the well-known dark brown spike. A dwarf variety that loves soggy soil, but can also be grown in a container submerged 10 cm beneath the surface.

Back...

to the earth

For several years, now, the vegetable garden has been making a comeback. The popularity of fresh food and organic food – which started several decades ago – is reaching critical mass. There is no doubt, the back to the earth movement is gaining ground... right in our backyards. So much the better.

Creating a vegetable garden means playing by mother nature's rules. And profit from her rewards! And what a reward it is to chow down on fresh vegetables grown by oneself. This year's harvest was too plentiful? No worries. Simply share the bounty with family and friends.

But the vegetable garden is not just spreading, it's also improving. People no longer feel constrained to align their vegetables in rows like soldiers going to war. With shrinking acreage, the vegetable garden is playing a new role by adding to visual aesthetics. Some vegetables and herbs are now getting their due for their ornamental value: just think of the magnificent foliage of the Swiss Chard, carrots and some of the lettuces, and the vibrant colours of peppers. Many are now planting them amongst aromatic plants and edible annual flowering plants. Surrounded by their new friends, they contribute to your health... and provide a visual display!

Lycopersicon esculentum
Tomato

From theory to practice

The only thing more gratifying than harvesting vegetables from your own garden is harvesting vegetables from your own well-planned garden, and vegetable gardens profit more from planning and care than do flower beds. It's thus important to think hard about the requirements of the vegetable garden before laying that bed.

Space

You'll find it works better to create the space to meet your needs than to try to meet your needs from an arbitrary space. For example, a family of four would require a vegetable garden of approximately 2 x 4 m. Calculate the space required for each vegetable and its neighbours. Drawing a plan is a good plan!

The Soil

All vegetables do not have the same nutritional needs (nitrogen, phosphorus, potassium). So, it is important to amend and fertilize the soil. To know the specific needs of your soil, think of a soil analysis that any BOTANIX garden center can perform.

Planting and Companionship

You can start some vegetables inside and transplant them to the garden in spring. You can also buy seedlings.

To create a healthy biodiversity for your vegetable garden, it's best to intersperse aromatic plants and flowering plants with your vegetables such that they attract insects useful to their neighbours, repel deleterious ones, or distract predators. This is not, of course, an infallible technique, but judiciously practiced, it will improve results and ease mainte-nance. Plus it's good for the environment. Annual flowers such as Alyssum draw useful insects to your garden, while the Nasturtium will sacrifice itself by attracting aphids, which prefer it to your vegetables.

Edible flowers will enhance the beauty of your vegetable plot, fit in with the culinary theme, provide variety in your diet and beautify your table.

BOTANIX Experts by nature

Tips and Tricks

- Planting your own seeds indoors can be tricky. The simple solution: buy seedlings in divided trays. Tomatoes, peppers, eggplant, cabbage, leeks, celery and squash are all available in this manner.
- Not all vegetable plants have the same frost resistance. Some, including lettuces, onions, leeks and cabbages can be planted **before the last frost** in spring because they are more cold-resistant.

  However, tomatoes, peppers, eggplant, ground-cherries, cucumber and squash should only be planted **when there is no more risk of frost**.

From theory to practice

Successive Seeding

It's possible to stagger your harvests to lengthen the season and avoid waste. For your first planting, rapid growing vegetables including radish, leaf lettuce, beans and kohlrabi are ideal as they mature quickly, giving you an early harvest, and they can easily be successively seeded. This means you're planting the seeds every two weeks, and getting smaller harvests more or less continuously throughout the season.

Plant Rotation

Not all vegetables have the same requirements, but they all require nourishment from the ground. In order to avoid nutritional depletion, as well as to maintain soil structure, do not plant the same vegetables at the same place for more than two years in a row. Your vegetable garden will look healthier and your stomach will thank you.

For a more detailed understanding of the steps to follow in creating your vegetable garden, go to **botanix.com.**

Container Culture

Not having a garden doesn't necessarily prevent you from growing your own vegetables. If you have a balcony, deck, window boxes or a place for pots, then by following certain basic rules, you can still grow your favourite vegetables. You won't have to worry about top dressing, but you'll have to water more consistently, and wait a little longer for your harvest. Here's how to go about it:

- Sufficient sunlight.
- Protection from cold and wind. Potted plants are more susceptible to temperature variations and the drying forces of wind. Also, the wind could knock your pots over.
- Appropriate pot sizes.
- Good drainage. Water must be able to escape from the bottom of the pot.
- High-quality soil.

Allium cepa
Onion

Artichoke — *Cynara scolymus*
Type: Flowering vegetable.
Soil: Rich and well-drained.
Maturity: 100 to 120 days.

Remarks: Annual. **Good companions:** tomato, zucchini.

Asparagus — *Asparagus officinalis*
Type: Root vegetable.
Soil: Sandy, rich and well-drained.
Maturity: 3 years after planting.

Remarks: Perennial. Highly decorative foliage. Can produce for over a dozen years. **Good companions:** basil, chicory, lettuce, parsley, radish, tomato.

Bean — *Phaseolus vulgaris*
Type: Legume
Soil: Light and well-drained. No manure.
Maturity: 42 to 55 days.

Good companions: eggplant, beetroot, carrot, cabbage, corn, potato, savory. **Poor companions:** garlic, fennel, leek, peas, onion.

Beet — *Beta vulgaris*
Type: Root vegetable.
Soil: Well-drained soil.
Maturity: 55 to 70 days.

Remarks: The leaves are also delicious raw or cooked. **Good companions:** garlic, carrot, cabbage, kohlrabi, onion, thyme.

Broccoli — *Brassica oleracea italica*
Type: Flowering vegetable.
Soil: Fertile, rich in calcium and well-drained.
Maturity: 70 to 95 days.

Good companions: cucumber, potato, onion. **Poor companions:** strawberry, climbing beans.

Solanum melongena esculentum
Eggplant

Brussels Sprouts — *Brassica oleracea, var. gemmifera*
Type: Flowering vegetable.
Soil: Rich but carefully dosed with nitrogen, amended with ripe compost.
Maturity: 90 to 120 days.

Good companions: thyme, sage, cucumber, lettuce, potato. **Poor companions:** strawberry, climbing beans.

Cantaloupe — *Cucumis melo, var. cantaloupsis*
Type: Fruit
Soil: Rich, deep and damp.
Maturity: 70 to 90 days.

Good companions: corn, zucchini, marjoram. **Poor companion:** chamomile.

Carrot — *Daucus carota*
Type: Root vegetable.
Soil: Light and well-drained.
Maturity: 50 to 70 days.

Remarks: Can be seeded every two weeks until the end of July. **Good companions:** garlic, beetroot, sage, rosemary, radish, coriander, onion, leek, tomato, chives.

Phaseolus vulgaris
Bean

Cauliflower — *Brassica oleracea, var. botrytis*
Type: Flowering vegetable.
Soil: Rich, fertile and amended with ripe compost.
Maturity: 50 to 80 days.
Good companions: tomato, dwarf beans, lettuce, cucumber, potato. **Poor companions:** strawberry, climbing beans.

Cherry Tomato — *Solanum lycopersicum cerasiforme*
Type: Fruit
Soil: Rich, without too much nitrogen.
Maturity: 65 to 75 days.

Remarks: Annual. Don't seed directly into your vegetable garden. **Good companions:** basil, garlic, artichoke, eggplant, cauliflower, pepper, asparagus. **Poor companions:** potato, beans, corn, cabbage, kohlrabi.

Cucumber and Pickle — *Cucumis sativus*
Type: Fruiting vegetable.
Soil: Fertile, rich in nitrogen, damp and well-drained.
Maturity: 48 to 70 frost-free days.

Good companions: corn, spinach, beans, tomato, lettuce, cabbage, anice, marjoram, chives.

Eggplant — *Solanum melongena esculentum*
Type: Fruiting vegetable.
Soil: Rich in potassium and well-drained.
Maturity: 55 to 80 days.

Remarks: **Good companions:** basil, spinach, beans, lettuce, pepper, tomato. **Poor companions:** Potato.

Garlic — *Allium sativum*
Type: Stem vegetable.
Soil: Well-drained. Little compost.
Maturity: 120 to 150 days.

Remarks: Separate cloves before planting. **Good companions:** beetroot, carrot, cucumber, spinach, tomato. **Poor companions:** Beans, Peas.

Ground-Cherry — *Physalis pruinosa*
Type: Fruit
Soil: Slightly damp. Little compost. Carefully dosed nitrogen.
Maturity: 75 days.

Remarks: Annual. Reseeds naturally. Care similar to tomato.

Head Lettuce, Iceberg Lettuce — *Lactuca sativa, var. capitata*
Type: Leafy vegetable.
Soil: Rich, deep and damp.
Maturity: 55 to 65 days.

Italian Tomato — *Solanum lycopersicum esculentum*
Type: Fruit
Soil: Rich, without too much nitrogen.
Maturity: 65 to 75 days.

Remarks: Annual. Don't seed directly into your vegetable garden. **Good companions:** basil, garlic, artichoke, eggplant, cauliflower, pepper, asparagus. **Poor companions:** potato, beans, corn, cabbage, kohlrabi.

Leaf Lettuce — *Lactuca sativa*
Type: Leafy vegetable.
Soil: Light and rich.
Maturity: 40 to 55 days.

Remarks: Successive seeding possible.

Leek — *Allium porrum*

Type: Stem vegetable.
Soil: Light, rich, well-drained and amended with ripe compost.
Maturity: 70 to 105 days.

Good companions: carrot, cabbage, kohlrabi, celery, celeriac. **Poor companions:** beans, peas.

Onion — *Allium cepa*

Type: Stem vegetable.
Soil: Well-drained. Little compost.
Maturity: 60 to 115 days.

Good companions: beetroot, lettuce, carrot, pepper, tomato, cabbage, chamomile, savory. **Poor companions:** beans, peas.

Paprika — *Capsicum annuum*

Type: Fruiting vegetable.
Soil: Rich and well-drained.
Maturity: 50 to 80 days.

Remarks: Paprika is a mild pepper. The colour of paprika and peppers changes as they mature. **Good companions:** eggplant, carrot, okra, onion, peas, tomato, basil. **Poor companions:** kohlrabi, beans.

Peas — *Pisum sativum, var. sativum*

Type: Legume
Soil: Well-drained. No compost.
Maturity: 55 to 80 days.

Good companions: eggplant, beetroot, cabbage, carrot, zucchini, fennel, corn, potato, savory. **Poor companions:** garlic, onion, leek.

Pink Tomato — *Solanum lycopersicum esculentum*

Type: Fruit
Soil: Rich, without too much nitrogen.
Maturity: 65 to 75 days.

Remarks: Annual. Don't seed directly into your vegetable garden. **Good companions:** basil, garlic, artichoke, eggplant, cauliflower, pepper, asparagus. **Poor companions:** potato, beans, corn, cabbage, kohlrabi.

Potato — *Solanum tuberosum*

Type: Root vegetable.
Soil: Light, rich, sandy and slightly acidic.
Maturity: 55 to 80 days.

Remarks: Plant the tubers, not the seeds. **Good companions:** cabbage, spinach, beans, radish, corn, thyme. **Poor companions:** beetroot, celery, zucchini, tomato, melon.

Pumpkin — *Cucurbita pepo*

Type: Fruiting vegetable.
Soil: Rich, deep and well-drained, amended with fresh compost.
Maturity: 85 to 100 days.

Remarks: Plant on slope. **Good companions:** corn, marjoram. **Poor companions:** potato.

Radish — *Raphanus sativus*

Type: Root vegetable.
Soil: Light, rich and well-drained.
Maturity: 21 to 35 days.
Remarks: Successive seeding possible. **Good companions:** asparagus, carrot, cucumber, beans, spinach, lettuce, peas. **Poor companions:** potato.

Lactuca sativa
Leaf Lettuce

Red Tomato — *Solanum lycopersicum esculentum*

Type: Fruit
Soil: Rich, without too much nitrogen.
Maturity: 65 to 75 days.

Remarks: Annual. Don't seed directly into your vegetable garden. **Good companions:** basil, garlic, artichoke, eggplant, cauliflower, pepper, asparagus. **Poor companions:** potato, beans, corn, cabbage, kohlrabi.

Romaine Lettuce — *Lactuca sativa, var. longifolia*

Type: Leafy vegetable.
Soil: Light and rich.
Maturity: 65 to 80 days.

Round Cabbage — *Brassica oleracea capitata*

Type: Leafy vegetable.
Soil: Fertile and well-drained.
Maturity: 60 to 110 days.

Remarks: Successive seeding possible. **Good companions:** thyme, sage, chamomile, savory, beetroot, celery, cucumber, spinach, lettuce, onion. **Poor companions:** tomato.

Solanum lycopersicum cerasiforme
Cherry Tomato

Slicing Cucumber — *Cucumis sativus, var. sativus*

Type: Fruiting vegetable.
Soil: Fertile, rich in nitrogen, damp and well-drained.
Maturity: 60 days.

Good companions: beans, tomato.

Spinach — *Spinacia oleracea*

Type: Leafy vegetable.
Soil: Light and well-drained.
Maturity: 45 to 60 days.

Good companions: asparagus, celery, cabbage, cucumber, beans, lettuce. **Poor companions:** potato.

Squash — *Cucurbita maxima*

Type: Fruiting vegetable.
Soil: Rich and well-drained.
Maturity: 80 to 100 days.

Good companions: corn, marjoram, savory, onion. **Poor companions:** potato, cabbage.

Swiss Chard — *Beta vulgaris cicla*

Type: Leafy vegetable.
Soil: Rich, fertile and well-drained.
Maturity: 55 to 70 days.

Remarks: Highly ornamental. **Good companions:** garlic, onion, carrot, cabbage.

Watermelon — *Citrullus lanatus*

Type: Fruit
Soil: Rich, fertile and damp.
Maturity: 70 to 110 days.

Good companions: zucchini, spinach, corn, marjoram, radish.

Zucchini — *Cucurbita, var. melo pepo*

Type: Fruiting vegetable.
Soil: Rich and well-drained.
Maturity: 42 to 52 days.

Good companions: corn, marjoram, onion.

BOTANIX Experts by nature

LA MARQUE DE CONFIANCE∗THE BRAND YOU CAN TRUST

BOTANIX

100% Natural Fertilizer
Here's health!

Let's be...

sense-able

Aromatic plants – or herbs as they are also popularly known – are synonymous with pleasure and gourmet delight. With their varied textures and shades, they are also valuable ornamentals that often give off singular, agreeable, volatile aromas – particularly when being watered or rubbed.

Aromatic plants not only please the senses, they also reward our common sense, contributing in so many ways, including warding off insects that love to lunch on your vegetables. Please see the vegetable-garden section for more details.

Cuisine Gardening
Aromatic plants can be ingested as liquids (mint and chamomile teas are but the tip of the iceberg) or solids: secretly enhancing a favourite flavour, adding a distinct timbre to an orchestrated taste sensation, or dominating a dish. The only limit, it seems, is one's own imagination.

Some herbs can be grown indoors, for the rest, try to grow them in the ground or in containers as close to the house as possible, so you'll always have them at hand for your favourite recipes or experiments. What a pleasure it is to make one's own bouquet garni and simmer it into an autumnal sauce... allowing that incomparable aroma to pervade the indoor atmosphere!

Salvia officinalis
Sage

Different tastes, different techniques

Aromatic plants can be grown with a variety of care in a variety of soils, but all have in common that they thrive on direct sun.

- Create a thematic planting comprising only herbs, for a visual and olfactory blend.

- Plant your herbs in the front or last row of annual or perennial flower beds, or in your rockery. In fact, with their multi-sensate ornamental value, you'll want to plant them anywhere the sun shines.

- Use them as a ground cover to release their distinct aromas as you walk. Thyme, in particular, lends itself well to this use. It's undemanding, and looks so natural tumbling over a low wall or sprouting between patio stones.

- Grow your aromatic plants in pots so you can enjoy their fragrance on your balcony or deck, and inside when a warm summer breeze wafts their aromas indoors.

- In your house, grow Basil, Tarragon, Bay Laurel, Rosemary, Lemon Verbena or any other herbs that can tolerate your indoor conditions.

The right soil for the right results

Although aromatic plants are not demanding, they do appreciate a light, sandy soil that's well-drained and moderately fertile. If the soil contains too much nitrogen, the foliage will be luxuriant, but the taste weaker. These ones like poor, dry soil: Borage, Oregano, Rosemary, Savory and Thyme.

Some of the aromatic plants prefer damp, fertile soil as they must grow to great heights rapidly. Basil, Chives, Lemon Balm, Lovage and Parsley are among these.

For container growing, it's best to amend the soil with a bit of sand, and use clay pots to counteract root-rot.

BOTANIX Experts by nature

Tips and Tricks

- Before you buy: verify! Is it an annual, perennial or non-hardy perennial? Non-hardy perennials such as Rosemary can't be left outside during our boreal winters. Grow them in a pot outdoors in summer, and bring indoors after a few cool nights.

- Invasive herbs like Mint and Lemon Balm are also better cultivated in pots, which can be placed on your balcony or buried up to their necks in the garden.

- Keep this in mind: With the aromatic plants it's even more important to use natural fertilizers and soil amendments, because they're going to end up inside your body.

Flavours to savour

Aromatic plants, most of which are herbs, enhance the flavours of various dishes in unique and unforgettable ways. In order to optimize their subtle variations, chef Nicole-Anne Gagnon provides us with a bit of background and best-use practices for some of the most interesting herbs.

Let's be sage and start with sage

Spicy, full-bodied, strong and slightly woody tasting, sage is best used in small quantities, without boiling or prolonged cooking – so add it near the end of the cooking period.

Sage works best with pork, chicken and veal, whether part of a slow-simmer meal or quickly prepared, e.g. chicken salads, osso buco, roast pork, stuffed fowl or game-birds. Also tasty with vegetable gratins.

COOK LIKE A PRO: Lightly oil the sage leaves before grilling it for a few seconds. Sprinkle on your thick soups, stuffed pasta, grilled vegetables or mashed root or tuber.

Lemon Balm

As with all herbs that have delicate foliage, add this towards the end of cooking, as its intense flavour, spicy highlights and lemon undertones are highly volatile. Also, like most herbs, use the leaves before flowering.

Used especially for appetizers and desserts, where it's chopped leaves add freshness to any dish and substitute well for coriander in Asian stir-fry recipes. Also adds contrast to fish marinades, salad dressings, and rice, fruit or seafood salads.

COOK LIKE A PRO: Make a syrup by heating up equal quantities of sugar and water until the sugar dissolves. Chill and add a dozen Lemon Balm leaves. Use in fruit salads or as a sweetener for iced tea.

Rosemary: the subtle aroma of conifers

A spicy taste and pronounced, resinous flavour. This is an indispensable ingredient for Provencal cooking, where, with Thyme and Oregano it's one of the three basic ingredients in herbes de Provence – which also often contains other herbs such as lavender, depending on the local variation.

The flavours in Rosemary are stable enough to maintain their integrity despite prolonged cooking, in fact it's best to use Rosemary parsimoniously as it can have an overpowering flavour.

The ideal companion to lamb, game-birds, grilled fish, eggs and poultry, and an intriguing accent in red-wine or Port-based sauces.

COOK LIKE A PRO: Grind the Rosemary leaves with sea salt and refrigerate, sprinkling on grilled meats and tomato dishes, especially pan-fried tomatoes in olive oil.

BOTANIX Experts by nature

Unbeatable Basil

Depending on the variety, it may have a hint of Lemon, Camphor, Jasmine, Anise or Thyme. It's typical of the delicate-leaved herbs as the leaves should be removed before the flowers emerge in order to get the most taste out of them, and the flavour doesn't last well if the leaves are cooked for a long time. Therefore, add it towards the end of the cooking period.

Basil leaves oxidize quickly, becoming sour, so it's best not to cut the leaves until the last moment. Basil does not freeze well for long periods, but to freeze for short periods, simply place the leaves together and wrap them in aluminum paper, avoiding defrosting before use.

Ideal for salads, egg-based dishes, cheese, pasta, soups and stews. Not terribly good with vinegar and other herbs, but particularly tasty with lemon juice and olive oil. Basil butter is great on grilled salmon, and it adds an unexpected, unusual taste to sweet dishes.

COOK LIKE A PRO: Surprise your guests with a Basil-flavoured chocolate mousse, or sprinkle a few leaves in a fresh fruit salad.

Parsley equals freshness

A well-known and much loved herb that's ironically underused. Will add a touch of colour and freshness to mostly any dish, particularly the flat-leaf variety which has a stronger taste than the curly. Add after cooking, as its delicate texture disappears when heated. Chop finely and toss it in a salad, rice, couscous, or quinoa dish just before serving.

Conserve by wrapping leaves on stems in damp paper and refrigerating.

COOK LIKE A PRO: For a delicious pesto that will last several days in the refrigerator, mix Parsley with a bit of olive oil, Chives, salt and pepper – and, optionally, pine nuts or almonds. Spread on grilled bread – or use as a topping for a thick soup instead of sour cream, for an unforgettable experience.

Anise — *Anethum graveolens*

☀ ↔ 50 cm ↕ 50 cm   Annual

Cultivation:	Rich. Well drained soil. Reseeds easily.
Conservation:	Freeze in a liquid.
Usage:	Marinades. Salads. Fish. Seafood.

Basil — *Ocimum basilicum*

☀ ↔ 60 cm ↕ 60 cm   Annual

Cultivation:	Damp soil. Don't allow to flower.
Conservation:	Freeze in a liquid.
Usage:	Salads. Pasta. Fish. Chicken. Vegetables. Pesto. Olives.

Bay Laurel — *Laurus nobilis*

☀ ↔ 50 cm à 1 m ↕ 1 à 3 m   Perennial Not hardy

Cultivation:	Also grows in pots. Bring inside in fall.
Conservation:	Dry.
Usage:	Soups. Meat. Fish. Required ingredient of bouquet garni.

Borage — *Borago officinalis*

☀ ☁ ↔ 30 cm ↕ 60 cm   Annual

Cultivation:	Light, dry soil. Prefers full sun. Ornamental blue flowers.
Conservation:	Freeze in a liquid.
Usage:	Infusions. Salads. Soups. Use flowers to decorate desserts.

Camomile — *Matricaria recutica*

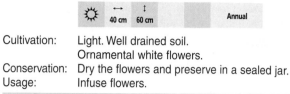

☀ ↔ 40 cm ↕ 60 cm   Annual

Cultivation:	Light. Well drained soil. Ornamental white flowers.
Conservation:	Dry the flowers and preserve in a sealed jar.
Usage:	Infuse flowers.

Helichrysum italicum
Curry plant

Chervil — *Anthriscus cerefolium*

☁	↔ 20 cm	↕ 60 cm		Annual

Cultivation: Light. Well drained and slightly acidic soil. Don't allow to flower.
Conservation: Freeze for maximum flavour.
Usage: Salads. Soups. Sauces. Poultry.

Chives — *Allium schoenoprasum*

☀	☁	↔ 30 cm	↕ 30 à 50 cm	ZONE 2

Cultivation: Multiply quickly.
Conservation: Freeze.
Usage: Salad dressings. Mayonnaises. Sauces. Salads. Don't cook.

Coriander — *Coriandrum sativum*

☀	☁	↔ 25 cm	↕ 70 cm	Annual

Cultivation: Sandy soil. Don't allow to flower.
Conservation: Freeze.
Usage: Salads. Soups. Sauces.

Curry plant— *Helichrysum italicum*

☀	↔ 50 cm	↕ 65 cm	ZONE 5	Annual

Cultivation: Rich. Well drained soil. Sheltered area.
Conservation: Dry and preserve in a sealed jar.
Usage: Soups. Vegetables. Rice dishes. Chicken. Butters and mayonnaises.

Ocimum basilicum
Basil

Fennel — *Foeniculum vulgare* 'Rubrum'

☀	↔ 45 cm	↕ 80 cm		Annual

Cultivation: Also grows in pots. Bring inside in fall.
Conservation: Preferably frozen or dry.
Usage: Salads. Soups. Fresh or smoked fish.

Lemon Balm — *Melissa officinalis*

☀	☁	↔ 45 cm	↕ 50 cm	ZONE 4

Cultivation: Cool. Clay-rich soil. Invasive.
Conservation: Dry and preserve in a sealed jar.
Usage: Marinades. Drinks. Desserts.

Aromatic Plants

Melissa officinalis
Lemon Balm

Lemon Verbena — *Aloysia triphylla*

☀	↔ 40 cm	↕ 1.5 cm	Perennial Not hardy

Cultivation: Fertile. Well drained soil. Bring indoors at seasons end.
Conservation: Dry and preserve in a sealed jar.
Usage: Infusions. Marinades. Fish. Poultry.

Marjoram — *Origanum majorana*

☀	↔ 40 cm	↕ 40 cm	Perennial Not hardy

Cultivation: Seed in early spring in well drained soil. Don't allow to flower.
Conservation: Dry and preserve in a sealed jar.
Usage: Infusions. Vegetables. Poultry. Fish. In Herbes de Provence.

Oregano — *Origanum vulgare*

☀	↔ 40 cm	↕ 30 cm	ZONE 5

Cultivation: Spreading growth habit. Divide every 2-3 years to limit growth.
Conservation: Dry or freshly picked.
Usage: Sauces. Stuffing. Salad dressings. Vegetables. In Herbes de Provence.

Parsley — *Petroselinum crispum*

☀ ☁	↔ 30 cm	↕ 30 cm	Biannual

Cultivation: Well drained and slightly acidic soil.
Conservation: Preferably frozen or dry and preserve in a sealed jar.
Usage: Salads. Soups. Meat. Poultry. Fish. Required ingredient of bouquet garni.

Peppermint — *Mentha piperita vulgaris*

☀ ☁	↔ 30 cm	↕ 45 cm	ZONE 3 to 5

Cultivation: Cool soil. Invasive. Better to grow in pots.
Conservation: Dry or freeze.
Usage: Infusions. Salads.

Rosemary — *Rosmarinus officinalis*

☀	↔ 90 cm	↕ 50 cm to 1 m	Perennial Not hardy

Cultivation: Well drained soil. Can be brought indoors at season's end.
Conservation: Dry and preserve in a sealed jar.
Usage: Lamb. Pork. Chicken. Game. In Herbes de Provence.

Sage — *Salvia officinalis*

☼	↔ 35 cm	↕ 50 to 80 cm	ZONE 4	

Cultivation:	Pinch off terminal-buds regularly to encourage branching.
Conservation:	Freeze or dry and preserve in a sealed jar.
Usage:	Vegetables. Meat. Fish. Cold cuts.

Summer Savory — *Satureja hortensis*

☼	↔ 30 cm	↕ 45 cm		Annual

Cultivation:	Well drained soil.
Conservation:	In refrigerator as soon as picked, or dry and preserve in a sealed jar.
Usage:	Soups. Stews. Game. Fish

Tarragon — *Artemisia dracunculus*

☼	↔ 30 cm	↕ 60 cm	ZONE 4	

Cultivation:	Also grows indoors.
Conservation:	More pronounced taste when dried or frozen as soon as picked.
Usage:	Soups. Poultry. Veal. Marinades. Sauces.

Thyme — *Thymus vulgaris*

☼	↔ 30 cm	↕ 20 to 30 cm	ZONE 4	

Cultivation:	Sandy, chalky soil. Slow grower.
Conservation:	Refrigerate as soon as picked, or dry and preserve in a sealed jar.
Usage:	Meat. Poultry. Fish. Stews. Required ingredient of bouquet garni.

Aromatic Plants

Thymus vulgaris
Thyme

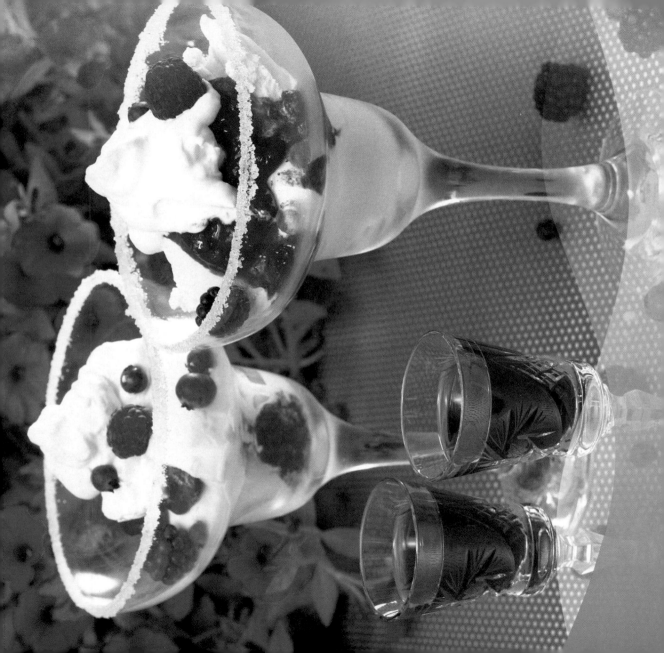

Anyone up for
seconds?

To grow small-fruit plants is to discover the pleasure of eating the product of your own land... biting into sweet, juicy, sun-ripened, tasty fruit of unsurpassed freshness. What ineffable joy to fill a bowl with nature's little treasures grown on your own land!

In our gardens, we cultivate fruit for this gourmet pleasure, yes, but they also reward our visual and olfactory senses while they are growing. Small-fruit plants are increasingly used as perennials, not grown in isolation, adding a touch of originality and a lot of colour to your garden experience.

Intending to make your own wine? The grape vines now available produce a plethora of fruit in many flavours, and some of the new cultivars were created specifically to weather our winters.

Whatever you plan to do with your berries, big or small, let your imagination rule... and your taste buds exalt!

Rewarding labour

If you've never tried growing small fruits, the first thing that will surprise you is how easy and rewarding they are. They are hardy, versatile and aesthetically pleasing, plus you can stagger their ripening periods so you're getting fresh fruit throughout the summer and into fall.

The eclectic garden

Because they're so ornamental, small fruits fit into a flower bed among your favourite perennials, smooth-over a corner of your house, or reward you when you take out your compost. Here are a few placement suggestions:

- A border of Strawberries in a blooming flower bed.
- An edible Honeysuckle or Raspberry behind a flower or bush arrangement.
- A Rhubarb in your vegetable garden.
- A few Cranberries as a groundcover at the foot of a bush.
- A Grapevine crawling up a trellis or covering a pergola.
- A Red Currant hedge.
- An intermingling of Blueberries and Cranberries for colour contrast and their love of acid soil.
- A Strawberry or Blueberry-dwarf in a pot on your balcony or deck.

Vaccinium 'Heaven'
'Heaven' Cranberry

A grape way to enjoy your garden

Few things conjure up the laid-back warmth of the Mediterranean countryside like a Grapevine. Fortunately for us, there are several cultivars adapted to our Nordic climate, and more are being developed every year to fruit abundantly despite our frigid winters. Thus, our climbing plants can perform an additional function: providing fruit for eating off the vine or drinking in a wine.

Purely from a visual point of view, Grapevines are rewarding, though, with their interesting leaf shapes, red autumnal foliage and bunches of grapes in varied colours.

The way you trim your vine depends on where you live. In colder climates, they should be cut back to the ground for winter protection. Where it's warmer, they can be left to cover trellises and pergolas all year.

Vitis 'Marechal Foch'
'Marechal Foch' Vine

Did you know?

- Most small-fruit plants are self-fertilizing, meaning you only need one plant to produce fruit, although having a second one nearby often fosters more abundant fruiting. Some species, such as *Vaccinium nigrum* 'Augusta' ('Augusta') are self-sterile. These dioecious plants require another plant in the proximity or they simply won't produce fruit.
- Some species, such as Raspberries and certain Strawberries, bear fruit in the summer and once again, in the fall.

American Hazelnut
Corylus americana

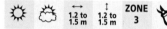

| | | ↔ 1.5 m | ↕ 3 m | ZONE 5 | |

An actual bush with upright branches and many stems bearing small fruit. The foliage turns yellow in fall.

'Illini Hardy' Blackberry
Rubus fruticosus 'Illini Hardy'

| | | ↔ 1.2 to 1.5 m | ↕ 1.2 to 1.5 m | ZONE 3 | |

In summer, this thorny plant produces sweet, succulent, red berries that resemble Raspberries. Attach to a support in order to make it easier to pick the fruit. Requires a rich, well-drained soil. Self-fertile.

'Patriot' Blueberry
Vaccinium corymbosum 'Patriot'

| | ↔ 1.25 m | ↕ 1.5 m | ZONE 3b | |

An early fruiting cultivar that will provide you with firm, sweet blue berries in early and late summer. Plant in highly acid soil and don't let its roots stay wet for too long. It's arching stems with their lustrous foliage is very attractive. Can be planted alone, as it's Self-fertile. Trailing.

'Augusta' Lowbush Blueberry
Vaccinium nigrum 'Augusta'

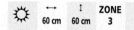

| | ↔ 60 cm | ↕ 60 cm | ZONE 3 | |

Has many large berries in summer. Requires a light, acidic, rich and well-drained soil. Plant close to other varieties to ensure pollinating. Self-fertile.

Cranberry
Vaccinium macrocarpon

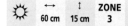

| | ↔ 60 cm | ↕ 15 cm | ZONE 3 | |

From the end of summer to early fall, you can pick the sour, red fruit that's renowned for being so vitamin-rich. The contrast between the fruit and the foliage – which turns red in fall – is a real delight. Requires acid soil. Self-fertile.

Ribes rubrum 'Red Lake'
'Red Lake' Red Currant

'Red Lake' Red Currant
Ribes rubrum 'Red Lake'

| | | ↔ 90 cm to 1.1 m | ↕ 90 cm to 1.2 m | ZONE 2 | |

A highly rustic, spreading bush that produces many red berries, which ripen between early summer and late summer. An interesting addition to your cooking repertoire. Self-fertile.

'Resista' Red Currant
Ribes rubrum 'Resista'

This upright Red Currant has many dark, scented fruit that ripen late. A good-sized bush that's disease-resistant. Self-fertile.

'White Pearl' Red Currant
Ribes rubrum 'White Pearl'

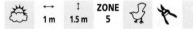

An extremely hardy cultivar that will bear a cornucopia of large, tasty, greenish-white fruit in bunches. Would make a nice hedge, but also, being self-fertile, can be planted alone. Self-fertile.

'Captivator' Gooseberry
Ribes grossularia 'Captivator'

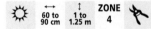

Gooseberries grow to be attractive bushes that produce succulent, transparent red, juicy, acidic fruit. Great for jams, sauces and sprinkling in among your sweeter fruit in a bowl. Likes rich, well drained soil and good air circulation. Self-fertile.

Grapevine (European or North American)
Vitis vinifera, labrusca

Depending on the variety, it produces grapes for winemaking or eating. The red colours of the leaves in fall add to its ornamental value. In cold areas, it should be cut back to the ground to ensure winter protection. See chart for available cultivars.

'Issaï' Kiwi
Actinidia arguta 'Issaï'

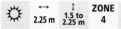

A twining plant that's perfect to cover the chain-link fence around your pool with its decorative foliage, and the greenish yellow, smooth, fuzzy fruit that arrives at the end of summer. This is a self-fertile variety that likes well-drained soil.

'Pathfinder' Raspberry
Rubus 'Pathfinder'

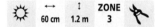

A prolific Raspberry with short stems bearing delicious, fragrant, red berries all summer. In early spring, cut back to the ground all stems that bore fruit.

'Early Sweet' Black Raspberry
Rubus ideaus 'Early Sweet'

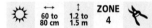

In summer, harvest the delicious, black fruit for desserts, jams, sauces and salad dressing. Afterwards, cut back the stems that bore fruit. Raspberries have stolons and require light, rich, well-drained particulate soil.

'Festival' Trailing Raspberry
Rubus 'Festival'

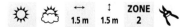

This highly prolific Raspberry gives you two harvests comprising a multitude of succulent, pale red berries. It's a hardy escape artist with unremitting runners. Cut back to the ground for a better harvest the next year. Excellent right off the plant or in jams. Trailing.

Small-fruit Plants

Rubus fruticosus
Blackberry

Rhubarb
Rheum cultorum

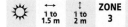

☀ | ↔ 1 to 1.5 m | ↕ 1 to 2 m | ZONE 3

Other than the un-reproducible taste, Rhubarb is popular because it grows quickly and easily. If you want to harvest the stems all summer, don't let it flower. Great for the back of your flowerbed or to add an exotic touch to your pond-area with its oversized leaves. Likes fertile, constantly damp soil.

'Rosalyne' Strawberry
Fragaria 'Rosalyne'

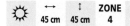

☀ | ↔ 45 cm | ↕ 45 cm | ZONE 4

The only Canadian Strawberry with large pink flowers. From spring until the final frost, you'll get juicy, sweet fruit that taste like field berries. Replace your plants every three to five years. Also enjoy their foliage, flowers and fruit in a pot or flower box.

'Berry Blue' Sweetberry Honeysuckle
Lonicera caerulea, var. edulis 'Berry Blue'

☀ | ↔ 1 m | ↕ 1.5 m | ZONE 7

An astonishing, oval, 2-cm long, blue fruit that's sweet with a touch of sour. One of the first to ripen every year. This vigorous and productive bush is self-sterile so you'll need two varieties to get fruit.

'Blue Belle' Sweetberry Honeysuckle
Lonicera caerulea, var. edulis 'Blue Belle'

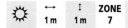

☀ | ↔ 1 m | ↕ 1 m | ZONE 7

Were it not for the darker, slightly smaller fruit, you'd be forgiven for mistaking this for 'Berry Blue'. Don't: the berries are tastier. It is self-sterile, though, so you'll need another variety nearby to obtain fruit.

'Heritage' Trailing Raspberry
Rubus ideaus 'Heritage'

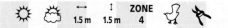

☀ | ☁ | ↔ 1.5 m | ↕ 1.5 m | ZONE 4

Expect the delicious, bright red, firm and slightly sour fruit twice a year. A hardy plant with aggressive runners. Cut back to the ground in winter for a better harvest the following year. Excellent right off the plant or in jams. Trailing.

Name	Zone	Fruit	Maturity	Uses	Remarks
North American Cultivars					
Vitis labrusca 'Canadice'	4	Red, seedless	Autumn	Wine/table	Vigorous grower.
Vitis labrusca 'Concord'	4	Blue, sour, seeds	Autumn	Juice, jellies and desserts	Extremely vigorous grower.
Vitis labrusca 'Himrod'	5	White, seedless	Autumn	Wine	
Vitis labrusca 'Ste-Croix'	4	Blue, very sweet	End of summer	Wine/table	Very productive and very hardy.
Vitis labrusca 'Suffolk Red'	5	Red, seedless	End of summer	Table	
European Cultivars					
Vitis vinifera 'Catawba'	4	Red	Autumn	Wine/table	Middling productivity and hardiness.
Vitis vinifera 'Eona'	4	White	Autumn	Wine/table	Very productive and hearty, even in northern climates.
Vitis vinifera 'Kay Gray'	4	White, high-quality	Autumn	Table	
Vitis vinifera 'Sabrevois'	4	Red	End of summer	Wine	Vigorous and very hardy. Disease-resistant.
Vitis vinifera 'Seyval'	5	White	Autumn	Wine/table	Very productive.
Vitis vinifera 'Valiant'	4	Blue	Summer	Table	Very hardy.
Vitis vinifera 'Vandal-Cliche'	4	White	End of summer	Wine/table	Good choice for northern climates.
Vitis labrusca 'Vanessa'	5	Red, seedless	End of summer	Table	Crunchy flesh and tender skin. A vigorous grower.
French Hybrid Cultivars					
Vitis vinifera 'Marechal Foch'	4	Blue	Autumn	Wine/table	Hardy. A vigorous grower. Needs a net for bird-protection.
Vitis 'Somerset'	4	Reddish orange, sweet, tasty	End of summer	Table/Juice	Very hardy and very disease-resistant.

BOTANIX helps you

garden greener

A successful garden depends, above all, on our understanding of the environment, our grasp of the fact that we have to adapt to nature, not the other way around. In order to help you become a greener gardener, BOTANIX proposes a range of services and products to help you change your landscape as you desire without destroying the environment. The following pages address these topics:

- **Soil analysis**: determining the soil composition and recommending the appropriate amendments.

- **Lawns** that are green in every sense of the word are becoming increasingly popular. Judicious advice on seading and maintaining will allow you to have a beautiful natural carpet that requires less synthetic products.

- The **Plant Protection Centre** resolves your phytosanitary problems within the parameters of government regulations on pesticides, and it's a BOTANIX exclusive.

- The **high-quality** products in all BOTANIX garden centres are made from high-performance organic and mineral elements.

BOTANIX

Experts by nature

After 30 years as a respected business, BOTANIX's reputation is solid. We are considered to be a leader in ornamental horticulture, with unquestionable expertise and superior client services. We're BOTANIX, experts by nature.

The BOTANIX network means:

- A team of specialists to advise you on every step of your landscaping projects;
- A soil and analysis service;
- Landscaping services available in many centres;
- Delivery service available in most centres;
- A Plant Protection Centre – exclusive to BOTANIX – with FREE consultation;
- An incomparable choice of plants from all categories;
- Superior quality, plants warranties;
- BOTANIX exclusives;
- A vast choice of new horticultural arrivals;
- High-end, proven BOTANIX products;
- Hard-to-find garden decorations and accessories.

Working...

from the ground up

All BOTANIX garden centres can do soil analysis. After your soil is analyzed in the lab, a specialized staff member will help you interpret the results and recommend solutions.

Why analyze the soil?

Soil composition varies enormously from one area to another, and influences the soil-temperature in different seasons as well as its capacity to retain water and minerals. Soil type also impacts plant growth and your plants' resistance to insect-attacks and diseases. Therefore, analyzing the soil gives you an exact picture of its chemical composition so you can appropriately amend it, if required, and know which plants best grow in it.

How?

1) Remove the grass or scratch the soil surface. Take out stones, weeds and other debris, then take about a cup (250 ml) of soil from a depth of 10 to 15 cm.

2) Use a brown paper bag or one of our special bags available at your BOTANIX garden centre. For each sampling area, fill a bag from under the grass (if you have any) and one from the garden. For the grass, several soil samples are required, and could be placed in the same bag.

3) Bring the bag(s) to your BOTANIX garden centre. As soon as the lab results get back, you'll receive your analysis report. Don't forget to note the size of the affected area in order to calculate how much new soil, amendments or fertilizer you'll need.

The laboratory analysis

When your soil sample gets to the lab, the experts will analyze it in several steps: granulometry, pH, pH buffers, and nutritional element composition.

Granulometry is a visual evaluation of the soil type. Is it a sandy, silty, organically rich or clay-loam?

The **pH** is the reading of acid and alkaline ratios in the soil. Most plants thrive in soil that's neutral or slightly acidic.

The **pH buffers**, tested on acid soils, involve adding a chemical product to evaluate the exact quantities of lime required to correct soil acidity.

The **nutritional element composition** measures the nitrogen (N), phosphorus (P) and potassium (K) content of your soil.

Nitrogen, phosphorus and potassium

- **N (1st number) = nitrogen.** Required for good development of foliage and other above-ground plant members. Stimulates growth.

- **P (2nd number) = phosphorus.** Required for a healthy root system, but also plays an important role in flowering and fruiting.

- **K (3rd number) = potassium.** Increases disease-resistance, improves the flavour of fruit and intensifies colours.

Results of the analysis present the three nutritional elements in your soil in the same order as they're presented on fertilizer packaging, so you know right away which fertilizer to use in your garden. For example, if the analysis shows a lack of nitrogen, the first number in the appropriate fertilizer will be higher than the others; if the potassium is low you'll be looking for a fertilizer where the last number is highest.

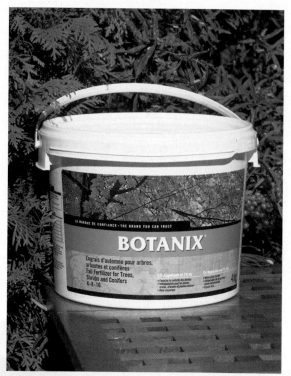

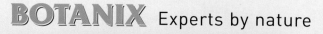

BOTANIX Experts by nature

Amendment and fertilization

Sometimes, you'll need to amend a poor soil that's deficient in minerals and organic matter. Good soil fosters your plants' performance and growth by providing their essential minerals. By looking at the results of your soil analysis, your BOTANIX counsellor will be able to recommend the right product to improve your loam. You'll then be able to grow plants that are appropriate for the soil and vice versa. The following indexes, which are at the end of the guide, will help you choose your plants:

- List of plants for acidic soil
- List of plants for dry soil
- List of plants for damp soil
- List of plants that are ecologically valuable
- List of groundcovers to replace grass
- List of plants to revitalize shorelines

Endophytes and mycorhizae

These bacteria and mushrooms live in symbiosis with plants. They live in the soil, helping the plant capture water and minerals. Two of these microorganisms have been reproduced and marketed. They are part of the endophytes family and act as biostimulants for plants.

Mycorhizac are microscopic mushrooms that team up with the roots of the plants and form a network of filaments that help bring nutriments to the plants. However, the amount of mycorhizac has dramatically decrease due to human activities, so the plants cannot longer profit from them.

Mychorizae can be spread like granular fertilizer. The granules that contain mychorizae just need to be in contact with roots. For plants that are benefiting from this symbiotic relationship however, excess fertilization must be strictly avoided. A fertilizer containing more than 10% of a mineral element may actually kill endophytes and mychorizae, so to be safe, it's better to use 100% natural fertilizer.

Soil Analysis

A respectful solution
for the environment

- better drougth tolerance
- increases plant survival
- faster plant establisment
- better phosphorus uptake

AVEC **MYCORRHIZE** INSIDE

When you buy trees, shrubs and perennials*

Ask for your
MYKE® warranty

3-month or 1-year warranty.
See details in store.

100 % growth
Warranty conditions:

- **Retail sales only**

- **Return your dead plant during the warranty period**

- **Return plant identification label and invoice**

If these conditions are met, we will refund the plant at its purchase price. We do not offer refund for plants damaged by rodents or extreme climatic conditions. Annuals and perennials are not included in this warranty.

BOTANIX
Experts by nature

For a healthy,

"green" lawn

More and more people want their lawn be natural, and are turning towards ecological maintenance methods. If you, too, are looking for a dense, green and healthy lawn – that's environmentally sound –here's some maintenance advice to help you develop and maintain the light, fertile soil that a healthy lawn requires. These are simple solutions developed to avoid dangerous treatments that are deleterious to the environment and our health.

A small step for man, a giant step for the environment!

Your lawn is composed of small grasses that require a lot of sun. There's really not much point in trying to grow them in shaded areas. For your shaded areas, there are simple, practical, ecological solutions that replace boring old grass with interesting groundcovers, as the BOTANIX turnkey gardens so beautifully illustrate. Unlike lawns, they're low-maintenance with a big reward. Some even have scented flowers, or leaves that produce a fragrance when walked upon. At the end of this guide, you'll see a list of our top 10 ground covers. In heavy traffic areas, you can replace your lawn with interesting natural materials such as mulch, small decorative stones, duckboard or flat stones.

If you decide to keep your lawn in some areas though, regular maintenance will reduce weed problems so you don't have to resort to pesticides. Such chores include aeration, dethatching, top dressing, fertilizing, mowing and watering.

Seeding

Seeding is an inexpensive solution that requires more time and patience than laying sod. Using grass seed allows you to choose the seed mix that best meets your needs and available light. The best times to seed are in spring and late summer when cool temperatures facilitate germination. Follow these five steps:

1) Prepare the soil by turning it over, topping it up nutritionally and eliminating weeds. Add a rooting fertilizer with a broadcast spreader.

2) Level the ground by raking the surface until it's uniform and then compressing it with a roller that's a third full of water.

3) Seed by hand or with a spreader, crossing the ground in two perpendicular directions for a cross-hatching effect that will give you the most uniform spread.

4) Keep the seed on the ground by raking the surface over with a leaf rake. The idea is not to bury the seed: it should stay on the surface. In order to maximize the seeds' contact with the dampness of the soil, roll over the surface again with the roller that's one third full of water.

5) For the following two weeks, water lightly – being careful not to push the seeds around. You should begin to see the sprouts coming up. Throughout this period, don't let the ground dry out at all.

Reseeding

Reseed every two or three years for denser grass coverage and to fill bald patches that could be invaded by weeds. This is a natural method of combating weeds, and one that can be done at any time during the season.

BOTANIX 100% Natural 4-step fertilization program.

BOTANIX Experts by nature

Aeration

Annual aeration at the beginning and end of the season involves piercing the grass mats and soil surface to increase porosity, so air and water can more easily reach the roots. It also makes it more difficult for weeds to grow. Leave the little carrots that the aerator pulls out on the surface; in a few days they'll disappear.

Dethatching

The purpose of this operation is to eliminate the blanket of thatch on your lawn, using a dethatching rake or a power dethatcher, so more water gets to the roots.

Top dressing

Every year, simply scatter a fine layer of organic material such as BOTANIX top soil to nourish the soil and improve its structure. After analyzing the loam, you may also wish to add granulated lime to rebalance the pH. To increase penetration of this organic material in the soil, dethatch before top dressing.

Fertilizing

Fertilizing is all about giving your lawn the necessary nutrients. You'll want large quantities of three nutrients: nitrogen (growth and greening factor), phosphorus (disease resistance and improved rooting), and potassium (cold and disease resistance). The percentage of each of these elements is represented by a three-number code on the packaging. 10-4-8, for instance, means there's 10% nitrogen, 4% phosphorus and 8% potassium. Ask about the four-step BOTANIX program that uses a range of synthetic fertilizers or 100% natural products in store or at **botanix.com**.

Mowing

Lawn mowing can actually compromise the health of your lawn. Never cut more than a third of the height of your grass at a time, and leave the leaf cuttings on the soil to trickle nitrogen into it. During heat waves, your lawn is dormant, so don't mow it at all.

Clean cuts heal more easily, using less of the grasses' energy. Roll-type mowers, which are usually push-mowers, are the most effective... plus they're quiet! Just make sure the blades are sharp.

Watering

Watering intelligently means maximizing the water that reaches the roots when and where it's needed, and minimizing the amount of water used. It's better to water deeply and less often; ideally 1 inch (2.5 cm) early in the morning. To measure the depth, place a leak-proof container on the lawn surface. Did you know that if you water at midday, 50% of the water evaporates before it can do your grass any good?

Information to count on!

At **BOTANIX** ,

you will find usefull specification
sheets to help you choose plants
that are suited for your needs.

Echinacea 'Sundown'
'Sundown' Coneflower

BOTANIX

Perennials

Its fall-flowering inflorescences boast
sunset colours that contrast sharply with
the foliage of vines and the blue of globe
thistle. A dynamic plant that makes
excellent cut flowers.

Zone	Exposure	Flowering	Color	Flower Diam.	Pruning	
4-9	☀	MidSummer , Late Summer	Orange	N/A	N/A	24"

© DSD International Inc. - www.soft3D.com Printed in Canada

Distributed by Botanix

Echinacea 'Sundown'
Échinacée 'Sundown'

BOTANIX

Vivaces

La saison de jardinage se termine en
beauté avec cette échinacée. Les
inflorescences portent les couleurs d'un
coucher de soleil. Une plante vigoureuse
qui crée des contrastes étonnants avec
le feuillage des graminées et le bleu des
chardons bleus. Elles font d'excellentes
fleurs coupées.

Utilisations: Massif, plate-bande, fleurs
coupées

					Hauteur	Étalement	Forme	Intérêts
				N/A	24"-30'	20'-24'		

Zone	Exposition	Floraison	Coloris	Diam. fleur	Taille	
4-9	☀	Mi-été, fin été	Orange	N / A	N / A	

© DSD International Inc. - www.soft3D.com Printed in Canada

Distribut par Botanix

BOTANIX
Experts by nature

PLANT PROTECTION CENTER
A way to restore the *health* of your *plants*

BOTANIX

Involved with the

prevention of risks

related to the use

of pesticides, **BOTANIX**

offers an exclusive

and free service:

the Plant Protection Centre.

BOTANIX
Experts by nature

Complete presentation of the concept on page 330.

The Plant Protection Centre:

Protection and control

You're having a problem with one of your trees? You want advice about maintaining your grass? Simply contact one of the Plant Protection Centre (PPC) experts at your BOTANIX garden centre. This exclusive BOTANIX service is completely free. Our experts will answer any questions you may have about your plants, soil, and diagnosing or treating disease or insect problems, always keeping in mind your personal situation.

Le PPC was set up in April 3, 2003, when the pesticide management regulations came into effect in Quebec. These rules govern the sale, reduction and the use of pesticides, as well as health and environmental risk prevention. The centre is ideally situated to offer you the best natural solutions for phytosanitary issues.

The PPC databank contains over 300 information sheets illustrated with colour photos to facilitate identification. These files are updated regularly to reflect new regulations and products. They contain information required for the diagnosis and help the advisor offer solutions to mitigate, master and prevent the problem while reducing the use of pesticide.

Here's an example of an information sheet a PPC counsellor might give out:

The PPC at work

1) Bring as many clues as you can: a piece of a branch with leaves still on it or dead leaves from the ground, and a few live insect specimens from the plant in a plastic bag would be helpful – as would a photo of the plant in question.

2) At the PPC, your counsellor will give you the information sheet indicating the probable causes of the problem and the concomitant solutions.

3) With the help of your samples and a few well-directed questions, the counsellor will be able to diagnose the problem and recommend solutions: either preventive measures or the use of products that don't endanger health or the environment. If no innocuous solutions are known, you'll be pointed towards the required chemicals and shown how to use them safely.

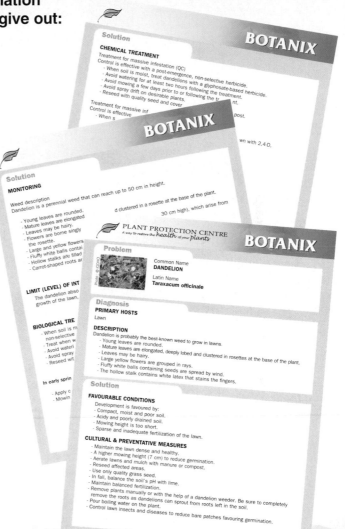

BOTANIX

Solution

CHEMICAL TREATMENT
Treatment for massive infestation (QC)
Control is effective with a post-emergence, non-selective herbicide.
· When soil is moist, treat dandelions with a glyphosate-based herbicide.
· Avoid watering for at least two hours following the treatment.
· Avoid mowing a few days prior to or following the treatment.
· Avoid spray drift on desirable plants.
· Reseed with quality seed and cover

Treatment for massive inf
Control is effective
· When s

BOTANIX

Solution

MONITORING

Weed description
Dandelion is a perennial weed that can reach up to 50 cm in height.

· Young leaves are rounded.
· Mature leaves are elongated
· Leaves may be hairy.
· Flowers are borne singly
the rosette.
· Large and yellow flowers
· Fluffy white balls contai
· Hollow stalks are filled
· Carrot-shaped roots ar

LIMIT (LEVEL) OF INT
The dandelion abso
growth of the lawn,

BIOLOGICAL TRE
· When soil is m
non-selective
· Treat when w
· Avoid wateri
· Avoid spray
· Reseed wit

In early sprin

· Apply c
· Mowin

d clustered in a rosette at the base of the plant.

30 cm high), which arise from

PLANT PROTECTION CENTRE
A way to restore the health of your plants

BOTANIX

Problem

Common Name
DANDELION

Latin Name
Taraxacum officinale

Diagnosis

PRIMARY HOSTS
Lawn

DESCRIPTION
Dandelion is probably the best-known weed to grow in lawns.
· Young leaves are rounded.
· Mature leaves are elongated, deeply lobed and clustered in rosettes at the base of the plant.
· Leaves may be hairy.
· Large yellow flowers are grouped in rays.
· Fluffy white balls containing seeds are spread by wind.
· The hollow stalk contains white latex that stains the fingers.

Solution

FAVOURABLE CONDITIONS
Development is favoured by:
· Compact, moist and poor soil.
· Acidy and poorly drained soil.
· Mowing height is too short.
· Sparse and inadequate fertilization of the lawn.

CULTURAL & PREVENTATIVE MEASURES
· Maintain the lawn dense and healthy.
· A higher mowing height (7 cm) to reduce germination.
· Aerate lawns and mulch with manure or compost.
· Reseed affected areas.
· Use only quality grass seed.
· In fall, balance the soil's pH with lime.
· Maintain balanced fertilization.
· Remove plants manually or with the help of a dandelion weeder. Be sure to completely remove the roots as dandelions can sprout from roots left in the soil.
· Pour boiling water on the plant.
· Control lawn insects and diseases to reduce bare patches favouring germination.

High-end

products

The success of a garden depends, to a large extent, on soil quality. Good soil, composed of the right mix of nutritional elements, both organic and mineral, ensures the balanced growth and health of your plants. Specially formulated fertilizers supply any additional nutrients required.

Your BOTANIX centre provides a vast range of high-quality, proven products that are easy to use, meet specific needs and adapt to various soil and plant types. They improve poor soils, lighten heavy ones, amend soils with missing elements or stimulate the growth and flowering of plants.

There are six categories of products at BOTANIX, each containing a list and description of the respective mixes for the gardening steps (preparing the soil, planting and maintenance).

Soil-amending products

- BOTANIX SHRIMP COMPOST: A microorganism-rich, seafood-enhanced compost that supply all the elements required for growth, and regenerates the soil with its organic components.

- BOTANIX SHEEP MANURE: This organically-rich material regenerates impoverished soil.

- BOTANIX PEAT MOSS: This organic material increases water and nutritional elements retention, while maximizing root development.

Soils

- BOTANIX BLACK EARTH: A nutritionally-rich soil that nourishes poor and sandy loam, increasing water and mineral retention. Used with shrimp compost, it enriches the soil of flower beds and vegetable gardens.

- BOTANIX TOPSOIL: This weed-less mix lightens heavy and clay soils while increasing the amount of organic material they hold. It's pH balance facilitates plant-absorption of minerals.

- BOTANIX 3-IN-1 PLANTING MIX: Made from compost, black earth and peat moss, this mix is good for all types of planting: vegetable gardens, flower beds, trees, shrubs, conifers, roses and climbing plants.

- BOTANIX BALCONY MIX: A light, pH-balanced soil for increased water and mineral retention. Also a good choice for potted perennials and vegetables.

- BOTANIX PERENNIAL MIX: A rich mix that promotes the healthy growth of perennials, with a lot of organic matter to continuously provide nutrients. Also good for roses.

- BOTANIX INDOOR POTTING MIX: A light potting soil consisting mainly of organic material and fertilizers, to provide a well aerated soil that will give your plants an immediate boost. Suitable for green plants, flowering plants and seedlings.

Garden fertilizers

- BOTANIX 15-5-15 CONIFERS AND CEDAR HEDGES FERTILIZER: Increases annual conifer growth, vigour and disease resistance. A rich formula that's an excellent fertilizer, providing your conifers with exactly what they need.

- BOTANIX 15-6-12 TREE AND SHRUB FERTILIZER: Stimulates the growth of trees and shrubs, while increasing their vigour and disease resistance. Composed mainly of slow-release nitrogen to ensure continuous, prolonged fertilization.

- BOTANIX 4-8-16 TREE AND SHRUB FALL FERTILIZER: The iron and magnesium in this fertilizer prepare your plants for winter cold and harsh conditions. Also suitable for perennials and roses.

- BOTANIX SOIL ACIDIFIER: Used to correct soil that's too alkaline, in order to grow acid-loving plants like Hydrangeas, Poppies and Rhododendrons.

Flower fertilizers

- BOTANIX 5-10-5 ROSEBUSH FERTILIZER: A mix of organic materials supplying all the elements required for the growth and flowering of your roses. Also increases their resistance to insect-attack and disease.

- CLIMBING PLANT FERTILIZER 16-12-8: The formula that best meets their nutritional needs for growth and abundant flowering.

- BOTANIX 8-12-10 ANNUAL AND PERENNIAL FERTILIZER: A balanced fertilizer for abundant, colourful blooms.

Organic fertilizers

- BOTANIX 100% NATURAL 4-3-8 ANNUALS, PERENNIALS AND ROSE FERTILIZER. This fertilizer is ideal for annual and perennial flowers as well as roses. It enriches the soil for nearly 6 weeks with minerals and calcium that help perennials and roses resist fungal diseases. Fertilize annuals more often, especially if they're container-grown.

- BOTANIX 100 % NATURAL 4-5-7 TOMATOES AND VEGETABLES FERTILIZER: This mix improves growth, flowering and fruit-setting. Contains not only nitrogen, phosphorus and potassium, but also 6% calcium for stronger growth and disease resistance.

- BOTANIX GRANULAR LIME: Lime corrects pH in acidic soils, increasing the calcium and magnesium in the soil, and improving the structure of heavy loams. The amount to apply varies with soil-type.

- BOTANIX 2-14-0 BONE MEAL: bone meal is primarily used to help plants deal with the trauma of transplanting. The high organic phosphorus content promotes root development. Especially suitable for tomatoes, peppers and eggplant.

Decorative groundcovers

Just like the materials that naturally gather on the forest floor, mulch discourages weeds, protects surface roots and maintains soil dampness so less watering is required. During heat waves, it keeps the soil cool, and stops your flower bed soil from being carried away by strong rains. A good coat of mulch also prevents mud from being splashed up on your windows and walls. In flower beds, a layer at least 10 cm thick covering all the soil is recommended. In order to maintain this quantity, add a bit of mulch every year. Where you have perennial groundcovers, though, it's best not to add mulch, so the plant can spread and grow.

- MULCH: Your BOTANIX expert can propose a range of products: natural Cedar mulch, Red Cedar mulch and Hemlock mulch. They have the advantage that they decompose slowly, so they are long-lasting.

- WHITE PEBBLES: These little stones are not only attractive, but also improve drainage. In order to avoid them getting mixed up with the soil, you might want to place the stones on a geotextile sheet.

Vivid color.
Green thumb
not required.

The so called "experts" say shrubs are the backbone of the garden. I disagree.

I plant shrubs in mixed containers, side by side with my perennials, right out front.

I'm no expert, but with ColorChoice® flowering shrubs, I don't have to be. My neighbors agree — the yard looks fantastic.

ColorChoice shrubs from Proven Winners. They give you all the color of perennials—without all the work.

Color is easy with ColorChoice.

ColorChoice featured plant is My Monet™ Weigela.

PW
PROVEN
WINNERS®

COLOR CHOICE®
FLOWERING SHRUBS

Horticultural calendar

Here's a little memory-jog for seasonal tasks in the garden. Here, we've used zones 4 and 5 as our example. You'll want to adjust the dates according to your hardiness zone. These tasks don't include regular garden maintenance, such as soil digging and hoeing, deep watering, weeding, and keeping a constant eye out for diseases and harmful insects.

	Spring			Summer			Autumn		
	March	April	May	June	July	Aug.	Sept.	Oct.	Nov.
Plan your plant beds									
Transplant, prune; cuttings of indoor plants	•	•	•	•	•				
Plan your landscaping	•	•							
Enrol in the local 'Flowering homes' contest				•					
Deciduous trees, shrubs and conifers									
Shrub maintenance pruning (before the buds open)	•								
Prune fruit trees and fruiting vines (before the buds open)	•								
Spray with dormant oil, as needed	•								
Remove winter protection		•							
Trim Rose bushes and climbing Roses		•							
Cut back Clematis to the ground, as needed		•							
Trim midseason flowering shrubs, as needed		•	•						
Plant and transplant		•	•	•	•	•	•		
Reposition climbers that spent the winter on the ground			•						
Apply preventive treatment against oidium, as needed			•						
Fertilize			•	•	•				
Prune spring flowering shrubs (after flowering)				•					
Prune Cedars and upright Junipers				•					
Shorten the candles of your Mountain Pines (before the needles open)				•					
Prune leafy hedges (without interesting flowers)					•				
Stop fertilizing your trees						•			
Severely cut back the less hardy Roses						•			
Install winter protection								•	•
Annuals and perennials									
Start annual seedlings indoors	•	•							
Replace flower bed borders		•							
Cut back perennial and ornamental grass foliage		•							
Start your summer bulbs indoors		•							

BOTANIX Experts by nature

	Spring			Summer			Autumn		
	March	April	May	June	July	Aug.	Sept.	Oct.	Nov.
Plant and transplant perennials		•	•	•	•	•			
Replace or rejuvenate flower-box and planter soil			•						
Fertilize perennials			•	•	•				
Fertilize annuals			•	•	•	•	•		
Divide perennials that flower at summer's end			•						
Plant annuals			•	•					
Acclimatise your indoor-seedlings outdoors			•	•					
Deadhead spring bulbs		•	•	•					
Bring your interior plants out gradually				•					
Divide spring flowering perennials after flowering				•					
Pinch stems of autumn Asters and Chrysanthemums				•					
Perennial seedlings					•				
Bring in indoor plants						•	•		
Plant spring flowering bulbs								•	
Maintenance									
Analyze the soil		•	•						
Amend and break-up flower bed soil		•	•						
Install or replenish mulch			•					•	
Collect dead leaves for mulching or composting								•	
Lawn									
Abundantly water areas exposed to road salt		•	•						
Aerate and top dress the lawn		•	•						
Fertilization: first step		•	•						
Reseed damaged areas			•						
Fertilization: second step			•	•					
Seed the new grass			•			•			
Fertilization: third step				•	•				
Fertilization: fourth step						•			
Vegetables									
Seed and transplant cold-tolerant vegetables		•	•						
Seed and transplant cold-sensitive vegetables			•	•					
Successively plant seedlings			•	•	•				
Harvest herbs and vegetables				•	•	•	•		
Protect the last vegetables against frost							•	•	
Plant garlic								•	

Hardiness

zones

Agriculture Canada has published a map of Canada depicting the hardiness zones right across the country. There are ten zones, each given a number from 0 to 9, with 0 being the coldest and 9, the warmest. Each zone has been divided into subzones, with sub-zone 'a' slightly colder than subzone 'b'.

To consult the complete list of canadian cities and their respective hardiness zone, visit **botanix.com**.

This map has been reproduced with the permission of Public Works and Government Services Canada, courtesy Natural Resources Canada (2007).

© Her Majesty the Queen in Right of Canada, 2007.

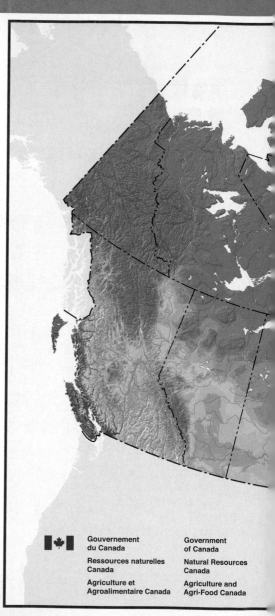

Gouvernement
du Canada

Ressources naturelles
Canada

Agriculture et
Agroalimentaire Canada

Government
of Canada

Natural Resources
Canada

Agriculture and
Agri-Food Canada

BOTANIX Experts by nature

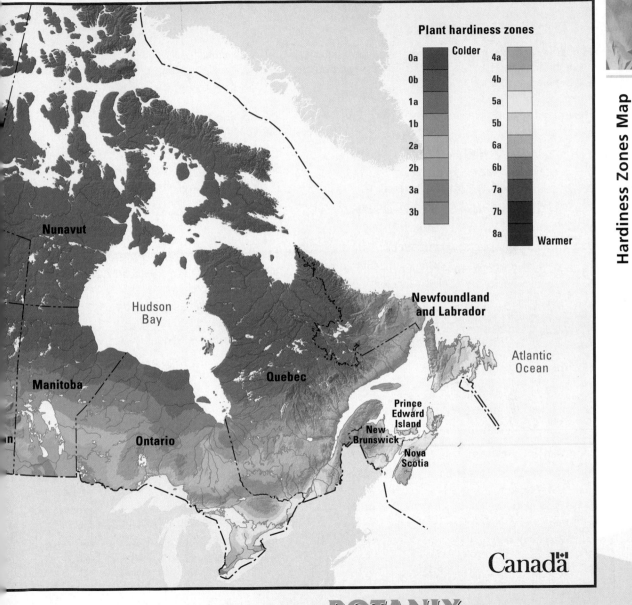

Plant hardiness zones

Colder
0a 4a
0b 4b
1a 5a
1b 5b
2a 6a
2b 6b
3a 7a
3b 7b
    8a
Warmer

Nunavut

Hudson Bay

Manitoba

Ontario

Quebec

Newfoundland and Labrador

Atlantic Ocean

Prince Edward Island

New Brunswick

Nova Scotia

Canada

Amazing plants

In order to help you more easily determine the ideal plants for various situations, BOTANIX has created a top 10 of the most resistant and popular plants, in various categories. Some of them aren't in this Guide, and are still available at your local BOTANIX.

Perennial groundcovers to replace grass

1. *Asperula odorata (galium)* / Sweet Woodruff
2. *Ajuga reptans* / Bugleweed
3. *Lamium maculatum* / Dead Nettle
4. *Thymus serpyllum* / Creeping Thyme
5. *Pachysandra terminalis* / Japanese Pachysandra
6. *Vinca minor* / Vinca/Periwinkle
7. *Thymus pseudolanuginosus* / Woolly Thyme
8. *Lysimachia nummularia* / Creeping Jenny
9. *Houttuynia cordata* 'Tricolor' / 'Tricolor' Chameleon Plant
10. *Aegopodium podagraria* 'Variegatum' / Bishop's Weed

Shrubs on standards

1. *Amelanchier ovalis* 'Pumila' / Cotoneaster
2. *Caragana arborescens* 'Walker' / Weeping Peashrub
3. *Euonymus alatus* 'Compactus' / Compact Winged Euonymus
4. *Hydrangea paniculata* 'Limelight' / 'Limelight' Hydrangea
5. *Malus sargentii* 'Tina' / Sargent's Crabapple
6. *Viburnum lantana* 'Mohican' / 'Mohican' Wayfaringtree

7. *Physocarpus opulifolius* 'Summer Wine' / 'Summer Wine' Ninebark
8. *Prunus cistena* / Purple-leaf Sandcherry
9. *Salix integra* 'Hakuro Nishiki' / 'Hakuro Nishiki' Dappled Willow
10. *Syringa meyeri* 'Palibin' / 'Palibin' Dwarf Korean Lilac

Conifers on standards or weeping

1. *Picea pungens* 'Glauca Globosa' / Dwarf Colorado Spruce
2. *Picea abies* 'Little Gem' / 'Little Gem' Norway Spruce
3. *Tsuga canadensis* 'Pendula' / Weeping Canadian Hemlock
4. *Juniperus scopulorum* 'Tolleson's Blue Weeping' / 'Tolleson's Blue Weeping' Rocky Mountain Juniper
5. *Chamaecyparis nootkatensis* 'Pendula' / Weeping Nootka Falsecypress
6. *Larix décidua* 'Pendula' / Weeping European Larch
7. *Picea pungens glauca* 'Pendula' / Weeping Colorado Blue Spruce
8. *Picea abies* 'Pendula' / Weeping Norway Spruce
9. *Pinus strobus* 'Pendula' / Weeping White Pine
10. *Pinus strobus* 'Nana' / 'Nana' White Pine

Plants for revitalizing the shoreline

1. *Cornus stolonifera (sericea)* / Red Osier Dogwood
2. *Diervillea lonicera* / Bush Honeysuckle
3. *Myrica gale* / Bayberry
4. *Parthenocissus quinquefolia* / Virginia Creeper
5. *Physocarpus opulifolius* / Ninebark
6. *Salix discolor* / Pussy Willow
7. *Sambucus canadensis* / American Elder
8. *Spiraea latifolia* / Meadowsweet
9. *Acer rubrum* / Red Maple
10. *Larix laricina* / Eastern Larch (Tamarack)

Ecological-champion plants

The following plants are good environmental choices as they resist dryness and don't need any maintenance, support or fertilizer.

Trees and shrubs

1. *Celtis occidentalis* / Common Hackberry
2. *Betula nigra* 'Heritage' / 'Heritage' River Birch
3. *Gleditsia triacanthos var. inermis* 'Skyline' / 'Skyline' Thornless Honeylocust
4. *Malus* 'Sugar Tyme' / 'Sugar Tyme'™ Crabapple
5. *Ulmus* 'Accolade' / 'Accolade' ™ Elm
6. *Berberis* 'Aurea Nana' / 'Aurea Nana' Barberry
7. *Rhus typhina* 'Tiger Eyes' / 'Tiger Eyes' Staghorn Sumac

8. *Spiraea arguta* 'Grefsheim' / 'Grefsheim' Spiraea
9. *Hippophae rhamnoides* / Seaberry
10. *Potentilla fruticosa* 'Gold Star' / 'Gold Star' Cinquefoil

Perennials

1. *Calamagrostis acutiflora* 'Karl Foerster' / Feather Reed Grass
2. *Sedum spectabile* 'Autumn Joy' / Showy Stonecrop/Sedum
3. *Perovskia atriplicifolia* / Russian Sage
4. *Hemerocallis* 'Stella de Oro' / 'Stella de Oro' Daylily
5. *Rudbeckia fulgida* 'Goldsturm' / 'Goldsturm' Coneflower
6. *Armeria maritima* / Sea Pink
7. *Echinops ritro* 'Blue Globe' / 'Blue Globe' Globe Thistle
8. *Achillea millefolium* 'Red Beauty' / 'Red Beauty' Yarrow
9. *Potentilla* 'Gibson Scarlet' / 'Gibson Scarlet' Potentilla
10. *Lythrum salicaria* 'Terra Nova' / 'Terra Nova' Purple Loosestrife

Index by Theme

Trees

	Quick growing	Slow growing	Distinctive flowering*	Colourful autumn foliage	Tolerates acid soil	Tolerates dry soil	Tolerates damp soil	Attract birds	Attract butterflies
Acer freemanii	•			•		•			
Acer ginnala				•		•		•	
Acer negundo	•					•			
Acer platanoides				•				•	
Acer rubrum				•	•		•		
Acer saccharum				•				•	
Betula papyrifera	•							•	
Betula pendula	•								
Catalpa speciosa			•			•			
Celtis occidentalis				•		•		•	
Elaeagnus angustifolia	•					•		•	
Fraxinus americana	•			•					
Fraxinus pennsylvanica				•			•		
Ginkgo biloba				•					
Gleditsia triacanthos var. inermis	•			•		•			
Liriodendron tulipifera			•						
Prunus virginiana								•	•
Quercus				•					
Quercus macroparca					•			•	
Quercus palustris	•			•				•	•
Quercus robur		•							
Quercus rubra	•			•	•			•	
Robinia pseudoacasia			•	•		•			•
Salix alba	•						•		
Sorbus aucuparia				•				•	
Sorbus thuringiaca			•					•	
Syringa reticulata			•						•
Tilia americana	•		•						
Tilia cordata	•		•			•			
Ulmus	•		•				•		

Grafted trees

	Quick growing	Slow growing	Distinctive flowering*	Colourful autumn foliage	Tolerates acid soil	Tolerates dry soil	Tolerates damp soil	Attract birds	Attract butterflies
Amelanchier canadensis			•					•	
Amelanchier ovalis		•	•					•	
Caragana arborescens						•		•	
Catalpa bignonioides		•		•					
Cercidiphyllum japonicum			•	•					
Fraxinus excelsior			•						
Ginkgo biloba		•							
Halimodendron halodendron	•		•			•			
Maackia amurensis			•			•			
Magnolia loebneri			•	•					
Magnolia soulangiana			•	•					
Magnolia stellata			•	•					
Morus alba	•							•	
Prunus cerasifera			•			•		•	•
Robinia pseudoacacia			•	•					
Salix caprea	•								
Syringa juliana			•						•
Syringa meyeri			•						•
Ulmus glabra			•	•					

Crabapple Trees

	Quick growing	Slow growing	Distinctive flowering*	Colourful autumn foliage	Tolerates acid soil	Tolerates dry soil	Tolerates damp soil	Attract birds	Attract butterflies
Malus			•					•	
Malus sargentii			•					•	

* Distinctive flowering means flowers are abundant or spectacular, or long-lasting.

	Quick growing	Slow growing	Distinctive flowering*	Colourful autumn foliage	Tolerates acid soil	Tolerates dry soil	Tolerates damp soil	Attract birds	Attract butterflies
Decorative Conifers									
Abies balsamea					•		•		
Microbiota decussata					•	•			
Picea abies					•				
Picea glauca					•				
Picea strobus					•	•			
Pinus					•	•			
Pinus mugo					•	•			
Tsuga canadensis					•				
Upright Conifers									
Juniperus chinensis	•								
Larix decidua	•						•		
Picea abies					•				
Picea glauca					•				
Picea pungens					•				
Picea pungens glauca					•				
Pinus cembra					•	•			
Pinus nigra austriaca						•			
Pinus strobus					•	•			
Thuja occidentalis 'Brandon'	•						•		
Thuja occidentalis 'Fastigiata'	•						•		
Thuja occidentalis 'Pyramidalis'	•						•		
Tsuga canadensis					•				
Shrubs									
Acer palmatum					•				
Aralia elata				•				•	
Aronia melanocarpa				•	•			•	•
Azalea					•	•			•
Berberis thunbergii						•			
Buddleja davidii			•						•
Clethra alnifolia			•	•			•		•

	Quick growing	Slow growing	Distinctive flowering*	Colourful autumn foliage	Tolerates acid soil	Tolerates dry soil	Tolerates damp soil	Attract birds	Attract butterflies
Cotinus coggygria							•		
Daphne cneorum		•	•						
Euonymus alatus				•					
Forsythia			•						
Genista lydia			•			•			
Hibiscus syriacus			•						
Hydrangea arborescens	•		•						
Hydrangea macrophylla			•		•		•		
Hydrangea paniculata	•		•				•		
Hydrangea serrata			•		•				
Hypericum kalmianum			•			•			
Kolkwitzia amabilis			•					•	
Philadelphus virginalis			•						•
Physocarpus opulifolius								•	
Potentilla fruticosa			•			•			
Rhus typhina				•		•			
Salix integra	•						•		
Sambucus canadensis							•		
Sorbaria sorbifolia	•						•		
Spiraea arguta			•						
Spiraea bumalda			•						•
Spiraea japonica			•						•
Spiraea nipponica			•						•
Spiraea van houttei	•		•						•
Spiraea van houttei 'Gold Fountain'			•						•
Stephanandra incisa	•								
Syringa		•	•						•
Syringa meyeri		•	•						•
Syringa patula			•	•					•
Syringa prestoniae			•						•
Syringa vulgaris			•						•

	Quick growing	Slow growing	Distinctive flowering*	Colourful autumn foliage	Tolerates acid soil	Tolerates dry soil	Tolerates damp soil	Attract birds	Attract butterflies
Tamarix ramosissima	•		•			•			
Viburnum dentatum							•	•	•
Viburnum lantana	•			•			•	•	•
Viburnum sargentii							•		•
Viburnum trilobum				•				•	•
Weigela			•					•	
Weigela florida			•						•
Weigela hybrida			•						•
Evergreen Shrubs									
Andromeda polifolia					•				
Arctostaphylos uva-ursi		•			•	•			
Calluna vulgaris			•		•				
Cotoneaster		•	•				•		
Erica carnea			•		•				
Gaultheria procumbens					•				•
Ilex meservaea					•				
Pieris japonica				•	•				
Rhododendron			•		•				•
Rhododendron catawbiense			•		•				•
Yucca filamentosa			•			•			
Hedges									
Caragana arborescens	•					•			
Cotoneaster acutifolia				•					•
Lonicera xylosteoides						•			
Physocarpus opulifolius nanus				•			•		
Ribes alpinum						•			
Rosa rubrifolia						•			
Salix purpurea	•						•		
Sambucus canadensis	•						•	•	
Spiracea japonica			•						

	Quick growing	Slow growing	Distinctive flowering*	Colourful autumn foliage	Tolerates acid soil	Tolerates dry soil	Tolerates damp soil	Attract birds	Attract butterflies
Symphoricarpus albus								•	
Thuja occidentalis	•						•		
Climbing Plants									
Clematis			•						
Campsis radicans			•					•	
Celastrus scandens	•							•	
Humulus lupulus	•								
Hydrangea petiolaris			•						
Lonicera			•					•	
Parthenocissus quinquefolia	•		•					•	
Parthenocissus tricuspidata			•						
Polygonum aubertii			•				•		
Vitis riparia	•						•	•	
Wisteria macrostachya			•						
Roses									
Hybrid Tea			•						
Floribunda			•						
Hardy Shrubs			•						
Perennials									
Acanthus spinosus						•			•
Achillea clyopetala			•			•			•
Achillea millefolium			•			•			•
Aconitum cammarum			•						
Aconitum napellus			•				•		
Aegopodium podagraria	•						•		
Ajuga reptans			•						
Alcea rosea									•
Alchemilla mollis							•		
Alyssum saxatile							•		
Anemone hybrida			•						
Anemone pulsatilla							•		
Anthemis tinctoria			•						•

BOTANIX Experts by nature

	Quick growing	Slow growing	Distinctive flowering*	Colourful autumn foliage	Tolerates acid soil	Tolerates dry soil	Tolerates damp soil	Attract birds	Attract butterflies
Aquilegia alpina									•
Aquilegia hybrida			•				•		•
Aquilegia vulgaris			•						•
Arabis caucasica						•			•
Arenaria montana						•			
Armeria maritima			•			•			•
Artemisia schmidtiana						•			
Artemisia stelleriana						•			
Aruncus dioicus	•		•		•				
Asclepias incarnata							•		•
Asclepias tuberosa						•			•
Aster alpinus									•
Aster dumosus			•						•
Aster novae-angliae			•						•
Astilbe arendsii							•		•
Astilbe chinensis			•						•
Astilbe japonica							•		•
Astilbe simplicifolia									•
Astilbe taquetii	•						•		•
Astilbe thunbergii			•						•
Astilboides tabularis							•		•
Astrantia major			•				•		
Baptisia australis						•			•
Belamcanda chinensis						•		•	
Bellis perennis			•						
Bergenia cordifolia							•		•
Brunnera macrophylla				•			•		
Campanula									•
Campanula carpartica			•						•
Campanula cochlearifolia			•						•
Campanula glomerata			•						•
Campanula lactiflora			•						•

	Quick growing	Slow growing	Distinctive flowering*	Colourful autumn foliage	Tolerates acid soil	Tolerates dry soil	Tolerates damp soil	Attract birds	Attract butterflies
Campanula latifolia macrantha		•							•
Campanula persicifolia		•							•
Campanula portenschlagiana (Muralis)		•				•			•
Centaurea dealbata						•			•
Centaurea montana						•			•
Cerastium tomentosum	•					•			
Chelone obliqua		•					•		•
Chrysanthemum	•	•							
Chrysanthemum arcticum		•				•			•
Chrysanthemum coccineum						•			•
Cimicifuga ramosa				•			•		•
Convallaria majalis						•			
Coreopsis		•				•			•
Coreopsis grandiflora		•							•
Coreopsis verticillata		•				•			•
Crocosmia		•							•
Delphinium		•							•
Dianthus		•							•
Dianthus barbatus									•
Dianthus deltoides		•							•
Dianthus gracianopolitanus		•				•			
Dianthus plumarius		•				•			•
Dicentra formosa		•				•			
Dicentra spectabilis	•							•	•
Digitalis purpurea		•				•			•
Echinacae		•				•			•
Echinacea purpurea		•				•			•
Echinops ritro		•				•			•
Erigeron hybridus		•							•
Eryngium planum						•			
Eupatorium rugosum							•		

BOTANIX Experts by nature

Index by Theme

Index

BOTANIX Experts by nature

BOTANIX Experts by nature

British Columbia

Abbotsford
Revy Home & Garden
34530 McConnell Rd
(604) 504-5000

Rona Revy Home Centre
32073 South Fraser Way
(604) 853-2286

Burnaby
Rona Revy Home Centre
7260 Edmonds Street
(604) 524-9771

Chilliwack
Rona Revy Home Centre
45656 Yale Road West
(604) 792-1351

Coquitlam
Rona Revy Home Centre
2798 Barnet Highway
(604) 464-5522

Rona Revy Home Centre
425 Lebleu
(604) 931-2085

Hope
Rona Revy Home Centre
840 - 5th Avenue Box 818
(604) 869-5692

Kamloops
Rona Revy Home Centre
416 Mt. Paul Way
(250) 372-2236

324 Mt.Paul Way
(250) 372-3969

Kelowna
Revy Home & Garden
1711 Springfield Rd
(250) 762-7389

Madeira Park
Rona Revy Home Centre
12390 Sunshine Coast Hwy
(604) 883-9551

Maple Ridge
Rona Revy Home Centre
21213 Lougheed Highway
(604) 466-0004

Mission
Rona Revy Home Centre
32290 Lougheed Highway
(604) 826-6248

North Vancouver
Rona Revy Home Centre
915 West First Street
(604) 985-3000

Rona Revy Home Centre
1160 East 3rd
(604) 984-1892

Pemberton
Rona Revy Home Centre
7456 Prospect St.
(604) 894-5812

Prince Rupert
Rona Home Centre
405 East 3 rd. Avenue
(250) 627-7011

Quesnel
Rona Revy Home Centre
450 Johnston Ave
(250) 992-2155

Richmond
Revy Home & Garden
3000 Sexsmith Road
(604) 273-8985

Rona Home Centre
7111 Elmbridge Way
(604) 273-4606

Salmon Arm
Rona Revy Home Centres
2430 Highway #1 West
Box 99
(250) 832-7044

Squamish
Rona Revy Home Centre
39009 Discovery Way
(604) 892-3551

Surrey
Rona Revy Home Centre
19550 - 92nd Avenue
(604) 882-6226

3165 King George Hwy
(604) 535-9888

6965 King George Hwy
(604) 591-5050

16659 Fraser Highway
(604) 576-2955

Vancouver
Revy Home & Garden
2727 East 12th Avenue
(604) 253-2822

Rona Revy Home Centre
1503 Kingsway
(604) 877-1171

2727 E 12th Ave
(604) 254-2355

Vernon
Rona Revy Home Centre
2201 - 58th Ave
(250) 545-3332

Victoria
Revy Home & Garden
850 Langford Parkway
(250) 478-6680

Rona Home Centre
220 Bay Street
(250) 595-1225

Whistler
Rona Revy Home Centre
1350 Alpha Lake Road
(604) 932-3620

Williams Lake
Rona Revy Home Centre
298 Proctor St
(250) 392-7767

Alberta

Calgary
Revy Home & Garden
12330 Symons Valley Rd
NW
(403) 274-9897

9630 MacLeod Trail S
(403) 212-4875

2665 - 32nd Street NE
(403) 219-5800

90 Crowfoot Way NW
(403) 239-5850

Rona Revy Home Centre
3303 - 57th Avenue SE
(403) 236-2055

3005 Ogden Rd SE
(403) 265-5651

300 Stewart Green SW
(403) 242-4477

Edmonton
Revy Home & Garden
10450 - 42nd Avenue
(780) 437-8080

17303 - 100 Avenue
(780) 481-8080

9603 -165 Avenue NW
(780) 406-8600

Rona Revy Home Centre
9651 - 51 Avenue
(780) 437-7910

13851 - 127 Street
(780) 456-1111

Fort McMurray
Rona Revy Home Centre
8408 Manning Ave
(780) 743-4666

Leduc
Rona Revy Home Centre
5202 Discovery Way
(780) 986-5904

Medicine Hat
Rona Revy Home Centre
3010 Dunmore Road SE
(403) 526-2125

Red Deer
Rona Revy Home Centre
2610 - 50th Avenue
(403) 343-1764

Sherwood Park
Rona Revy Home Centre
222 Baseline Rd
(780) 449-0808

Spruce Grove
Rona Revy Home Centre
175 Highway 16A
(780) 960-3140

Saskatchewan

Prince Albert
Rona Revy Home Centre
800 - 15th Street East
(306) 763-7662

Regina
Revy Home & Garden
3710 Quance St. East
(306) 522-7662

Saskatoon
Rona Revy Home Centre
286 Venture Crescent
(306) 933-1903

Manitoba

Altona
Rona Revy Home Centre
142 Centre Ave East
(204) 324-6407

Winkler
Rona Revy Home Centre
295 Cargill Road
(204) 325-8999

Winnipeg
Revy Home & Garden
1636 Kenaston Blvd
(204) 487-7662

775 Panet Road
(204) 663-7389

1333 Sargent Ave
(204) 774-7389

Newfoundland

Wabush
Rona Home Centre
6 First Street
(709) 282-6222

BOTANIX Experts by nature

The Plant Protection Centre:

Protection and control

You're having a problem with one of your trees? You want advice about maintaining your grass? Simply contact one of the Plant Protection Centre (PPC) experts at your BOTANIX garden centre. This exclusive BOTANIX service is completely free. Our experts will answer any questions you may have about your plants, soil, and diagnosing or treating disease or insect problems, always keeping in mind your personal situation.

Le PPC was set up in April 3, 2003, when the pesticide management regulations came into effect in Quebec. These rules govern the sale, reduction and the use of pesticides, as well as health and environmental risk prevention. The centre is ideally situated to offer you the best natural solutions for phytosanitary issues.

The PPC databank contains over 300 information sheets illustrated with colour photos to facilitate identification. These files are updated regularly to reflect new regulations and products. They contain information required for the diagnosis and help the advisor offer solutions to mitigate, master and prevent the problem while reducing the use of pesticide.

PRO-MIX ®

MYCORISE ® «INSIDE»

PRO-MIX ® FOR OUTDOOR PLANTING / POUR PLANTATION

PRO-MIX ® FOR LAWN CARE / POUR PELOUSE

PRO-MIX ® ULTIMATE ORGANIC MIX / ULTRA TERREAU BIO

ROOTS **GROW BEST** in **PRO-MIX** ®

Premier Horticulture